LINGUISTIC DIVERSITY AND SOCIAL JUSTICE

LINGUISTIC DIVERSITY AND SOCIAL JUSTICE

An Introduction to Applied
Sociolinguistics

Ingrid Piller

OXFORD
UNIVERSITY PRESS

OXFORD
UNIVERSITY PRESS

Oxford University Press is a department of the University of Oxford. It furthers
the University's objective of excellence in research, scholarship, and education
by publishing worldwide. Oxford is a registered trade mark of Oxford University
Press in the UK and certain other countries.

Published in the United States of America by Oxford University Press
198 Madison Avenue, New York, NY 10016, United States of America.

© Oxford University Press 2016

First Edition published in 2016

Library of Congress Cataloging-in-Publication Data

Names: Piller, Ingrid, 1967- author.
Title: Linguistic diversity and social justice : an introduction to applied
sociolinguistics / Ingrid Piller.
Description: Oxford ; New York : Oxford University Press, [2016] |
Includes bibliographical references and index.
Identifiers: LCCN 2015030016| ISBN 9780199937264 (pbk. : alk. paper) |
ISBN 9780199937240 (hardcover : alk. paper) |
ISBN 9780199937257 (ebook) | ISBN 9780190267414 (online content)
Subjects: LCSH: Multilingualism—Social aspects. | Linguistic change—
Social aspects. | Linguistic minorities—Social aspects. | Sociolinguistics.
Classification: LCC P115.45 .P55 2016 | DDC 306.44/6—dc23
LC record available at http://lccn.loc.gov/2015030016

3 5 7 9 8 6 4 2

Printed by Webcom, Canada

CONTENTS

ACKNOWLEDGMENTS

I would like to acknowledge the Darug and Guringai people, the traditional custodians of the land on which much of the work for this book was carried out. I would like to pay my respects to their elders, both past and present, and extend that respect to all other Aboriginal and Torres Strait Islander people.

Linguistic Diversity and Social Justice is part of an ongoing conversation. To begin with, it is part of an academic conversation in applied sociolinguistics and I am indebted to all the researchers on whose work I draw here. It is also a continuation of a conversation about inequality in intercultural communication that emerged from my previous book *Intercultural Communication* (Piller, 2011). I would like to thank all those who engaged with that book and provided feedback.

Many of the conversations that feed into this book have taken place online through the *Language on the Move* network and I extend my heartfelt gratitude to all the team members, contributors, translators, and readers who have made *Language on the Move* such a vibrant and rewarding forum. Many of the conversations have also taken place in the 'Language and Globalization' Reading Group at Macquarie University and I thank all its members, past and present, for their contributions and dedication.

As always, my international family and friends have been central to the conversations that have shaped my thinking about linguistic diversity and social justice and I am truly blessed to have you all in my life.

I have decided against providing a long list of individuals because I would be bound to exclude more than I can include. However, I would like to individually thank Angela Turzynski-Azimi for proofreading the full manuscript; Sadami Konchi for her artwork; and Hallie Stebbins from Oxford University Press for her patience.

LINGUISTIC DIVERSITY AND SOCIAL JUSTICE

Chapter 1

Introduction

LINGUISTIC DIVERSITY

I live in Sydney, Australia, and one of the stories that contemporary Sydneysiders like to tell about their city is that it is one of the most linguistically diverse in the world. A 2014 newspaper article, for instance, boasted: 'From Afrikaans to Telugu, Hebrew to Wu, the depth and diversity of languages in Sydney rivals some of the world's largest cities.' Not to be outdone, Melbourne—Sydney's eternal rival for urban preeminence in Australia—declared itself 'justifiably proud of its linguistic diversity' because 'more languages are spoken in Melbourne than there are countries in the world.' These two Australian cities are not alone in their rivalry over the greater number of languages spoken in their communities. Across the Pacific, Canadian media, too, tally the linguistic diversity of Canadian cities and find 'Toronto leading the pack in language diversity, followed by Vancouver and Montreal.' Similarly, the media of Canada's southern neighbor suggest that US cities, too, compete in some kind of multilingualism championship: 'New York remains the most multilingual city in the country, with 47% of its massive population speaking at least two languages.' Continuing our journey east across the Atlantic, British media play the same game: we learn that Manchester has been 'revealed as the most linguistically diverse city in western Europe' while London is celebrated as the 'multilingual capital of the world.'[1]

Simultaneously with media reports such as these, which fete linguistic diversity as a desirable attribute of a polity, there is another set of media reports that paint a darker picture. In Australia, media reports also dating from mid-2014 showed that youths from 'culturally and linguistically diverse backgrounds' were more likely to be unemployed than their Australian-born peers despite being better qualified. At the same time in the USA, children from minority backgrounds were reported to outnumber white children in schools for the first time in US history. However, this was not seen as a cause for celebration. On the contrary, white middle-class parents chose to move away from diverse neighborhoods or opted to send their children to private schools with lower levels of racial and linguistic diversity. The result is segregation, not diversity. Meanwhile in Britain, the media regularly report concerns about the high and rising cost of linguistic diversity. This is because British institutions are required by national and international law to provide—and thus pay for—interpreting services for clients who do not speak English.[2]

These two sets of media reports raise a conundrum: on the one hand, the fact of linguistic diversity in many societies around the world is well-recognized, frequently enumerated, and even celebrated. However, on the other hand, linguistic diversity is associated with a range of social ills and seen as something that needs to be contained, possibly even something to be fearful of. In the space between these two contradictory discourses of linguistic diversity as inherently good but socially problematic, there is currently a distinct absence of any public discussion of what the fact of linguistic diversity might actually mean for our social organization. How does linguistic diversity structure societies at institutional, local, national, and global levels? How does linguistic proficiency mediate social participation? In short, how is language related to inequality?

Questions such as these which explore the intersection between linguistic diversity and social justice are currently rarely being asked and they are certainly not at the center of any sustained public debate. As a consequence of this lack of debate, we are faced with a celebration of linguistic diversity in the abstract that clashes with the patent existence of social problems associated with linguistic diversity: minority youths being disadvantaged in the Australian job market, schools with diverse populations underperforming in the USA, or barriers to health and legal services faced by migrants in the UK. In fact, the media texts from which I have drawn these examples are relatively hazy about what the precise nature of the problem might be. Are 'culturally and linguistically diverse' youths in Australia excluded from the job market because they do not have the required proficiency in English, or are they being discriminated against on the basis of their race or country of origin? Are diverse US schools underperforming because multilingualism is incompatible with the provision of a good education or because of the low socioeconomic status of minority children? Are migrants who cannot be bothered to learn English to blame for spiraling interpreting costs in the UK, or is the provision of language mediation services the price a society has to pay for the economic benefits that come from globalization and freedom of movement in the European Union?

None of these questions have easy answers since language intersects with race, socioeconomic status, legal status, and gender in complex ways. However, this complexity is rarely acknowledged in public debates and the sophistication of public debates about language and inequality is relatively low. Therefore this book is intended to serve as a systematic exploration of the social consequences of linguistic diversity. It is also a clarion call to start thinking about linguistic disadvantage as a form of structural disadvantage that needs to be recognized and taken seriously, and that warrants a sustained public debate as to how it can best be mitigated.

SOCIAL JUSTICE

The front cover of this book depicts Lady Justice, a traditional allegory for the rule of law. Customarily, Lady Justice has been portrayed wearing a blindfold as a metaphor for her impartiality. The idea is that blind Lady Justice will not be affected by bias because the physical characteristics and appearance of those before her—their clothes as an indicator of their social status or their skin color as an indicator of their race—remain invisible to her. In the cover image, the artist, Sadami Konchi, has added earmuffs to indicate that Lady Justice would have to be deaf as well as blind to be truly impartial. This is so because the way we speak is an integral part of who we are. Some of those who come before Lady Justice will be able to make their case in eloquent Standard English—or the standard of whichever language we imagine Lady Justice to speak—while others will make their case haltingly, searching for the right words, or in the accents of those who have not had the privilege of formal education. As long as Lady Justice can hear, she will be able to form a view of the speaker's socioeconomic status, their level of education, their ethnicity, their gender, their age, and their country of origin. Indeed, the great English Renaissance playwright Ben Jonson pointed out that our language is even more revealing than our appearance: 'Language most shows a man: Speak, that I may see thee.'[3] Without earmuffs Lady Justice's blindfold is, in fact, pointless.

Of course, Lady Justice does not exist. In reality, the idea of impartial justice is a fiction; a fiction that reminds us what it is that we should strive for. As the conventional blindfold keeps us alive to the fact that appearance is a factor in inequality that we should strive to eliminate, the earmuffs highlight the fact that linguistic diversity, too, is a factor in inequality that we should strive to redress.

Language is an important aspect of our social position and the way we use language—be it in speech, in writing, or in new media—can open or close doors. For sociolinguists this is, in fact, old news. It has long been known that speakers of non-standard varieties are frequently deprived of equal opportunities. However, our understanding of the relationship between language and inequality in the highly linguistically diverse societies of the early twenty-first century is less systematic. It is one aim of this book to fill this gap and provide an overview of contemporary research into the intersection between linguistic diversity and social justice.

The second aim of this book is to put linguistic diversity on the map of contemporary social justice debates. Engagement with social justice focuses principally on disadvantage and discrimination related to gender, race, ethnicity, sexual orientation, religion, and age. It is extremely rare for 'language' to feature as a basis on which individuals, communities, or nations may be excluded.[4] However, if we do not understand how linguistic diversity intersects with social justice and if we are unable to even recognize disadvantage and discrimination on the basis of language, we will not be able to work toward positive change.

Social justice has been thought of as the master virtue that undergirds all others since ancient times.[5] In *The Republic* Plato put forward a view of justice as being fundamental to all other virtues, arguing that it is only by overcoming institutional injustice that it will be possible for other social and individual virtues to flourish. The understanding of social justice adopted here draws on the work of the philosopher Nancy Fraser and conceives of social justice as constituted along three dimensions, namely, economic redistribution, cultural recognition, and political representation.[6] This book therefore pursues three principal lines of inquiry: first, an exploration of the relationship between linguistic diversity and economic inequality; second, an exploration of the relationship between linguistic diversity and cultural domination; and, third, an exploration of the relationship between linguistic diversity and imparity of political participation.

My focus will be on linguistic diversity and injustice —how linguistic diversity relates to economic inequality, cultural domination, and imparity of political participation—because our ideas about justice are formed by the experience of injustice. This is a pragmatic approach that is not concerned with 'perfect justice' or 'transcendental justice' but is focused on seeking solutions and exploring alternatives to existing problems and injustices. It is an exploration of justice that is 'realization-focused,' as the economist Amartya Sen has called it.[7]

My inquiry is informed by the assumption that it is desirable to keep inequalities between individuals, communities, and nations within relatively narrow margins. This broad commitment to social justice is a product of the labor movement and the European revolutions of the nineteenth century. Social justice was an important policy goal of the broad left-to-centrist political spectrum for much of the twentieth century but was abandoned with the advent of Reaganomics in the USA, Thatcherism in the UK, and, since the fall of the Berlin Wall and the end of the Cold War, across most parts of the globe. The consequences of the neoliberal abandonment of the commitment to social justice have been skyrocketing levels of inequality between individuals, communities, and nations in the late twentieth and early twenty-first centuries.

It is only recently that the tide has begun to turn as we begin to recognize, once again, that ever-widening gaps between the haves and the have-nots are not only immoral but may threaten the very survival of humanity as they are closely tied to the depletion of natural resources, climate change, and the escalation of global violence and wars. The United Nations has warned that 'neglect of the pursuit of social justice in all its dimensions translates into de facto acceptance of a future marred by violence, repression and chaos.' Or, as philosopher Brian Barry has pithily put it, the challenge of our time is 'justice or bust.'[8]

OVERVIEW

Understanding and addressing linguistic disadvantage must be a central facet of the social justice agenda of our time. As mentioned above, I will explore this by focusing on the linguistic dimensions of economic inequality, cultural domination, and imparity of political participation. To do so, I employ a case-study approach to real-world instances of linguistic injustice as they are reported in existing research and the media.

This book starts with an exposition of the linguistic facts of life by establishing that linguistic diversity is universal. However, linguistic diversity is rarely neutral and tends to be accompanied by linguistic stratification (Chapter Two). Chapter Three then goes on to explore why linguistic diversity is so frequently associated with social problems and examines the processes of linguistic subordination. Chapters One to Three thus constitute the conceptual foundations of the ways in which linguistic diversity intersects with social justice. The following chapters then go on to examine the connection between linguistic diversity and inequality in specific contexts.

According to the United Nations, key domains where social justice policies are needed to redress social injustice—and, conversely, where the experience of social injustice can be assumed to be concentrated—include work and remunerated employment; education and knowledge; health services, social security, and a safe environment; and civic and political participation.[9] Chapters Four to Six each explore the role of linguistic diversity in one of these areas, namely work (Chapter Four), education (Chapter Five), and human security and participation (Chapter Six).

The framework within which social justice is understood has typically been that of the modern nation-state. It is the nation-state that is charged with safeguarding the rights of its citizens as individuals and in groups. Consequently, Chapters Four to Six focus on the intersection between linguistic diversity and social justice within the nation-state. Most of the discussion centers on nation-states that are organized as liberal democracies because the recognition and accommodation of diversity—which is at the heart of the intersection between linguistic diversity and social justice—is the essence of liberal democracy.[10]

Although the nation-state is the key framework within which social justice is organized today, 'there is clearly a universal dimension to social justice, with humanity as the common factor.'[11] The most disadvantaged are often the citizens of nation-states with very limited capacity to redress injustice. Inequalities exist not only between individuals and groups within a state but also between states. The inequalities between the rich nations of the global north and the poor nations of the global south constitute a fundamental injustice in addition to the challenges posed by inequalities between individuals and groups within states. Chapter Seven therefore changes the perspective to justice between states and explores the role of linguistic diversity in global injustice.

While much of the analysis in this book focuses on language as a means of exclusion, discrimination, and disadvantage, the concluding chapter asks what the positive content of linguistic justice might be.

JOIN THE CONVERSATION

This book is part of an ongoing conversation. Many of the arguments and analyses brought together here were first published as research blog posts on the sociolinguistics portal *Language on the Move* at www.languageonthemove.org. Therefore, you can join the conversation at any time while reading this book and I cordially invite you to do so. Watch out for the 'Join the conversation' notes. These contain a URL that takes you directly to the relevant *Language on the Move* entry, where you can join the conversation through various social media tools. Often, you will also find additional images, audio, and video on the site.

Some 'Join the conversation' notes also contain suggestions for further research and invite you to collect your own data and analyze them. In such cases, you are welcome to submit your findings as a research blog post to *Language on the Move* for consideration for publication. Our submission and review policy is available at www.languageonthemove.com/language-on-the-move.

Chapter 2

Linguistic Diversity
and Stratification

LANGUAGE, MULTILINGUALISM, LINGUISTIC DIVERSITY

You may have been wondering why this book is not called 'language and social justice' or 'multilingualism and social justice.' After all, it deals with different languages being used in the same space and so seems to involve bi- or multilingualism. The short answer to this question is that it is not always easy to know where one language ends and where another language begins, and that social justice issues arise just as often in relation to the use of one single language that is used in different ways—think of 'speaking with an accent'[1]— as they do in relation to the use of clearly distinct languages. I will now explain this point in some more detail.

For a while now, sociolinguists have expressed concern that terms such as 'bilingualism,' 'trilingualism,' or 'multilingualism' can be misleading because they suggest that languages are clearly separate and can be easily counted and compartmentalized.[2] At one level, this is, of course, exactly the case, and the borders between languages are patently obvious, as, for instance, in the example of the headline about Sydney's linguistic diversity mentioned in the Introduction, which read 'From Afrikaans to Telugu, Hebrew to Wu, the depth and diversity of languages in Sydney rivals some of the world's largest cities.' Afrikaans, Telugu, Hebrew, and Wu are clearly different languages: Afrikaans is an Indo-European language of South Africa, Telugu is a Dravidian language of India, Hebrew is a Semitic language of Israel, and Wu is a Sinitic language of China. An individual with proficiency in these four languages is clearly multilingual (or quadrilingual if one wishes to highlight the exact number of languages) and a city where these four languages are spoken is clearly multilingual.

However, as soon as languages come into contact the apparent clarity of this situation starts to change—both on the level of language categorization and on the level of the individual. This works in two ways. First, while Afrikaans, Telugu, Hebrew, and Wu are clearly distinct from one another, each is related to other languages where the boundary is much fuzzier. Afrikaans, for instance, is closely related to Dutch—up to 95% of Afrikaans vocabulary overlaps with Dutch—while Wu is widely regarded as a 'dialect' of Chinese rather than a 'language' in its own right.[3] Therefore, it is debatable whether we should consider an individual who speaks both Afrikaans and Dutch or Wu and Mandarin Chinese as bilingual in the same way we would consider someone with proficiency in Afrikaans and Wu as bilingual.

Second, the relationships between Afrikaans and Dutch or Wu and Mandarin Chinese are the result of past migrations (e.g., people from the Netherlands moving to southern Africa) and past language contact (e.g., the roughly 5% of Afrikaans vocabulary that is not Dutch in origin comes from contact languages in Africa). But processes of language contact and language change that are so clear when we look at them from a historical perspective are always ongoing, as individuals use language to communicate rather than for the sake of speaking a particular language. The Afrikaans of a present-day Sydney resident will bear traces of new language contacts; what is more, it may not even be possible at any given moment to determine whether the person is speaking Afrikaans, English, or a mixture of both, or is switching rapidly between these two languages.

Conversely, migrants from South Africa—whether Afrikaans speakers or not—are having an effect on the communicative repertoires of people in Sydney who may not even be aware that 'Afrikaans' is becoming part of their repertoire. For instance, the supermarkets and grocery stores in the suburb where I live all stock *biltong*, a type of cured meat that is said to have been invented by the *voortrekkers* ('pioneers') who left the Cape Colony in the 1830s to occupy land further inland. Today considered a traditional food of South Africa, the word *biltong* ultimately derives from two Dutch words, namely *bil* ('buttock, hindquarter') and *tong* ('tongue'). That *tong* and 'tongue' share an even longer common history is readily apparent.[4]

As is obvious from the example, in real life and everyday usage languages are not usually as neatly compartmentalized as our usage of language names suggests. At an abstract level, it seems clear what 'Afrikaans,' 'Telugu,' 'Hebrew,' or 'Wu' refer to but as soon as we encounter a mundane language item such as 'biltong' in a Sydney supermarket the neat borders fall away immediately: is this an Afrikaans word? A South African word? A Dutch word? A Germanic word? An English word? An Australian word? A global word? The fact that a case could be made for any of these—and probably more—suggests that the question itself is not an analytically productive one.

Socially, the way an Afrikaans-speaking Sydney resident speaks Afrikaans (e.g., interspersed with lots of English or trying to keep the two languages separate) is probably relatively inconsequential. What is socially relevant in Sydney is the traces of Afrikaans in English and how these are evaluated vis-à-vis other ways of speaking English. This means that, in Sydney, it is mostly not multilingualism per se that is socially relevant but diversity within English, distinguishing not only 'native' ways of speaking English from those ways of speaking English that bear obvious traces of language contact (e.g., in the form of a foreign accent) but also ordering different contact varieties hierarchically.

In sum, my concern here is with linguistic difference—specifically, linguistic difference that becomes socially relevant—and not the number of languages present in a society per se. My use of the term 'linguistic diversity' is intended to highlight the fact that such difference may or may not be tied to what is conventionally labeled a language with a name. The unique ways in which each and every one of us uses the linguistic resources at our disposal to communicate in context constitute the basic fact of 'linguistic diversity,' irrespective of whether that linguistic diversity involves Afrikaans and Wu, a mixture of the two, or internal variation within each.

HIERARCHY IN DIVERSITY

Whether they understand and use the word 'biltong' or not is one of countless ways in which contemporary Sydney residents differ from each other. As in all societies, linguistic diversity is ubiquitous and each individual repertoire—formed in childhood and youth and undergoing bigger or smaller changes throughout life as we lose an accent, incorporate a new style, forget a term, or learn a new way of speaking—is a key aspect of our individual identity. Our language—meaning not a particular abstract Language X but the way we use the linguistic resources at our disposal to communicate—contributes to making us who we are in the same way as our physical appearance, our ideas and beliefs, and our way of life do. It is this diversity that each and every human society is made up of. As the philosopher George Herbert Mead observed: 'We are indefinitely different from each other, but our differences make interaction possible. Society is unity in diversity.'[5]

If linguistic diversity is ubiquitous and equally distributed in the population—everyone has their own individual repertoire but interaction is predicated on the considerable common ground that members of a society share—how can linguistic diversity raise social justice issues? The short answer to this question is that some languages are more equal than others and that linguistic difference is rarely neutral but more often hierarchically structured.

I will start the long answer with an example. Over the past few years, the media in Anglophone countries have regularly run reports about concerns that the populations of these countries are lacking the multilingual skills of the rest of the world and will therefore be left behind when it comes to the global economic opportunities of the future. There is concern that students are not studying foreign languages in school and that, as a result, they will miss out on job opportunities at home and abroad. Additionally, lack of foreign language capabilities is presented as diminishing opportunities for international trade, limiting global political influence, and threatening national security. The situation seems to be so dire that employers have to leave positions unfilled, secret services are missing out on crucial information, and policy makers simply throw up their hands in despair and fund students to study abroad even if they have no knowledge of the language in their destination nor any intention of studying it while there.[6]

Reading depressing news reports such as these one has to wonder how they can be squared with upbeat language news circulating in the media at the same time. The media items cited in the Introduction present the cities of Anglophone nations as hothouses of linguistic diversity where large numbers of languages are spoken by the population. And at the same time there is a widespread linguistic deficit?![7]

The answer to this conundrum lies in the fact that commentators and politicians bemoaning the fact that Americans, Australians, or Britons do not know languages other than English have a very different segment of the population in mind than those commentators who note their multilingualism.

Clive Holes, a professor of Arabic at Oxford University, explains the differential visibility of language skills with reference to Arabic in the UK[8]: there are few students who study Arabic at university—a language for which there is high demand both in the private and public sector—and those who do are mostly middle-class students who have no previous experience with Arabic. The kind of language they study is 'Arabic university-style,' a variety that is focused on written texts and a standard form that is quite different from the varieties of Arabic spoken across the Arab world.[9]

At the same time, Britain is also home to a large number of people who learned to speak Arabic in the home: 159,290 residents of England and Wales identified Arabic as their main language in the 2011 census.[10] According to Professor Holes these people have 'more useable language skills' than those who study Arabic at university without a background in the language. Even so, those who have Arabic as their main language are being overlooked for Arabic-language jobs: 'They are an incredibly valuable national resource that we are failing totally to use.'

The example demonstrates that language skills may be evaluated quite differently depending on the identity of the speaker. In linguistically diverse societies injustices arise because the ways in which people communicate are valued differently. The language practices of those who are disadvantaged in other ways—because of their legal status, their gender, their race, or their class—are usually the ways of speaking that are least valued, and language thus becomes one aspect of cumulative disadvantage in diverse societies.

In sum, diversity—including linguistic diversity—is a characteristic of all human societies. However, the principle of universal social diversity is complemented by the principle of stratification: the social meaning of linguistic diversity is rarely 'different but equal'; much more frequently linguistic diversity forms the basis for inequality, as the metaphor of the language pyramid explains.

LANGUAGE PYRAMIDS

In his book *Words of the World*, the sociologist Abram de Swaan describes the global language system as a pyramid-like organigram. The vast majority of languages cluster at the bottom of the pyramid. The languages at the bottom of the pyramid, which account for an estimated 98% of all the 5,000 to 6,000 languages in the world, are 'peripheral languages.' Peripheral languages are the languages of local communication, 'the languages of conversation and narration rather than reading and writing, of memory and remembrance rather than record.'[11] Above the huge layer of peripheral languages sits a thin layer of 'central languages.' Central languages are usually the official languages of a nation-state. They are used in elementary and sometimes secondary education, in the media and in national politics and bureaucracies. De Swaan estimates that there are around one hundred central languages. The next layer is occupied by about a dozen 'super-central languages,' which serve in international and long-distance communication. Finally, the apex of the pyramid is occupied by one single language, English, which de Swaan describes as 'hyper-central language.'

De Swaan's global-language-system pyramid is intended to demonstrate communicative reach: speakers of a peripheral language need to learn a central language to communicate outside their local community; speakers of a central language need to learn a super-central language to communicate internationally; and speakers of a super-central language need to learn the hyper-central language in order to communicate globally. The system is hierarchically ordered because the greater the communicative reach of a language, the more valuable the language is.

In the same way that the global language system can be conceptualized as a pyramid, local language systems are organized hierarchically, too. One way to understand the language hierarchy in a community is to compare private and public language use, as in the following example from the Sydney suburb of Auburn. Throughout Sydney, Auburn is known as an immigrant suburb with a highly diverse population predominantly of Middle Eastern origin and predominantly Muslim. In tune with the suburb's high level of diversity, the motto of the Auburn City Council, which can be found on signs throughout the suburb, is 'Many Cultures, One Community.' The iconic status of Auburn as a migrant and Muslim suburb is also evidenced by the fact that the acclaimed Australian TV police series 'East West 101'[12] is set there. 'East West 101' plays on the global conflict between East and West as well as the local opposition between Sydney's affluent eastern suburbs and its poorer western suburbs with their migrant populations.

Auburn's population speaks a wide variety of languages at home. According to the 2011 census,[13] Arabic is the most frequently spoken home language in Auburn (5,186 speakers), followed by English (4,455), Turkish (3,825), Mandarin (3,427), Cantonese (2,693), Persian (1,899), and Urdu (1,347). Other languages with more than one hundred speakers (in descending order of frequency) include Tamil, Hindi, Vietnamese, Filipino, Punjabi, Korean, Bengali, Italian, Greek, Spanish, Indonesian, Russian and Croatian. Furthermore, Thai, Polish, Samoan, Maltese, Sinhalese, Serbian, Hungarian, Macedonian, French, Assyrian, Portuguese, German, and Japanese are also spoken in more than twelve households each.

All these home languages sit at the bottom of the local language pyramid. Their communicative reach is restricted to the households where they are spoken. The next layer is occupied by public but unofficial languages. That means languages that can be heard on the street and languages that are visible in public space, such as on commercial signage (e.g., restaurant and shop names, fliers for events, community newspapers, for-rent notices). In Auburn, this layer is inhabited by English, Chinese, Arabic, Persian, and Turkish. The apex of the pyramid is formed by public and official languages: languages that are used on official signage (e.g., street names, directional signs to public institutions such as schools or the train station) and that are used in education and bureaucratic communication. In Auburn, the apex of the local language pyramid is occupied by one single language only, English.

The global and the local language pyramids complicate each other. A globally valuable language may not be very valuable in a specific local context. Japanese, for instance, is a valuable supercentral language in de Swaan's global pyramid. However, in Auburn, it is relegated to the bottom rung of home language. Conversely, the availability of home languages on satellite TV or the Internet raises the low local status of Auburn home languages in the global language pyramid.

Global connections mean that in Auburn official institutional communication is, in fact, not uniformly in English. The suburb's parking garage, which is operated by the Auburn City Council, dispenses multilingual parking tickets printed in German, English, Italian, and French (in this order). The English version of this quadrilingual text reads: 'Please do not leave the ticket in the car. Please take care not to fold or bring ticket in contact with direct heat. Please note that the parking conditions in operation are displayed within the car park.'

The parking ticket is issued in these four languages because it is not designed for the Australian market—let alone the local market of Auburn—but for the European market. It is produced by Designa, a parking management company headquartered in Germany.[14] In the context of Auburn, multilingual official communication such as this one complicates the language pyramid in two ways. The parking ticket can be interpreted as a challenge to the sole status of English as apex language. At the same time, it can be interpreted as further devaluing local home languages with a strong local presence—Arabic, Turkish, Chinese, Persian, Urdu—precisely because of their absence.

The language on a parking ticket may seem banal, mundane, and not worthy of further attention. However, language choice on such mundane texts is important because it is not only an expression of what is 'normal'—conforms to the norm—but also shapes our expectations of normalcy. The usual monolingual English parking tickets contribute to normalizing Australia as a monolingual English space. A German-English-Italian-French parking ticket sets up the dominant languages of Europe as the norm. In each case, there is a mismatch between the norm and actual multilingual realities. In each case, the effect is to devalue the actual local languages.[15]

The global language pyramid, which is undergirded by innumerous national, regional, and local language pyramids, is a central facet of inequality based on language. Speakers of languages higher up in the hierarchy enjoy more opportunities than speakers of languages lower in the hierarchy. The pyramid is based on a language's communicative value in the first instance. However, as we have seen in the example of the local language pyramid of Auburn, the communicative value of a language then becomes ideologically imbricated by the spaces—the home or the public domain; private or institutional; powerful or powerless institution—with which a language is associated. Another way to maintain linguistic hierarchies is through discourses that locate diversity exclusively on the lower rungs of the pyramid.

THE DIVERSITY OF THE OTHER

Talk about 'diversity' is everywhere these days and 'diversity' is mostly seen as a good thing. There is a broad discourse—often enshrined in institutional diversity policies—that embraces 'diversity' as a measure of how well an institution is doing in terms of 'inclusiveness' or even as a competitive advantage. However, such diversity discourses with their unquestioned underlying assumption that 'diversity is good' can often be quite confusing and leave the reader baffled about what 'diversity' actually refers to, as the following two examples show.

In Australia the term 'culturally and linguistically diverse,' or 'CALD' for short, is widely used by government agencies. The NSW Community Relations Commission defines 'culturally and linguistically diverse' as follows: 'a broad descriptor for groups and individuals who differ according to religion, race, language and ethnicity, but excluding those whose ancestry is Anglo-Saxon, Anglo Celtic, Aboriginal or Torres Strait Islander.'[16] The term was originally introduced as an expansion of the term 'non-English-speaking background' (NESB), which was deemed not to be sufficiently inclusive. Beyond language background, 'culturally and linguistically diverse' is intended to also capture 'the Australian-born descendants of immigrants, or people who come from countries where English is widely spoken but who may be unfamiliar with Australian governance and its structures (including many South Asian and African countries or other countries with British colonial histories).'

The term 'CALD' thus refers to a mélange of criteria related to language, race, ethnicity, and religion. A person who is considered

'CALD' is routinely assumed to have problems with English language proficiency as evidenced by fliers with titles such as 'What if a CALD client should walk in our door?' This particular guide instructs staff to be welcoming, to smile, to use plain English, to speak slowly, to pause and to remain calm.[17] The assumption underlying well-intentioned advice such as this is twofold: first, it is only the client that is conceived as potentially 'culturally and linguistically diverse' but not the service provider. Second, having to interact with a 'culturally and linguistically diverse' client is akin to an emergency situation ('Stay calm') because of the assumed language barrier. In fact, the vast majority of 'culturally and linguistically diverse' people in Australia speak English well. In some cases, such as the descendants of immigrants or those from countries with British colonial histories, 'CALD persons' may even be monolingual native speakers of English. Misdiagnosis of language proficiency can be highly detrimental to actual service provision as will be discussed in detail in Chapter Five. Here, I focus on the discursive effects of setting up a diffuse bureaucratic category that comprises new and long-term immigrants, first-generation migrants and the descendants of migrants, migrants from countries where English has no role, and migrants from countries where English is an official language.

Logically, and as discussed above, everyone is culturally and linguistically diverse. By exempting some English speakers—namely, those with an Anglo-Celtic heritage—from being diverse, 'diversity' becomes a euphemism for 'linguistically and racially/ethnically outside the mainstream.' In this way diversity discourses can easily become a binary and divisive mechanism that contributes to social stratification by setting some forms of language use up as the unremarkable default and others as 'diverse.'

It is easy to confuse the celebration of diversity with a progressive agenda. However, as the example of the CALD label shows, contemporary diversity discourses are part of social processes that reify difference, create boundaries and hierarchies, and undergird social inequality. Diversity discourses thus contribute to injustice precisely by concealing inequality at the same time that they create inequality by marking one group as 'normal' and the other as 'diverse.'[18]

Asking who it is that is considered 'diverse' and whether some people are exempted from being 'diverse' is a useful exercise not only with reference to diversity policies and bureaucratic terminology but also with regard to research design. A recent article about language education in the UK, for instance, makes a conceptual distinction between research participants who are examples of 'new diversity,' 'old diversity,' and 'very old diversity.'[19] In this research design, people who are marked by 'new diversity' are recent immigrants who have entered the UK since the 1990s and who come from backgrounds that did not have a strong presence in the UK prior to the 1990s. Members of groups who have a migration history that predates the 1990s are then considered 'old diversity.' 'Old diversity' is the outcome of the Commonwealth migrations of the twentieth century, and the author lists British Muslims and Sikhs as examples of 'old diversity.'

What is 'very old diversity' then? It turns out that Jews are considered exponents of 'very old diversity.'

While this periodization purports to be purely chronological, it is, in fact, simply another example of locating diversity in the people who are imagined to not fully belong. As it so happens, Jews first arrived in the British Isles from France with William the Conqueror in 1066. While subjected to anti-Jewish sentiment and repression over many centuries, Jews maintained a presence and must be considered an integral part of English history at least since the Tudor period. The two largest waves of Jewish immigration occurred in the fifteenth century from Spain and Portugal and in the nineteenth century from Eastern Europe.[20]

It is noteworthy that the descendants of other immigrant groups who arrived at around the same time as the Jews are not considered 'diverse.' Such 'non-diverse' immigrants and their descendants include the Roman conquerors of the first century AD; the Anglo-Saxons, who arrived from what is today northern Germany and southern Denmark from the fourth century onward; the Vikings, who invaded from Scandinavia in the eighth century; William the Conqueror's Norman invaders of 1066; and various European Protestants, including the Huguenots, who escaped persecution on the Continent in the sixteenth century.[21]

The 'diversity' concept in this example is undergirded by the unspoken assumption that only some people are 'diverse': here it is those who differ from an implicit white, Christian, and English-speaking norm who are considered to be 'diverse.' Furthermore, 'diversity' becomes an essential attribute of the individual: the descendants of Jews, Muslims, and Sikhs are forever marked by the migrations of their forebears, even if that migration took place centuries ago. By contrast, no such essential attribute is seen to mark the descendants of mobile whites.

The problem with the kinds of diversity discourses I have discussed here are twofold. First, they are factually wrong. Diversity is a feature of all human societies and to the extent that it is possible to speak of 'diverse individuals' or 'diverse groups' everyone is equally 'diverse.' Second, exempting socially dominant groups from being considered diverse—both internally vis-à-vis other members of the group and externally vis-à-vis people from other groups—contributes to the reproduction of the inequality between groups who are seen as 'default' and those who are seen as 'diverse.' If diversity discourses are nothing more than the unquestioned acceptance of boundaries between Us and Them, they not only lack analytical power but also blind us to our commonality.[22]

SEEING 'SUPER-DIVERSITY'

The Odyssey, the ancient Greek epic about the Trojan War dating back to the twelfth century BC, contains this description of the island of Crete: 'There is a land called Crete; ringed by the wine-dark sea with rolling whitecaps; handsome country, fertile, thronged with people well past counting; boasting ninety cities, language mixing with language side-by-side.'[23] This description is part of a recount of the many wonders the hero, Odysseus, has seen on his travels. As such, this 3,000-year-old boast about multilingual Crete is not particularly different from the kinds of contemporary grandstanding about multilingual cities we encountered in the Introduction.

Three thousand years of linguistic diversity confirm the point I have already repeatedly made: that diversity is a feature of all human societies, or as the anthropologist Ward Goodenough put it in 1976, 'multiculturalism is the normal human experience.'[24] However, there is a line of thought that linguistic diversity is relatively novel, that it is increasing, and that we are today confronted with an entirely new form of diversity, namely 'super-diversity.' The term 'super-diversity' was coined in 2007 by the anthropologist Steven Vertovec to underscore the fact that 'over the past twenty years globally more people have moved from more places to more places; wholly new and increasingly complex social formations have ensued.' The result is said to be 'a level and kind of complexity surpassing anything previously experienced in a particular society.'[25]

The idea of super-diversity has been embraced enthusiastically in many areas of the social sciences, including applied sociolinguistics, because it rings true with the everyday lived experience of many people, including social scientists. The economists François Grin, Claudio Sfreddo, and François Vaillancourt speak of an increase in 'subjective diversity.' They argue that 'objective diversity'—the number of languages spoken in the world—is in fact decreasing. However, more and more people experience linguistic diversity on a daily basis; hence, an increase in 'subjective diversity.' Put differently, it is not the level and complexity of diversity per se that has increased but the perception of that diversity.[26]

That super-diversity may indeed be more a matter of perception than actual social change is confirmed by migration researchers Mathias Czaika and Hein de Haas.[27] These researchers set out to investigate whether global migration really did increase in volume, diversity, geographical scope, and overall complexity—as the idea of super-diversity suggests—on the basis of data from the World

Bank's Global Bilateral Migration Database,[28] which covers the period from 1960 to 2000.

What the researchers found in terms of migration volume may seem counterintuitive to those seeing 'super-diversity' encroaching on their perception: between 1960 and 2000 there was actually a decrease in the percentage of international migrants. In 1960, 3.06% of the world's people were on the move internationally and by 2000 this figure had shrunk slightly to 2.73%.

One may wonder how it is possible that the 'subjective diversity increase' that many of us experience and that social scientists have dubbed 'super-diversity' is not actually borne out by global migration figures. The answer to this mystery lies in the data for countries of origin and destination countries. The researchers examined these to explore the diversification thesis, namely, the idea that international migration has increased not only in volume but also in complexity ('from more places to more places'). As regards countries of origin, it is indeed the case that international migrants come from an increasing array of countries, as countries that it was almost impossible to leave in 1960, such as those of the Soviet Bloc, became migrant-sending countries after the end of the Cold War. However, the diversification of countries of origin is juxtaposed with a concentration in destination countries. From 1960 to 2000, fewer international migrants headed for destinations in Africa, Asia, and Latin America and more and more headed for Australasia, Europe, and North America. The set of preferred destination countries thus shrank and by 2000 comprised the USA, Germany, France, Canada, Australia, and the Gulf countries.

As it so happens, these are the very countries where social scientists are now observing 'super-diversity.' As Czaika and de Haas point out, 'the idea that immigration has become more diverse may partly reveal a Eurocentric worldview':

> With declining European emigration toward other continents, there has been a major shift in global directionality of migration, with the transformation of Europe from a global source region of emigrants and settlers into a global migration magnet.

This has led to an increased presence of phenotypically and culturally distinct immigrants in Europe as well as settler societies
of European descent in North America and the Pacific. In other
words, rather than an increasing spread in terms of origin countries of migrants per se, the national and ethnic origin of immigrant populations has become increasingly non-European.[29]

There can be little doubt that there is a qualitative difference between diversity in a relatively isolated village society on a small Pacific
Island such as Romónum, on which Ward Goodenough's assertion
that 'multiculturalism is the normal human experience' was based,
and that of an immigration magnet such as ancient Crete or contemporary London.[30] But why is it that we look at the former as the imagined social default organization and the latter as something new and
special? Why should we consider the organization of Romónum with
its limited diversity as more typical of the human experience than
that of ancient Crete with its high level of diversity? Not to mention
that we imagine the village society of Romónum to be much more homogeneous and less diverse than Goodenough actually found it to be.

The idea of 'super-diversity' as a historically novel form of diversity can have unintended negative consequences, in the same way
that locating diversity only in people who are perceived as deviating
from some imaginary 'non-diverse' norm does. If the diversity of our
time seems unprecedented to us, attempts to 'reduce diversity' can
seem an entirely rational political response to contemporary social
problems. However, just as diversity itself is nothing new, attempts
to reduce diversity and to make populations fit an imaginary homogeneous norm are nothing new. In fact, attempts to eliminate diversity are a major form of injustice associated with linguistic diversity.

INVENTING HOMOGENEITY

In 2013 I had the opportunity to visit the Hagia Sophia museum
in Istanbul. That magnificent building has a long and checkered

history. It was originally built as an Orthodox church by Emperor Constantine in 360 AD. Emperor Constantine had only recently made the city where Hagia Sophia stands the capital of the Byzantine Empire and had changed the name of the former city of Byzantium to Constantinople. For more than a millennium Hagia Sophia served as a church before it was turned into a mosque following the Muslim Turks' conquest of the city in 1453. After almost five hundred years as a mosque, Hagia Sophia was converted again, this time into a museum, in 1935—by that time the name of the city where it is located had changed yet again, to Istanbul.

During my visit, I was keen to see the famous 'Halfdan' runes.[31] These are a set of obscure little graffiti on a parapet in Hagia Sophia's gallery written in Viking runes and dating back to the ninth century. All that is legible today is 'alftan,' which refers to the Norse name 'Halfdan' and which it is assumed was part of a formula such as 'Halfdan carved these runes'—the medieval equivalent of the modern graffiti formula 'XY was here.'

How did a medieval Viking get all the way from Scandinavia to what is today Istanbul and was back then Constantinople, the center of the Byzantine Empire and the most powerful metropolis on earth? It is generally assumed Halfdan was a mercenary in the Varangian Guards. The Varangian Guards were an elite army unit of foreign mercenaries serving as personal bodyguards of the Byzantine Emperor. Drawn from all over Northern Europe, the ethnic composition of the Varangian Guard was highly diverse and is known to have included Russians, Scandinavians, Germans, Englishmen, and Celts.[32] The Byzantine Emperors felt safer with foreigners as bodyguards who had no local loyalties. Little is known about the motivations of the young men who left Northern Europe to serve far from home in present-day Turkey but I imagine they were driven by the usual mixture of lack of opportunities at home and the lure of the metropolis—a lure so powerful that medieval Constantinople drew migrants from all across the known world to this multilingual and multicultural city.

One could consider the Viking graffiti in Hagia Sophia as evidence of 'super-diversity' more than a millennium ago. If evidence of past diversity is relatively easy to find, why do so many people experience an increase in 'subjective diversity'? In addition to the fact that people look in different places—say contemporary London instead of ancient Crete—a further explanation for the increase in 'subjective diversity' is the fact that (linguistic) diversity has been actively expunged from the historical record, as can be exemplified with an overview of the linguistic history of Istanbul.

To begin with, expunging linguistic diversity from the historical record is relatively easy because the linguistic record, by its very nature, is fleeting: spoken language disappears and, for most of human history, the written record has been the official record, bearing few traces of everyday language practices. Today, researchers collect evidence for linguistic 'super-diversity' by audio-recording informal conversations, by collecting mundane texts in the linguistic landscape such as handwritten room-for-rent notices, by being participant observers in diverse communities, or by sampling digital communication on social media.[33] Few if any of these data types that provide evidence for linguistic diversity in everyday language use are available from earlier periods. Where it has survived, evidence of linguistic diversity in the historical record has often been overlooked and ignored. The 'Halfdan graffiti' are, in fact, a case in point. Despite the relative durability of language etched in stone, it had been ignored for over a millennium and was only 'discovered' in 1964 by Elisabeth Svärdström.

The transient nature of everyday language is one part of the story of why we fail to see linguistic diversity in the historical record. The other part of the story is that evidence of linguistic diversity has been systematically erased from the historical record.

When Halfdan wrote his graffiti in Old Norse runes and, presumably, spoke some form of Old Norse with those of his fellow Varangians who shared his dialect, the main language of Constantinople—and the lingua franca of its diverse population—was (medieval)

Greek. Latin was also widely used because the Byzantine Empire considered itself to be 'Roman' after all. And then there were the languages of all the city's migrants and visitors:

> The entire east Mediterranean was represented in the city's population. In late antiquity there were Greek-speakers from the Balkans, western Asia Minor, and Cyprus; Latin-speaking Italians, Illyrians, and North Africans; Germanic-speaking Gepids, Goths, and Herules from northern Europe; Armenians from the high eastern plateau; Aramaic-speaking Palestinians and Syrians; Jews; and Coptic Egyptians.[34]

Christian Constantinople was obviously 'super-diverse.'

The city's linguistic make-up changed on May 29, 1453 when the Ottomans under Mehmed II took the city: not only did the Christian city become a Muslim one, and the Hagia Sophia church a mosque, but the city's dominant languages also changed from Greek and Latin to Arabic, Persian, and Turkish. What did not change was the fact of the city's linguistic 'super-diversity.' Mehmed himself had been educated in the sciences and arts of the Islamic and Western world and, in addition to Turkish, had learned to read and write Arabic, Greek, Hebrew, Latin, and Persian. His head tutor had been a famous Kurdish professor, Ahmet Kurani.[35] In the new Ottoman capital, Arabic was the language of prayer and religion, Persian was the language of the court, and Turkish was the language of the troops. Greek found itself as the language of a now downtrodden and subjected population and, as before, many other languages were spoken by the city's diverse inhabitants. Mehmed II sought to repopulate the devastated city and 'sent his servants to all his lands, to say "Whoever wishes, let him come, and let him become owner of houses, vineyards and gardens in Istanbul." This, however, was not enough to repopulate the city. [He then] brought very many families against their will.'[36] The languages of these new voluntary and involuntary settlers included Armenian, Hungarian, Italian, Ladino, Russian, and Serbian.

The Turkish language, which came to predominate over the centuries as Istanbul's lingua franca, was itself a highly heteroglossic language. Ottoman Turkish was inflected particularly by Arabic and Persian but also by all the other languages of this great melting-pot city.

The city's multilingualism and the multilingual character of Turkish officially came to an end with the proclamation of the Turkish Republic in 1923. The new Turkey wanted to sever its links with its Ottoman and 'Eastern' past and aspired to become modern and European.[37] The multilingual laissez-faire of the past was now seen as decidedly 'backward' and 'Eastern.' Languages other than Turkish started to be repressed, with Kurdish as the best-known victim of the new repression of linguistic diversity by the state. Not only was Turkey going to have only one language—Turkish—but that language was going to be 'modernized,' that is, rid of the traces of other languages, particularly linguistic traces associated with 'the East,' i.e., Arabic and Persian; such was the explicit aim of the Turkish Language Reform.[38]

The most widely known aspect of the Turkish Language Reform is the abolition of the Arabic script and its replacement with the Latin script. In one fell swoop, modern Turks lost access to their written historical record. Another target of the language reformers was Arabic and Persian vocabulary. Such words were replaced with 'Turkish' ones or loans from 'modern' European languages.

The futility of this undertaking—even if lost on everyone but the philologist—is neatly encapsulated in the word for 'city.' Ottoman Turkish used شهر (şehir). Because of its obvious association with Persian شهر (šahr) the language reformers saw no place for it in 'Modern' Turkish and cast around for a 'pure' Turkish word. They found it in the ancient 'kent.' The irony is that 'kent' is itself a much older loanword from Sogdian, the lingua franca of Central Asia before the Islamic Conquest.

The reform was 'a catastrophic success,' as the Turkologist Geoffrey Lewis has put it.[39] As a result, most contemporary Turkish speakers are cut off from their linguistic and cultural heritage predating the 1930s. A famous—and also ironic—example of the monolingualization of Turkish is the fact that a major 1927 speech by Atatürk, the founder of the Turkish Republic, has had to be 'translated' repeatedly into contemporary Turkish so as to remain comprehensible to contemporary Turks.

During my visit to Istanbul, I found the contemporary examples of 'super-diversity' impossible to ignore: the Russian скидка ('sale') signs in the shop windows, the menus in the tourist restaurants available in all the languages of countries with strong currencies, the handwritten Arabic للإيجار ('for rent') signs, or the Kurdish music stalls. By contrast, the fact that 'super-diversity' has been a characteristic of Istanbul aka Constantinople aka Byzantium since time immemorial is easy to overlook.[40]

The invention of linguistic homogeneity may seem of merely historical interest. However, the normalization of linguistic homogeneity continues to affect us today and constitutes a form of representational injustice as it has helped to create the linguistic homogeneity of the standard language as the imagined ideal against which the diverse repertoires of individual speakers are judged.

SUMMARY

This chapter has been concerned with the ways in which we think about linguistic diversity and the injustices these representations give rise to. While linguistic diversity in the abstract is widely seen as a good thing, we have few ways of speaking and thinking about linguistic diversity that do not consist of imagining a series of neatly delineated codified languages. However, each language with a name is an idealistic abstraction that may not have all that much to do with the diverse linguistic repertories of individual speakers. Repertoires that deviate from the imagined standardized norm, and particularly repertoires characterized by language contact and language change, are usually rendered invisible.

Linguistic diversity is not only widely ignored but also stratified. Some languages and their speakers are often seen and presented as more valuable than others resulting in yet another form of linguistic domination. In fact, 'linguistic diversity' has in some contexts become a euphemism for linguistic subordination.

Yet another injustice of representation is constituted by the fact that linguistic diversity is widely regarded as a novelty of our age when, in fact, it has been the normal human experience all along. We do not just fail to see linguistic diversity in the historical record because of ideological blinkers but also because it has oftentimes been actively expunged from the historical record in an attempt to deny legitimacy to subordinated groups.

In sum, the erasure of linguistic diversity—where the linguistic repertoires of individuals come to be seen through the lens of an imagined language with a name—and the stratification of linguistic diversity—where repertoires are ordered hierarchically and only some repertoires come to be seen as diverse—are widely held beliefs about language. I have already hinted at some of the injustices these beliefs about linguistic diversity give rise to. The next chapter will explore those linguistic injustices in detail.

Chapter 3

The Subordination
of Linguistic Diversity

The previous chapter showed that everyone has their own unique linguistic repertoire and that diversity is inherent in language use. However, the ubiquity of linguistic diversity all too frequently remains obscured and we come to accept that having one particular standardized language is normal and deviations from the norm are problematic. This chapter explores in detail the discursive processes through which this happens. It first asks how it is possible that linguistic diversity—ubiquitous as it is—is so often obscured from view. How can linguistic diversity remain hidden in plain sight? In a second step it examines how linguistic diversity is ascribed to only some speakers and what consequences this ascription has for their social position.

Language sociologists explain the relative invisibility of linguistic diversity by saying that linguistically diverse societies are oftentimes characterized by a 'monolingual habitus' or a 'monolingual mindset.' The term 'monolingual habitus' was introduced by the education researcher Ingrid Gogolin to explain the monolingual institutional organization of schooling in Germany in the face of the fact that significant numbers of students speak a language other than German at home. The concept of the 'habitus' draws on the work of sociologist Pierre Bourdieu, who describes habitus as 'systems of durable, transposable dispositions' and as 'principles which generate and organize practices and representations.' In English, the term 'monolingual mindset' is used more widely than 'monolingual habitus.' It was introduced by the linguist Michael Clyne to describe the mismatch between the fact of widespread multilingualism in Australia and the idealized representation of Australia as a monolingual English-speaking nation.[1]

A monolingual habitus or mindset does, of course, not appear out of nowhere. It is maintained through a wide range of practices and discourses in an ongoing process of discursive creation and recreation. Institutional and public elements in this process—the ways in which institutions organize linguistic diversity and the ways in which linguistic diversity is talked about in the media—are particularly powerful, and this chapter explores some of these institutional and public discourses that serve to subordinate linguistic diversity, first by obscuring it and second by problematizing it.

The focus in this chapter is on contemporary processes of linguistic subordination and the case studies you will encounter in this chapter all date from the early twenty-first century. However, before we proceed, it is worth bearing in mind that the discursive construction of a monolingual mindset is nothing new, certainly not in the Anglophone tradition, as a famous quote about medieval English by the writer and translator John of Trevisa (1342–1402) demonstrates:

> [. . .] by comyxtioun and mellynge [mixing and mingling] firste wiþ Danes and afterward wiþ Normans, in meny þe contray longage is apayred [damaged], and som vseþ straunge wlafferynge [stammering], chiterynge [twittering], harrynge [making a harsh roaring or snarling sound], and garrynge [chirping] grisbayting [gnashing of teeth].[2]

A text such as this serves to render some ways of speaking—those characterized by 'mixing and mingling' with Danes and Normans—problematic. Trevisa describes speech in which linguistic diversity is too obvious and impossible to ignore as if it constituted a language impairment ('wlafferynge') or was equal to animal sounds ('chiterynge,' 'harrynge,' 'garrynge') or to an involuntary physical reaction ('grisbayting').

Trevisa's text is one little instance in the long history of the discursive construction of linguistic diversity as exceptional and problematic. So how does this process work in contemporary institutional and public discourses?

THE TERRITORIAL PRINCIPLE

One way in which we come to see monolingual standard languages as the norm and deviations from that imagined monolingual standard language—and remember each individual repertoire is a deviation but repertoires characterized by multilingualism and language contact tend to be characterized by greater deviation—as problematic is through the close association between language and place.

You will have seen maps that map language onto territory. You probably can conjure up in your mind a map of the Americas where almost all of North America is coded for English except for a bit of French in Eastern Canada; more than half of Central and South America will be coded for Spanish; the other big chunk (Brazil) for Portuguese; and three tiny pockets of English, Dutch, and French where the states of Guyana, Suriname, and French Guiana are located. In addition to maps based on the national language of a state, you will be able to find more fine-grained maps that map traditional minority languages onto a particular territory.

Language maps do not only inform us about global language distributions, they also fulfill a particular discursive function: they establish a link between language and territory as a central and normal way to think about language use. The territorial principle is foundational to most thinking about linguistic justice because it undergirds linguistic legislation.

Where legislation exists that is specifically concerned with linguistic diversity, such legislation is usually based on the territorial principle and links a particular language to a particular territory. Typically, the territory to which such language legislation applies is a nation-state. Article 2 of the French Constitution provides a case in point: 'La langue de la République est le français.' ('The language of the Republic shall be French.')[3]

Even polities that accord legal rights to more than one language often do so on the basis of the territorial principle. Well-known examples of multilingual states that have enshrined the territorial principle fixing a particular language to a particular place include Belgium, Canada, and Switzerland. Belgian legislation, for instance, divides the country into various language territories based on historical settlement patterns. There are two large monolingual territories (Flanders with Dutch and Wallonia with French), one bilingual territory (Brussels with Dutch and French), and various territories that are defined as monolingual but where another language enjoys certain protections (Dutch regions where French is protected; French regions where Dutch and/or German are protected; and a German region where French is protected). Complicated as this may sound, it is still a significant abstraction from Belgium's actual linguistic diversity. To begin with, individual speakers may be located in the 'wrong' territory. In that case—say a French-speaking family living in Flanders—the family would enjoy none of the legal protections their French-speaking compatriots in Wallonia enjoy. Second, the legislated languages are not actually the local Belgian varieties of that language but standard languages standardized elsewhere. Traditionally, it is not standard Dutch or standard German that have been spoken in Belgium but Flemish and Alsatian. Assigning Standard Dutch and Standard German to certain territories has resulted in a shift away from Flemish and Alsatian in those territories. Finally, languages and varieties not 'traditionally' spoken in Belgium are left without any legitimate place. Languages such as Arabic, Berber, Italian, Portuguese, Spanish, and Turkish, for instance, have been spoken in Belgium by significant numbers of speakers since the 1960s but because they have not been assigned to a particular historical territory they continue to be seen as 'out of place.'[4]

Even where legislation is specifically designed to protect linguistic diversity and to promote minority languages, the logic of such legislation has followed the territorial principle, as is the case in the *European Charter for Regional and Minority Languages*. Widely seen as one of the most progressive pieces of linguistic justice legislation globally, the Charter was designed to protect and promote regional and minority languages and to enable speakers to use them in private and public life. Signatories commit to a range of measures to promote the use of the regional or minority language in the field of education, in the judicial arena, in public administration and public services, in the media, in cultural activities and facilities, and in economic and social life. However, the scope of the protection only applies to 'the territories in which those languages are spoken' and a relevant territory must correspond to 'the historical base' of the relevant language. As a result, two sets of languages are excluded from the scope of protection under the Charter: first, languages that have historically been spoken in Europe but have no historical association with a particular territory such as Yiddish and Romani; and, second, languages whose speakers arrived in a territory only after modern state formation and whose speakers did not settle in rural enclaves.[5]

In sum, the territorial principle is a collective belief that ties a particular abstract language to a particular place and that is enshrined in much linguistic-rights legislation. Given the fact that individuals do not speak a particular abstract language but have a range of repertoires at their disposal, the belief in the territorial principle results in at least two representational injustices: first, the real-life practices of real-life speakers may be rendered invisible (e.g., Flemish becomes Dutch and Alsatian becomes German). Second, the practices of speakers who are categorized as lacking 'historical ties' to a particular territory are rendered illegitimate. This gives rise to patently unfair situations where large 'new' minorities (also sometimes referred to as 'allochthonous minorities') are denied legal protection that is available to small 'historical' minorities (also termed 'autochthonous minorities'). For instance, the linguistic and cultural rights of Germany's 50,000 Danes and 60,000 Sorbs are protected under national and European legislation (including the European Charter for Regional and Minority Languages) but no such rights are available to Germany's three million Turks. An even more bizarre situation exists in Finland, where Russian speakers constitute both a 'historical' (pre-1945) and a 'new' (post-1989) minority. The former are accorded language and cultural rights under national and European legislation while no such rights are available to the latter.[6]

The territorial principle that fixes language practices as 'in place' or 'out of place' finds its clearest expression in language maps and in language legislation. However, for it to maintain the strong hold it has on our collective belief systems the territorial principle needs to be continuously created and re-created in a wide variety of mundane discourses. In the following, we will explore some of those discourses.

LANGUAGE SEGREGATION

Powerful as the belief in the territorial principle is, linguistic diversity, particularly in urban spaces, has become increasingly difficult to ignore. Even the Belgians, who have taken such pains to assign language to territory, obviously were stumped when it came to their capital city, Brussels, which is designated the country's only bilingual territory. Linguistic diversity and social complexity are characteristics of urban spaces and divvying up this complexity into neatly contained parcels is nearly impossible. Where it has been attempted, it is usually the product of extreme political, social, or economic violence and the result is the ghetto and genocide.

However, even in the most multicultural cities pockets of segregation persist. Somewhat ironically, some of the most clearly segregated spaces in many contemporary multicultural and highly diverse cities are cemeteries. It is not unusual to find that different communities have different cemeteries and even in the absence of separate cemeteries, different communities tend to occupy different plots within one cemetery. As an example I will describe the Catholic cemetery in Tehran in some detail.

Tehran has a number of cemeteries organized by religion: Muslim, Christian, and Jewish. The Catholic cemetery is part of the large Christian Doulab Cemetery complex, where various Christian denominations are located in adjacent but walled-off compounds. About three quarters of the Catholic cemetery is known as the 'Polish cemetery' and constitutes the final resting place of almost 2,000 Polish men, women, and children who died in Tehran between 1942 and 1945.

The story of the Poles lying in Iranian soil is one of the less well-known tragedies of World War II. In 1939 the area that was then Eastern Poland and is today part of Belarus and Ukraine was annexed by the Soviets. Around 1.5 million Poles were deported from the area to camps in Siberia. The vast majority of these died in the following months under horrific circumstances. Only around 250,000 of the deported Poles are known to have survived in Siberia. These survivors were released in 1941 when Germany attacked the Soviet Union so that they could join in the war effort against the Nazis. Making their way from Siberia, around 115,000 of these survivors managed to reach Allied-occupied Iran. For a few years, the Polish community flourished in Tehran. There were Polish radio stations and newspapers and study circles were set up, such as the Institute of Iranian Studies headed by Stanisław Kościałkowski, who had been Professor of History at the University of Vilnius until his arrest in 1941. Kościałkowski even wrote a history of Polish-Iranian relations throughout the ages during his time in Tehran.[7]

However, death was ever-present in this group of weakened survivors, as the 1,869 refugee graves in the cemetery demonstrate. Each of these graves has an identical headstone inscribed with a number, the Polish abbreviation 'Ś.P.' ('świętej pamięci,' 'in memory of'), a name, the year of birth, the year of death, and the Latin abbreviation 'R.I.P.' ('requiescat in pace,' 'may s/he rest in peace').

For the majority of the survivors, their stay in Iran was temporary and they later resettled in the UK, the Americas, Africa, and Australasia. However, some also chose to stay and to rebuild their shattered lives in Iran as is evidenced by the graves in the far corner of the Polish section. There, a number of tombstones have been erected to the memory of people born in Poland who died in Tehran as recently as 2002. Most of these commemorate women who married Iranian men, as is evidenced by their mixed Polish and Persian surnames. Sadly, these are all single graves and the Iranian husbands and/or families of these women thus must lie elsewhere; maybe in Tehran's huge Behest-e Zahra Cemetery, where the city's Muslims find their final resting place. The fact that none of these graves are family graves—despite the fact that the women obviously had new families in Iran—speaks to the fact that faith and nation continue to divide in death those who were joined in life.

In addition to the divisions of faith, national divisions are also set in stone within the Catholic cemetery. Although widely known as the 'Polish cemetery' because such a large number of Poles lie there, the cemetery was started in 1855 with a mausoleum for Dr. Louis André Ernest Cloquet, a Frenchman who died prematurely while serving as personal physician to the Shah. The memorial to this Catholic was placed close to—but outside of—the Armenian cemetery. Since then Catholics from most European countries have also found their final resting place there and the cemetery's sections are more or less clearly divided into national sections.

The banal nationalism of death is most obvious in the cases of the French and Italian dead who lie in the cemetery: their embassies have taken the trouble of placing little metal French or Italian flags at the foot of each French or Italian grave. While such flags are absent from the graves of other nationals lying in Doulab, the language of the tombstones is in most cases the language of the country of birth. None of the German graves I visited, for instance, shows any sign that the person lying there must have lived a transnational life and must, to a smaller or larger degree, have been part of the fabric not only of German but also Iranian society during their lives. The inscriptions on the tombstones bear no traces of a life partly lived in Iran.

Visiting a cemetery such as the Catholic Cemetery in Tehran constitutes an object lesson set in stone about the desire of the living to inscribe the boundaries of faith, nation, and language even on those who obviously led lives that transcended those very boundaries.[8] But the territorial principle rarely manifests as set in stone as it does in cemeteries. Usually, it is discursively constituted and subject to debate and contestation. In the following we will examine debates about the territorial principle in political discourse and media and social media discourse.

DEBATING THE TERRITORIAL PRINCIPLE

Political and media debates about the relationship between language and place enjoy a particularly wide reach and are highly influential in shaping the common-sense understanding that a nation should only have one language and that linguistic diversity is detrimental to social harmony and national unity. Even states that do not have an official language (or languages) codified in their constitution in the way that France and Belgium do usually operate on the territorial principle, elevating one language and its standard variety above all others.

This is true, for instance, in the case of the USA. The belief that English is the one and only language of the USA constitutes a central aspect of the national identity as an immigrant nation: the belief is that English constitutes an important cohesive device for the melting pot nation and that using English and English only is essential for social cohesion. A famous formulation of this language ideology can be found in a 1919 speech by President Theodore Roosevelt, who said 'we have room for but one language here, and that is the English language.'[9]

Despite the strength of the one-nation-one-language ideology, those disadvantaged by this particular language ideology—immigrants from non-English speaking backgrounds who, like most adults, have difficulties learning English to such high levels to be able to fully participate—have often struggled against it and won various concessions such as Section 203 of the Voting Rights Act. Section 203 is a provision for the full participation of non-English-speaking voters in the democratic process and thus mandates that election materials need to be printed in languages other than English in districts where population thresholds of other-language speakers are reached. First enacted in 1965 to eliminate the disenfranchisement of non-English speakers, it has been controversial ever since. This is not surprising given the strength of the one-nation-one-language ideology and the fact that even a relatively small and contained measure such as Section 203 has the potential to undermine the whole ideological complex of the territorial principle. Because Section 203 is the subject of such contention, it needs to be regularly extended by Congress. The most recent extension occurred in 2006 and the congressional debate that occurred on that occasion provides excellent evidence not only of the contested nature of the territorial principle but also the ways in which it is constituted and reconstituted in interaction.[10]

During the debate, speakers repeatedly extolled speaking English as a form of civic and patriotic virtue, as Mauro Mujica, the president of the language lobby group US English, who was invited to testify, did:

> When a person steps into a voting booth, he or she is exercising the highest civic duty. Yet, at that very moment the government sends a signal that English is not really necessary to join our national political conversation. Ironically, this message will not be sent to the Spanish speaker in Burlington, Vermont or the Chinese speaker in Wichita, Kansas. It will be sent only to those who live in high enough language concentrations to trigger Section 203's requirements. In short, it will be sent to the very immigrants who are likely to live in linguistic enclaves where an English-optional lifestyle is a real possibility.[11]

Practically, doing your civic duty means engaging in the life of your community and contributing to the common good: volunteer firefighters are often seen as the ideal example of civic service. Volunteer firefighting, like most other forms of civic participation, occurs on the local level, 'in linguistic enclaves where an English-optional lifestyle is a real possibility,' if you will.

Participating in elections, too, is a civic duty—as it is a civic right. However, in contrast to volunteer firefighting, voting requires participation not in a local community but in an imagined community. Promoting English as a civic duty only makes sense if civic participation is delinked from the local and is tied exclusively to the national level.

In the process, it is not only the meaning of speaking English that is transformed but also the meaning of civic participation. From being inextricably linked to participation in the real life of a real community, it becomes individualized. This is particularly clear in those arguments that contrast 'good' immigrants with their opposites. The following example by another speaker during the debate is a case in point. Here a 'good' individual immigrant from Russia who does his duty because he speaks 'good' English is contrasted with the community of Chinatown. Chinatown residents are implicitly coded as linguistic shirkers who fail to do their linguistic and national duty:

I just recently came from San Francisco. I was in Chinatown, and we talk about the enclaves. On my way to the airport I rode with a Russian immigrant who spoke probably as good English as I, though with an accent. And I asked him about Chinatown and he said they don't speak English there. You can't live there unless you are Chinese. And in walking in the streets, I heard all the young Chinese students speaking Chinese. That may work in San Francisco, but that would not work in Iowa. In order to participate in the community, you must speak English.[12]

This quote is patently absurd: an obviously existing community group is exhorted 'to participate in the community.' The reason its absurdity is not often called out lies in the hold the territorial principle that fixes language in place has on us: we come to share the belief that English is the one and only legitimate language of the USA and that national unity allows for only one single language to be legitimate.

The power of this belief is demonstrated by an egregious example of media discourse where the choice of the 'wrong' language in a high school speech was treated as a national scandal.[13]

In May 2012 the valedictorian of Orestimba High in Newman, a city of 10,000 in central California, chose to deliver his graduation speech in Spanish. Saul Tello Jr., the seventeen-year-old valedictorian, had won the honor to deliver the graduation speech because he was the top graduating student. More than three-quarters of the students at Orestimba High are bilingual in English and Spanish and the valedictorian therefore wrote his speech in English and Spanish. When he asked the principal's permission to deliver the speech in both languages, the principal argued that a bilingual speech would take too much time and asked the valedictorian to choose one language only in order to save time. Saul Tello Jr. chose Spanish because his parents, who are first-generation migrants from Mexico, do not have much English and he wanted them to understand his speech, where he spoke about always striving to do your best, holding on to your dreams, and acknowledging those who came before you.

Small-town high school graduation speeches are normally local events and their merits are judged by the school community. It is rare for a high school graduation speech to even make it into local media. However, as Saul Tello Jr. and the principal of Orestimba High were soon to find out, flouting the territorial principle that ties English to public speech on US territory was enough to catapult Saul Tello Jr.'s five-minute speech into the national media limelight.

Conservative political commentator Bill O'Reilly, who has a popular evening show on Fox News, denounced the choice of Spanish as evidence of falling educational standards in US schools and 'this whole self-esteem craziness.' Editorials in many media outlets across the country followed suit and widely decried the speech as evidence of rudeness and lack of respect for the United States. On many of these media websites, the public had the opportunity to weigh in, too, through social commentary.[14] Many of these comments directly invoked the territorial principle as a self-evident reason why the choice of Spanish at a US high school graduation speech was 'wrong.' For instance, commentators argued that 'Bill Oreilly is 100% correct. this is America not Mexico. He should of given his speech in english not Spanish' or that 'In America we speak English and to conduct the valedictorian speech in Spanish is wrong.' Another comment, which received the highest number of likes in the debate (an indicator that this view is widely shared among contributors) read, 'This was a flagrant insult to the United States of America which is an English speaking nation.'

The fact that a trivial event such as a short graduation speech by a high school student may gain national media coverage and condemnation is evidence of the power of the territorial principle. An 'incorrect' choice is seen as a problem of such proportions that it warrants national attention.

For national media to attack the language choice of a seventeen-year-old student while speaking in his local school is grossly unfair. The overall effect of national media scrutiny, criticism, and vilification of the choice of a language other than English is to reify English as the only legitimate language in the USA. That such media debates have consequences for individual speakers of other languages is obvious from frequent reports about service denial to people using a language other than English in the public space. These include reports of a college student being detained at an US airport because he was carrying Arabic vocabulary flashcards, an Orthodox Jew being removed from a plane because he was praying in Hebrew, or a young woman being denied service in an Apple store because she was speaking in Persian to an older relative. A survey of Asian-Americans found that 12% of respondents had experienced discrimination on the basis of language in a service encounter in the past two years. This was more than those who reported that they had experienced discrimination on the basis of race.[15] We will explore the consequences of·

experiencing language discrimination in detail in Chapter Six. The key point here is that political and media debates that keep reinforcing the self-evidence and legitimacy of the territorial principle have real-life consequences for those who deviate from the ideal of imagined linguistic homogeneity, whether by choice or not.

LINGUISTIC DIVERSITY AND PERSONAL RESPONSIBILITY

A key criticism of Saul Tello Jr., his family and, in fact, the whole group of 'Hispanics' or 'Latinos' that can be found again and again in the media debate about his high school graduation speech is the fact that they 'choose' not to speak English. As one Facebook commentator put it, 'If You choose not to learn english You dont belong here.' The reason for this 'choice against English' was widely attributed to lack of personal effort. Another comment sums up this view: 'You are just lazy if you don't learn it [=English].'

This section explores the issue of choice in linguistic diversity and asks whether people who deviate from a society's linguistic ideal do so willfully. In other words, are people whose linguistic practices are considered diverse partly to blame for their deviant choices? Victim blaming has always been an aspect of unjust regimes and I certainly would not wish to argue that linguistic subordination is defensible if speakers choose to differ from a society's imagined linguistic norm. Rather, the argument of this section will be that underestimating the effort involved in language learning, ascribing linguistic diversity to choice, and blaming certain speakers for their 'personal linguistic choices' is another central discourse through which the subordination of linguistic diversity is achieved.

We know that Saul Tello Jr. made a choice because he prepared his speech in both languages and we can assume that he could have delivered his speech with equal fluency in English because he would not have been the top student in a California high school if his English was not good. Saul Tello Jr. is bilingual in English and Spanish,

44

and to assume that he spoke in Spanish because he had not learned English and was lazy is obviously fallacious.

But what about his parents? The valedictorian claimed that he chose Spanish because he wanted to honor his parents, first-generation migrants from Mexico, who have little English. Have they been too lazy to learn English? Does a Facebook commenter such as this one have a point?

> Hell, if I can sit on a ferry boat and then a bus for 6 hours and learn enough French to get around Paris for 4 days, you can learn enough English in a few years to figure out your son's Valedictorian speech.

The idea that migrants who fail to learn the national language do so because they are too lazy, lack the will power required, or simply cannot be bothered is certainly not limited to US language debates. A 2011 German public awareness campaign, for instance, exhorted migrants and their descendants to speak German. The campaign's clever slogan 'Raus mit der Sprache!' (which literally translates as 'Out with language!' and means 'Speak! Confess! Out with it!') accompanied images of so-called German language ambassadors. These were German TV personalities, sports stars, or celebrities with a migrant background who posed with their tongue sticking out. The exposed tongue was painted in black, red and yellow, the colors of the national flag.

The campaign is based on a number of assumptions similar to those apparent in the debate about Spanish in the USA. To begin with, there is the assumption that migrants are unaware of the fact that most educational and job opportunities in Germany require German, and that therefore they need to be informed of that fact through public service advertising. The second assumption is that few migrants and their children learn German and, third, that they fail to do so by choice. Migrants are assumed to be too lazy to learn German, as is made explicit by one of the language ambassadors in a tabloid interview:

Q: Why is there so little desire to learn German?

A: Many people are too lazy. [. . .] I hope the campaign motivates some people to attend a language school. All you have to do is go to the campaign's homepage. There's a great database and it's easy to choose a school.

Q: And that's enough?

A: You can't make it any easier than that. All we can do is get people to think and then we have to say: 'Ok, you've got to do the rest by yourself.'[16]

Unfortunately, language learning is not as easy as choosing a language school from a database. The consensus in applied linguistics is that language learning takes a long time and that the precise duration and final outcome as measured in proficiency level are almost impossible to predict as they depend on many factors, most of which are outside of the control of an individual language learner, such as age, level of education, aptitude, teaching program, language proximity, or access to interactional opportunities.

Language learning is not at all a simple task and most people readily forget that it takes about twelve years to learn your first language. The first five or six years from birth are devoted to acquiring oral fluency and then another six years or so are needed to learn how to read and write, to acquire the academic and textual conventions of a language, and also to extend grammatical structures (e.g., the English passive is rare in spoken language and normally acquired through schooling), expand vocabulary (a process that continues throughout life whenever we enter a new field and acquire new specialist knowledge with its own terminology), and refine pragmatic conventions (e.g., young children tend to be oblivious to the rules for formal and informal forms of address).

First-language acquisition may take more time than you thought but its outcomes are relatively uniform (under the condition that schooling is universal in a population). By contrast, the outcomes of second-language learning and the time it takes to achieve those outcomes are much more variable. The US Foreign Service Institute

(FSI) estimates that it will take an adult learner with average language aptitude about 480 hours of instruction to achieve intermediate proficiency in an easy language (easy from the perspective of an English speaker, such as Dutch, French, Italian, or Spanish) and about 1,320 hours to achieve the same level of proficiency in a difficult language (difficult, again, from the perspective of an English speaker, such as Arabic, Chinese, Japanese, or Korean).

The Foreign Service Institute estimates are of hours of instruction that their clientele of future diplomats and other US service personnel preparing for missions abroad, i.e., highly educated foreign language learners, will need. Other than through formal language instruction, a language can also be learned informally, as is the case in the immersion contexts migrants typically find themselves in. These immersion contexts in themselves differ widely, as we will explore in the next section. The best estimates we have for immersion learners to acquire academic proficiency in a second language is four years and more, where 'and more' may well mean never.[17]

Putting a number on how long it takes to learn a new language is a popular exercise and estimates put forward range from the six hours mentioned by the Facebook commentator quoted above to the '10,000-hour-rule' provided by some Canadian educators. Curriculum designers, program developers and policy makers—just as language learners themselves—generally prefer to go by lower numbers. The UK government estimates that migrants will need 360 hours to reach 'fluency' in English, while the Australian government used to work on the assumption that it takes 1,765 hours but changed that estimate to 510 hours in the 1990s.[18]

How is it possible that estimates of how long it takes to learn a language can vary so widely?

To begin with, one needs to keep in mind that such estimates are often not based on the linguistic evidence but on practical considerations such as how many hours a typical course offered by a teaching institute takes or how much funding is available to cover the cost of a particular program. From a linguistic perspective, there are two problems with attempting to put a figure on how long it takes to learn a language: one is related to what is meant by 'fluency' and the other to learner variables.

'Fluency' is often thought of as conversational fluency—the ability to have an everyday conversation. Young learners in particular can achieve conversational fluency quite quickly. However, the conversational ease of young learners often fools us into overlooking that they may have continued difficulty with the kind of context-reduced and cognitively demanding language that is necessary to succeed in school. 'Children's second language acquisition *appears* superior largely because the structures and vocabulary they need for adequate communication are so much simpler than those required of adults.'[19] Conversely, the proficiency of post-puberty learners is often misjudged because even high-proficiency post-puberty learners tend to retain a 'foreign' accent.

Just as the fluency of children and adults is judged by different yardsticks, fluency will seem different for different people and different contexts. To be 'fluent' while shopping is different from being 'fluent' when undertaking university studies; to be 'fluent' as a supermarket check-out operator is different from being 'fluent' as a university student. Overall, the key point here is that 'fluency' means different things to different people and while we are often all too eager to pass judgment on the proficiency of those who have traces of complex language learning trajectories in their repertoires, our judgments are rarely particularly valid or reliable.

The problem that defining the endpoint of language learning is well-nigh impossible is compounded by the fact that a definite judgment on how much effort an individual will require to get to some point on the spectrum that is acceptable to those who pass judgment presents a problem of similar magnitude. Age makes a difference: adolescents and young adults have been found to learn faster than older adults. Prior education makes a difference: high school graduates have been found to learn faster than those who have not learned how to read and write in their first language. Socioeconomic status makes a difference: those who have the time and resources to set aside for dedicated language learning have been found to learn faster than those who struggle to make ends meet. Gender makes a difference: men in employment have been found to learn faster than stay-at-home housewives. Race makes a difference: European-looking students in Australian high schools have been found to learn faster than Asian-looking students. Religion makes a difference: Christian converts have been found to learn faster after conversion. Sheer luck makes a difference: learners with a caring landlady have been found to learn faster than those whose accommodation arrangements were less favorable.[20]

The list could go on and on. The general point is that your success at language learning is related to who you are and which hand you have been dealt in life. The factors listed above—age, prior education, socioeconomic status, gender, race, religion, luck—are by and large outside the control of the individual. What second-language learning research shows above all is that learning another language is not an easy feat. It requires a considerable investment of resources and it makes a huge difference whether you are learning in a supportive community or one that rejects you. The ultimate outcome of second-language learning efforts is not purely an act of willpower or the result of the learner's personal choices.

As Brian Barry explains in *Why Social Justice Matters*, a distinction between the deserving and the undeserving poor has long been a feature of capitalism but was tempered throughout most of the twentieth century by the arrangements put in place by the New Deal in the USA and strong welfare states in Western Europe.[21] Today, the distinction has made a comeback in the guise of neoliberal exhortations to exert 'personal responsibility' and has served to justify the widening inequalities of recent years. Mostly exhortations to take personal responsibility have targeted poor people but the wider abdication of social responsibility can also be seen in widely held views about the obesity epidemic that is gripping much of the world and, our focus here, in discourses about language learning.

Blaming individuals for having made choices outside their control is patently unjust. Not only is the stigma of lack of willpower and laziness unjust in itself but it also has unjust consequences. First, it makes inequality and discrimination seem fair as we can blame homelessness on the poor choices a person has made, obesity on a person's lack of fortitude, and inability to understand a speech in English on a person's laziness. Second, the shame that comes from victim blaming keeps those affected from seeking effective remediation and generally makes positive intervention more difficult.[22]

GRASSROOTS LANGUAGE LEARNING

In the previous section we learned that migrants are often blamed for their 'diverse' repertoires and are stigmatized for failing to meet the imagined ideal of a particular standard language. While we usually do not think much of it if foreign language learning in the classroom is unsuccessful, there is a special stigma attached to failing to learn a language in an immersion context. Immersion learners who fall short of the ideal are often accused not only of laziness but of self-isolation, of a failure to embrace their new community, of duplicitous disloyalty.

However, the immersion contexts that are conjured up in these discourses are more often than not imagined ideals, too. In real life, immersion learners do not normally encounter an army of language teachers who would like nothing better than to strike up helpful conversations with strangers that will allow those strangers to practice their communicative skills and this or that linguistic form. Usually, encounters in immersion contexts are with colleagues, employers, or service staff, that is people whose interest it is to get things done with words and not to act as language teachers. As likely as not, such encounters may leave learners frustrated and discouraged rather than providing the rich learning opportunities they are imagined to be. Ethnographic research has copiously documented that simply spending time with speakers of the target language does not necessarily result in language learning. For instance, local students have been found to be reluctant to engage with international students; local colleagues prefer to spend break times amongst themselves rather than include language learner colleagues who may be seeking language practice opportunities; and employers may prefer to assign language learners jobs that do not require interactions rather than jobs that would provide language practice opportunities.[23]

The repertoires that language learners have access to in immersion contexts can be quite different from those imagined, as a study of language practices in Guangzhou's Africa Town shows.[24] 'Africa Town' is the name of two suburbs in Guangzhou where the largest number of Africans in Asia resides. In 2011, there were around 20,000 Africans registered there. The number of Africans estimated to come there for short business visits and those without a legal status was assumed to be about ten times that number.

Africans come to Guangzhou to trade: at one end of the spectrum there is the so-called 'luggage bag trade,' which involves an African community pooling their financial resources. A member of the group then travels to China and purchases as many goods as possible. These are then shipped back home and sold for a profit. At the other end of the spectrum of African traders in Guangzhou are more established people who run their own shops, catering to bulk buyers, including the luggage bag traders.

The retailers of Africa Town include not only Africans but also rural Chinese migrants whose status may be as semi-legal as that of their African peers if they do not have an urban *hukou* (户口; 'residence permit') for Guangzhou.

English, as the global language of business, plays an important role in Africa Town. So does Mandarin as the national language. Additionally, Cantonese, the local language, and a number of other Chinese vernaculars are widely used in Africa Town, as are a number of African languages, including colonial languages such as French.

So, there are a lot of diverse repertoires being used in Africa Town but the preeminent power codes are English and Mandarin. The rich diversity of repertories characteristic of communication in Africa Town has been described as grassroots multilingualism or as fragmented, truncated, and incomplete repertoires.[25]

However, access to formal instruction in these power codes is rare and Africa Towners have to find other ways to learn whatever they can of these languages. As a result, a contact variety, which locals call 'Chinglish,' has developed. This kind of 'Chinglish' (not to be confused with unidiomatic Chinese English signage Westerners like to make fun of and which will be explored in Chapter Seven) is characterized by simple English vocabulary and sentence structures, repetition of key words, the mixing of Mandarin expressions, and the influence of Chinese syntax.

For example, Ibrahim, an urban middle-class male university graduate from Conakry, the capital of Guinea, mostly uses Chinglish, in addition to English, French, Susu, Pular, Mandinka, and Arabic. However, his impressive multilingual repertoire is of relatively limited value without access to Chinese, as he explains: 'Some factory they speak no French, they speak no English. So no Chinese, no business!'[26] However, immediate financial pressures in conjunction with a restrictive visa regime meant that his dream to attend formal Chinese language classes was beyond his grasp.

Ibrahim's immersion experience in Guangzhou is incredibly rich and diverse but the 'target language' he is predominantly immersed in is 'Chinglish' rather than Standard Chinese. Although Ibrahim is engaging in a lot of language learning, there is a mismatch between the 'target language' he is immersed in and the imagined 'target language' that he should be learning. Access to a power code such as Standard Chinese depends upon resources Ibrahim does not have: in order to study Chinese formally, he would need money, time, and legal status. The structural marginalization of the inhabitants of Africa Town, where money, time, and legal status are in short supply, results in their linguistic marginalization, too.

JUDGING SPEAKERS

Above I argued that stigmatizing the repertoires of second-language speakers is unjust because the yardsticks by which their 'fluency' or otherwise are measured in everyday judgments of their language are highly flawed. Another reason these everyday judgments about language proficiency are so problematic is related to the fact that language is never judged in isolation from the speaker. As the sociologist Pierre Bourdieu has pointed out 'speech always owes a major part of its value to the value of the person who utters it.'[27]

This means that people who are not expected to speak a particular language (well) may be heard not to speak that language (well) irrespective of their actual proficiency. For instance, Asians are often stereotyped as having low proficiency in English. Consequently, they may be heard not to speak English well even if they actually do. In a by-now-classic experiment conducted in the 1980s at a university in Florida researchers audio-recorded a science lecture aimed at undergraduate students.[28] The speaker on the tape was a native speaker of American English speaking in a standard American-English accent. The lecture was then played to two different groups of undergraduate students. In one case, the lecture was accompanied by the picture of a Caucasian woman and in the other it was accompanied by the picture of an Asian woman. Thus, the impression was created that a Caucasian woman was speaking in one instance and an Asian woman in another. Both women were shown in the same pose and had been rated as similarly attractive. So, we have one audio-recorded lecture spoken in Standard American English and two different visual signals: a Caucasian lecturer versus an Asian lecturer. The students who saw the Asian lecturer heard a 'foreign,' 'non-native,' or 'Asian' accent although none was present in the auditory signal. What is more, the perceived accent of the perceived Asian lecturer led to reduced comprehension. The students rated the quality of the lecture and the quality of their learning experience much lower when they thought it was delivered by a speaker with a foreign accent.

Stereotypes about the language proficiency of some groups can be so strong that deviations from the expectations may be taken as evidence that someone is not actually who they claim to be. This was for instance the case in an Australian media debate about a Sri Lankan asylum seeker who was alleged not to be a genuine refugee because he spoke English 'too well.'[29]

In October 2009 a patrol vessel of the Australian Customs Service intercepted a boat with seventy-eight asylum seekers from Sri Lanka on their way to Australia. The asylum seekers were being transferred to a detention center in Indonesia but refused to disembark for about a month, demanding resettlement in Australia. The asylum seekers' chief negotiator was widely discredited in the media on the grounds that he was using an English name (Alex), that he was 'well-spoken' and spoke 'English with an American accent.' None of these were expected of an asylum seeker. The following excerpt from a radio interview with presenter Mark Colvin provides an example:

MARK COLVIN: And the High Commissioner also said, I'll quote 'Alex's accent is quite a distinct American accent. It is not the accent of a Sri Lankan Tamil.'

ALEX: Does the Sri Lankan High Commissioner feel that people in Sri Lanka don't have American accents or British accents? Is there not international schools in Sri Lanka? Is there not people that do accent training for call centres and various other customer care services?

MARK COLVIN: So you trained in a call centre?

ALEX: Pardon me? I was trained in a call centre for an American call centre.[30]

In another media interview Alex took issue with the way in which his high level of English proficiency had come to discredit his claim to refugee status:

The spokesman of the group [. . .] has expressed surprise over the fact that how his American accent English could become a reason for the rejection of his refugee plea. 'Just because I speak English, and I was educated in an American boys mission school in my home town, and then I finished my BA, and then I finished my MBA in India, so does that mean I am not a refugee?'[31]

All the asylum seekers involved in the standoff, including Alex, were later found to be genuine refugees by the UNHCR and were resettled in a variety of countries.

The media story about Alex' accent being too American for him to be a genuine refugee shows yet another facet of the discursive subordination of linguistic diversity: debates about linguistic diversity are rarely concerned with purely linguistic matters but are about speakers. In making everyday judgments about linguistic diversity—which as we know by now most people are not very good at—media discourses create and recreate social boundaries. When we make everyday judgments about the language of Mexican immigrants in the USA, the language of migrants and their descendants in Germany, or the language of asylum seekers in Australia, what we are really doing is drawing boundaries between legitimate and illegitimate members of our communities. Judgments about language are ultimately judgments about speakers. Not only are these judgments about who is in and who is out; they also provide justifications for social boundaries when a person's linguistic repertoire becomes tied to moral worth.

LINGUISTIC DIVERSITY AND MORAL WORTH

As we saw above, multilingual repertoires are often associated with the stigma of laziness, the stigma of failure to take personal responsibility. In addition to the linguistic stigma directly related to language repertoires, language choice can also be constructed to undermine the moral worth of multilingual populations in other ways.

This is the case when language choice in instructions and prohibitions singles out a particular group as likely offenders. For instance,

I have collected a corpus of signage in Australian hotel rooms: information about the services available in the hotel, room service menus, instructions what to do in case of a fire or other emergency, and so forth. The vast majority of this signage is monolingual in English. In the minority of multilingual hotel room signage, Chinese figures rarely. Therefore, a Chinese-English sign (with Chinese above English to indicate priority) that I collected in a Sydney hotel room in 2006 stands out in my corpus because of its bilingualism and its language choice. The sign is a non-smoking sign and the English version reads 'This is a non-smoking room. An A$400 fine will apply for smoking in the room.'[32]

There can be no doubt that the sign is intended to send a message particularly to Chinese guests. The sign thus does double duty: not only does it alert guests to the prohibition against smoking, but it also positions Chinese guests as likely offenders.

Proponents of linguistic justice often make the facile assumption that multilingual signs by their very nature are more inclusive than monolingual ones. However, it all depends on the context. It is true that a sign such as the Chinese-English 'no smoking' sign includes Chinese readers as potential recipients of the message. However, at the same time, the sign excludes Chinese readers from polite society by singling them out as likely transgressors.

The ways in which signage directed at linguistically diverse populations can serve to impugn their good character is even more obvious in the next example.

As part of my work, I have over the years visited many English language schools across Australia. English language schools are obviously institutions characterized by a high level of linguistic and cultural diversity: many of the people from around the world who come to Australia for whatever reason—as new migrants, international students, or working-holiday makers—end up spending some of their initial time in Australia attending an English language school.

In many of these institutions I have discovered toilets to be flashpoints for intergroup tensions. This is because conventions for toilet use and for cleaning yourself after you have used the toilet differ around the globe. In Australia, toilets are designed for the user to sit down on and paper is provided for the user to clean herself (my observations are restricted to female toilets). Sit-down toilets are normal in western societies, even if, in public toilets, many women prefer to squat over them for hygienic reasons. Indeed, squat toilets where the user squats over a toilet bowl in the ground are the preferred design in most parts of the world. The Australian preference for toilet paper as a means of cleaning yourself after toilet use is not universal, either, and many societies have a preference for using water for this purpose. There are many more variations, of course, but the variations that matter for the present discussion are the ones between the provision of sit-down toilets and toilet paper, and the absence of squat toilets and water hoses.

The result of this one-size-fits-all approach is that some people will use the equipment provided in ways other than intended. People used to squat toilets may climb up on the toilet seat, place their feet on the toilet seat and use it as a squat toilet in that way. This can be dangerous as the toilet seat and/or bowl may break under the unusual distribution of weight and it usually has unpleasant consequences as the user may miss the hole, which is too small for this kind of use, or leave print marks of their shoes on the toilet seat. People used to cleaning themselves with water may fill a bottle, cup, or whatever other vessel is at hand in the sink and bring them into the cubicle. Again, the results can be unpleasant as some of the water may end up splashing here and there and the vessels are often left behind cluttering the cubicle. In sum, using the equipment provided in ways other than those they are designed for is problematic for the user and, even more so, for the next user. Furthermore, problems accumulate as the person who finds a public toilet slightly dirty will be less motivated to be careful themselves and the toilet may become quite quickly rather messy indeed.

Public toilet use constitutes a form of social contract: each user leaves it as they found it and considers not only their own needs and interests but those of the next user as well. In Asia and Europe, there are often public toilet attendants, who monitor user behavior and ensure cleanliness. This is not so in Australia, and in diverse institutions such as English language schools the social contract between public toilet users often breaks down. This can cause a lot of anger, frustration, and scapegoating of particular groups as is evidenced from many conversations I have had with administrators, teachers, and students. It is also evidenced from a corpus of toilet signage I have collected.[33]

For instance, in 2007 I recorded no less than nineteen individual pieces of signage in the female toilet of a suburban Sydney English language school catering mostly to new migrants from Africa and the Middle East. Five of these were located in each individual cubicle and the remaining fourteen were cluttered around the common wash area where sinks, a mirror, a paper towel dispenser, and a hand dryer were located. These signs contained a range of instructions, assertions, and prohibitions. The signage in the stalls consisted of instructions where to place toilet paper, tampons and sanitary pads, and other rubbish. Two of these signs were in English and two were in Arabic. In each case, one sign was text only and the other a combination of pictograms and text. The fifth sign was trilingual in Arabic, Chinese, and Vietnamese. In the wash area outside the toilet stalls, the wall on both sides of the sink and mirror was littered with a veritable plethora of bathroom etiquette: the disposal instructions featured in the stalls were repeated and there were also prohibitions against smoking, instructions to wash hands, a statement about the proper use of the sink and the towels ('for hands only'), and a prohibition against taking or leaving 'water, cups, or bottles.' As regards the language choice in these signs, seven used English text only, four English and pictograms, and one each used a pictogram, Arabic, Vietnamese, and trilingual Arabic-Chinese-Vietnamese.

Signage such as this is suggestive of a passive-aggressive running battle between different groups of users of this toilet. The language choices on the signage also suggest that Arabic-speaking women in particular and, to a lesser degree, Vietnamese- and Chinese-speaking women are singled out as offenders against toilet etiquette and as violators of the social contract of public toilet use.

Having to share a toilet with people who leave footprints on the toilet seat or water all over the floor is certainly aggravating. But is there a better way to reduce the incidence of these problems than plastering our public toilets with—more or less effective—signage that impugns the good character of specific user groups? Let's look at toilets in private schools, malls, and airports across Asia and the Middle East. Many of these institutions offer users the choice between sit-down toilets and squat toilets. And the provision of both paper and a water hose allows users flexibility in the way they wish to clean themselves. In Australia, too, the provision of different types of toilets in public spaces is, in fact, not uncommon. Institutions are required by law to provide toilets for the disabled. Additionally, malls often voluntarily provide mixed-sex family facilities (to cater for fathers with girls or mothers with boys) and miniature sit-down toilets for children. These examples prove that there are few practical obstacles to redesigning public toilets for an inclusive society.

Offering toilet choice in a diverse society would solve a concrete practical problem both for people who do not share dominant toileting habits as well as those with dominant toileting habits who would no longer have to put up with the unpleasantness created by improper toilet use. In addition to solving a practical problem, toilet choice would also send the inclusive symbolic message that, in a liberal democratic society, sitting or squatting on the toilet and cleaning yourself with paper or water are equally valid.

REMAKING LANGUAGE LEARNERS

At present, the symbolic message sent by no-choice toilet provision and toilet signage such as the one I have described above is one of exclusion. The message is that sitting down on the toilet and wiping yourself with paper is the only way—and hence the right and legitimate way—of doing things in Australia. If that is not how you prefer to toilet, then that turns you into an illegitimate offender against the social contract. When public institutions only provide sit-down toilets and toilet paper, they leave some people no choice other than to assimilate or transgress.

The effort to combine language instruction with personal transformation is not new. The toilet signage of Australian English language schools I have described here can be understood as an attempt to teach not only English but also to transform learners into new kinds of people by changing their toileting habits. Similarly, English language instruction during the Americanization movement in the early twentieth century also attempted to transform immigrants' diets and housekeeping habits. In yet another example, English language programs for Hispanic migrants in the USA are combined with parenting skills instructions.[34]

The deficit framing of migrant speakers that is apparent in impugning their toileting habits, their diet, or their parenting is unjust in at least two different ways. First, to impugn the good character and moral worth of language learners constitutes an unjust representation. Second, highly constrained institutional practices that allow only one way of doing things make it impossible for some people to do well. Above I argued that the provision of only one toileting option sets some people up for 'failure.' The same is true for language proficiency: inflexible communicative practices can distort proficiency and set up some speakers for failure.

As an example, let's consider the following incident reported by a court volunteer in an Australian Magistrates Court. Court volunteers help to work as a liaison between courts and laypeople who may find themselves before the court for the first time in their lives and may have little experience with the justice system. In a radio show about court volunteers, the following report appeared.[35] A court volunteer was mingling in the foyer of a Magistrates Court with various people waiting there and approached an Asian-looking couple to ask them why they were in court. The couple explained that they had been summoned for unpaid fines on their car. They also explained that they had sold the car prior to the fines being issued and showed the paperwork that they had brought along to document their innocence.

While the report does not comment in any way on the language proficiency of the couple, it is obvious that they were capable of explaining their situation in an informal one-on-one conversation with a stranger. Now, let's hear from the court volunteer what happened when the couple were asked to explain the exact same set of circumstances a few minutes later to the magistrate:

> When the magistrate actually asked the man if he had anything he wanted to say, just because of stress and I think the language barrier, he actually just stood up and said, 'No.' And so the magistrate then actually just started to make a judgement on orders as far as what he was going to have to do as far as paying back all these fines. And I thought, oh gosh, what am I going to do here? And so actually just said, 'Excuse me, Your Honour, but I'm really concerned that because of a language barrier you are not actually being advised of some critical information.' I should say, [. . .] we don't actually jump up like that on many occasions, but in that situation I just thought, well, we couldn't let that go.

In the example we see one and the same person having the English language proficiency to explain a problem in one context and lacking the exact same level of proficiency in another. The example thus complicates the notion of linguistic proficiency in yet another way: we have already seen that 'fluency' means different things to different people and that reaching a particular level of fluency is inextricably linked to the learner's identity and the ways in which that identity is (de)valorized in the target society. This example shows that, additionally, 'proficiency' is a function of inclusive or exclusive arrangements. Where a one-on-one informal conversation allowed this particular speaker to succeed, a formal context where the speaker had to speak in front of a group resulted in failure. Social arrangements that only allow for one type of performance to be valid—be it sit-down toilets or formal hearings in a Magistrates Court—while rendering all others invalid are obviously unjust.

SUMMARY

This chapter has explored the discursive processes through which linguistic diversity is dissimulated and subordinated. Linguistic diversity is rendered invisible through the territorial principle, which is inscribed in stone in the cemeteries of most multicultural cities and which is created and re-created—but also contested—in political and media debates. The territorial principle not only obscures the actual diversity of everyday language, but also, and with greater social consequences, sets some speakers up as legitimate 'default' members of a society while excluding others. Those who are being excluded, delegitimized, and subordinated are usually mobile speakers whose 'historical' ties to a territory are contested. One discourse about language that is central to their subordination is the construction of language learning as a matter of personal responsibility, where language learning is conceived of as a relatively easy and banal undertaking, and failure to measure up to an imaginary linguistic norm as a sign of laziness or self-isolation.

It is in debates about language that linguistic repertoires become markers of inclusion or exclusion, of legitimacy or illegitimacy. Language is ideally suited as a marker of distinction because unlike most other key bases for social stratification (e.g., class, gender, race) it is relatively fluid and—seemingly—not inscribed in the body. The discursive construction of language learning as an individual responsibility, however, conflicts with the experience of the relatively static linguistic habitus of adults. More so than most bases of social stratification, language thus dissimulates its operation.

As we have seen, it is not possible to draw a principled distinction between subordinating ways of speaking and/or subordinating speakers—one always also achieves the other. The injustices of cultural domination that are apparent in these processes are compounded in inflexible communicative spaces that institute the inequality between dominant and subordinated speakers. In the following chapters we will explore the results of linguistic subordination in specific domains.

Chapter 4

Linguistic Diversity at Work

The previous chapters have identified the general processes of linguistic stratification, subordination, and discrimination in diverse societies. This and the following chapters now go on to explore these general processes in specific domains that are known to be central to social justice. We begin with an exploration of linguistic barriers to adequate employment: how does linguistic diversity intersect with social justice at work?

In 2006, two years before the global financial crisis, the United Nations noted that '[e]mployment and work opportunities [. . .] have deteriorated, in both quantitative and qualitative terms, for the majority of people in the world.' The United Nations expressed particular concern about the fact that '[s]eemingly everywhere, wages and other forms of remuneration have become increasingly unequal within and between sectors, communities, countries and regions, and between nationals and immigrants, the skilled and the less skilled, and urban and rural residents.'[1] It is painfully obvious that since then, globally, access to adequate employment has continued to deteriorate while stark inequalities in opportunities for paid and fairly remunerated work have increased. This is true even in liberal democracies with relatively strong economies and meritocratic access. In these societies the greater vulnerability of some groups to unemployment and underemployment is relatively obvious and well-understood: youths, the unskilled or low-skilled, and those with a migrant background are overrepresented in the unemployment statistics. But how does language fit into the puzzle?

There are a number of widely held assumptions about the relationship between linguistic diversity and work: that migrants cannot find jobs at their level because their English (or other national language) is not good enough to enter the labor market; that linguistic diversity is a principal reason for problems in the workplace; that employers unscrupulously exploit those who do not speak the national language (well); or that the best way for migrants to improve their linguistic proficiency is at work. All of these assumptions contain a kernel of truth but, at the same time, are facile and overlook key aspects of the complex intersections of language and un- and underemployment in diverse societies. We will now explore these intersections.

LANGUAGE PROFICIENCY AS A BARRIER TO EMPLOYMENT

One of the most widespread assumptions around linguistic diversity and work is that it is lack of proficiency in the language of the destination country that constitutes the main barrier migrants face to finding work. Hence, policy makers as well as migrants themselves assume learning the language will bring employment. While it is obvious that proficiency in the dominant language is advantageous, these advantages accrue differentially and language proficiency in itself does not necessarily provide access to adequate employment, as this section shows.

The basic assumption that lack of language proficiency is the principal barrier to employment faced by migrants is easily disproved. As evidence let's examine what might be considered a natural field experiment in respect of the link between English language proficiency and settlement success as measured by employment outcomes in Australia.[2] The 'natural field experiment' is that of Iraqi translators and interpreters who worked for the Australian army during the 2003 invasion of Iraq and who were resettled in Australia when Australian forces withdrew from Iraq in 2008. In 2011, three years after they had been granted permanent residency in Australia, their employment outcomes were surveyed by a local newspaper, the *Sydney Morning Herald*.

As part of the program, 557 adult Iraqis were resettled in Australia. These included the translators and interpreters themselves as well as their family members. Two hundred twenty-three of these were surveyed for the study. According to conventional wisdom, finding employment and settling in Australia should have been a breeze for these people: as translators and interpreters, they were obviously highly proficient in English. They all had high levels of education: 135 of the 223 surveyed had completed tertiary education and all had prior experience in their profession. Furthermore, through their service they had obviously demonstrated their commitment to Australia.

As it turned out, the employment outcomes of this group of model migrants were no different from those who are so often exhorted by politicians and the media to learn English, to get an education, and to embrace Australian values so that they can find a job. After three years in Australia only nine out of 223 former Iraqi army translators and interpreters were in full-time employment. And only one single person of these was employed in their area of expertise. Thus, for this group, the Australian national unemployment rate of only 4.9% in 2011 was turned on its head and more or less constituted their rate of employment.

The personal testimony of the people interviewed for the story was heartbreaking. They spoke about how they could not return to Iraq, where they had seen their colleagues killed because of their work for the Australian troops and where they feared their names could still be found on the execution lists of terror commandos. At the same time, they spoke about seeing their life, skills, and self-esteem wasting away in Australia, where they survived by relying on welfare. One interviewee, a 28-year-old chemical engineer, said that 'coming to Australia was the worst decision of my life.'

The example clearly demonstrates that the assumption of a straightforward relationship between English language proficiency and access to the job market is overly simplistic. What it does show is that migrants' alleged language deficiencies can serve to hide systemic barriers to employment.[3] Obscuring systemic barriers through a focus on alleged individual language deficiencies is one language-related injustice when it comes to the operation of the labor market. However, are there others where language works more directly as a barrier to employment? There are two different ways of looking at this: one relates to assumptions about linguistic proficiency rather than actual language proficiency, that is, employers assume that a candidate with a migrant background might not speak the national language well and therefore exclude them already at the point of screening applications. The second perspective relates to intercultural communication and the fact that things can go wrong linguistically at the interview stage.

WHAT'S IN A NAME?

Do assumptions about the linguistic proficiency of a particular group constitute a more powerful barrier than any actual evidence about the linguistic proficiency of a particular individual applicant? In other words, is linguistic stereotyping to blame for the poor labor market outcomes of some groups? Were the Iraqi translators and interpreters never given an individual chance because potential employers simply assumed that the English language proficiency of Arabs is limited? Evidence for this hypothesis comes from experimental studies investigating the response rates to fictitious CVs and job applications. In this research design all details in the CV (education, qualifications, prior experience, etc.) are kept constant except for the applicant's name. The names that are assigned to the fictitious applicants are strongly associated with a particular ethnic group.

Studies with this design have found that job applicants with a name that suggests membership in a non-dominant ethnic group are less likely to receive a response or be invited for interview than candidates with a name that suggests membership in the dominant ethnic group. For instance, in a 2009 Australian study almost 5,000 fictitious applications were sent in response to ads for entry-level positions in wait-staffing, data entry, customer service, and sales. The fictitious applicants, whose high-school education was indicated to have been completed in Australia, were assigned Anglo-Saxon, Chinese, Indigenous, Italian, or Middle Eastern names. Applicants with Chinese and Middle Eastern names were least likely to be called back and invited for interview. Applicants with Indigenous names also suffered from a statistically significant level of discrimination while candidates with Anglo-Saxon and Italian names had similarly high callback rates. A similar Western Australian study comparing accountant job applicants with Middle Eastern and Anglo-Saxon names reached much the same conclusions, as did a German study with Turkish and German names.[4]

Converse evidence can be found from studies that compare the labor market outcomes of migrants from a particular ethnic group who changed their names with those who did not. Anglicizing stigmatized ethnic names is often considered typical of an earlier era of immigration when assimilation prevailed. In his book *The American Language*, which was first published in 1919, the linguist H. L. Mencken famously observed that European immigrants were likely to give up their distinctive names in America for 'protective coloration' in order to escape 'linguistic hostility' and 'social enmity':

> [. . .] more important than this purely linguistic hostility, there is a deeper social enmity, and it urges the immigrant to change his name with even greater force. For a hundred years past all the heaviest and most degrading labor of the United States has been done by successive armies of foreigners, and so a concept of inferiority has come to be attached to mere foreignness. [. . .] This disdain tends to pursue an immigrant with extraordinary

rancor when he bears a name that is unmistakably foreign and hence difficult to the native, and open to his crude burlesque. Moreover, the general feeling penetrates the man himself, particularly if he be ignorant, and he comes to believe that his name is not only a handicap, but also intrinsically discreditable—that it wars subtly upon his worth and integrity. [. . .] The immigrant, in a time of extraordinary suspicion and difficulty, tried to get rid of at least one handicap.[5]

It is certainly the case that Americanizing their names paid off for European immigrants to the USA in the 1930s. A recent comparison of the earnings of those who did or did not Americanize their names during that period found that a name change was indeed associated with earnings' gains of at least 14%.[6]

Similar findings pertain to a more recent group of immigrants to Sweden. There, a 2009 study found that Middle Eastern and Slavic migrants to Sweden who changed their names in the 1990s obtained a substantial increase in labor earnings over similarly qualified migrants from the same origin groups who did not change their name to a Swedish or neutral name (a 'neutral' name is one that is not particularly associated with any particular ethnic or national group).[7]

Being stereotyped as unlikely to fit into a workplace for which a candidate is well-qualified because of assumptions about linguistic proficiency or, more generally, cultural fit, is obviously discriminatory, and the introduction of anonymized CVs has been suggested as one way to overcome this disadvantage. Yet, it is still only one small piece of the linguistic-barriers-to-employment puzzle and we will now explore what it means to perform fluently in a job interview.

JOB INTERVIEWS

In the 2007 short film *The Applicant*, produced by a group of Sudanese Australians,[8] we see a black African man conscientiously preparing for a job interview as a computer engineer. He puts on a formal suit, a tie, and, after a last look at his immaculate appearance in the mirror, makes his way to the interview. When he is shown into the interview room, his prospective employer, a sloppily clad white man, cannot hide his surprise at the fact that the candidate whose excellent résumé he has before him should turn out to be African. The applicant and the interviewer exchange a few formalities and the conversation soon peters out. The applicant just sits there becoming increasingly fidgety and nervous while the interviewer repeatedly thumbs through the résumé, throws a bouncy ball and, after minutes of uncomfortable silence, eventually says, 'Sorry, mate, this is not going to work.' In a final shot, which is set weeks or months later, we see the interviewer despairing over a computer problem when the former applicant, now dressed in a cleaner's uniform and all but invisible to the white man, comes into the office and surreptitiously fixes the computer issue.

The film is a powerful artistic expression of racial discrimination in the job interview and its consequences for the social positions of African Australians as the applicant is transformed from a competent hopeful computer engineer to an invisible cleaner. In the course of 2007 and 2008 I attended a number of screenings of *The Applicant*, with audiences consisting predominantly of English language teachers. Everyone was struck by how uncomfortable the interview with its long silence was and at each screening some audience members asked whether it would not have been possible to achieve a different outcome despite the obvious racism of the interviewer. Could the applicant not have broken the silence? Could the applicant have been more proactive and talk about his accomplishments instead of acquiescing to the imposed silence of the encounter? Could the applicant have turned the situation around by making light of the interviewer's obvious discomfort and finding a humorous conversation starter? Some audience members felt that part of the problem was the applicant's lack of familiarity with Australian pragmatic norms, which would have called for the applicant to consider himself as an equal communication partner rather than one condemned to silence by the interviewer's inability to start a conversation with a black person.[9]

That mutual lack of familiarity with pragmatic norms and conventions may indeed be a more significant factor than racial discrimination was found in research in the UK, which compared the job interviews of white British-born applicants, non-white British-born applicants, and applicants born abroad.[10] The researcher, the sociolinguist Celia Roberts, and her associates recorded job interviews for low-skilled, low-paid work such as stacking shelves, packing factory products, or delivering parcels. For this kind of work employers hold 'assessment days' and interview large numbers of people with a view to taking on most of those who have applied. Around 70% of white and non-white British-born applicants are hired for these jobs and only around 30% are rejected. However, for applicants born abroad, the picture looks radically different: despite the fact that they are actually better qualified, less than half are hired and the majority are rejected.

These are surprising figures because English language proficiency can be assumed to be almost completely irrelevant to the ability to stack shelves, package products, or deliver parcels. Furthermore, the explanation that linguistic performance might be a pretext for racial discrimination does not hold in this case, either, because non-white British-born applicants were almost as successful as white British-born applicants. Also, if racist structures were to blame, they would presumably funnel migrants into low-skilled, low-paid work rather than exclude them from that particular segment of the labor market.

To begin with, the researcher explains that interviewers are guided by principles of equal opportunities and diversity management, and are perfectly aware that a good command of English is irrelevant to stacking shelves and similar monotonous and repetitive jobs. What they are looking for is evidence that applicants will be able to cope with repetition, monotony, and boredom and evidence that they are flexible individuals who will be capable of managing their own boredom.

How can you demonstrate that you are able to manage boredom and that you will be able to cope in a monotonous low-skilled job? By telling a good story! Candidates were expected to tell a vivid story of how they had worked in a boring job before and, ideally, inject a bit of humor. For instance, one candidate, who the interviewers really liked, told the panel about how he had once painted the 'giant walls' of a warehouse in one color for three weeks. He closed by joking that painting the ceiling in a different color was 'a bit of pleasure' because it broke the routine.

In another example, a successful candidate reflected on how he had coped previously when working a job consisting of 'complete mind numbingly same repetitive stuff' by reporting how he would not 'turn [his] brain on' and chat with coworkers while drilling and gluing a little piece of equipment onto another piece of equipment.

Both these (white British-born) successful candidates drew on a narrative structure that has been identified as typical of Anglo cultures and involves providing an orientation (setting, time, place, persons involved, etc.), a complicating action (series of events that took place), and an evaluation (the 'point' of the story).[11] As it so happens, this structure coincides with the structure of the evaluation form the interviewers had to fill in. That form is organized in a 'STAR structure' where they are asked to record the candidate's responses to 'Situation,' 'Task,' 'Action,' and 'Result.' Thus, 'the normative Anglo narrative and the institution's bureaucratic assessment form map on to each other precisely.'[12]

Candidates who produced stories about coping with monotonous work and who were able to reflect on the experience in order to project a credible, competent, and flexible personality did well during the interview, and interviews could become quite informal and friendly. This opened further spaces for the candidate to present themselves as having 'the right kind of personality.'

By contrast, migrants often did not know what to make of questions such as 'what would you tell me is the advantage of a repetitive job?' When they failed to produce an extended response, the interview usually became much more difficult: the interviewers became more controlling of the candidate's talk and turns; there was more negativity and interviewers became less helpful and sympathetic;

and the interviewers aligned more with formal participation roles so that the interview became more formal and more institutionalized. Such conduct was a response to the candidate's failure to produce the expected kind of discourse, but, crucially, it also served to make the interview much more difficult for them.

In sum, migrant candidates did fail because of language. However, it was not their accent, or their grammar, or their inability to produce 'Standard English.' What mattered was the ability to 'play a language game': to tell a story that would project the candidate as the kind of person who was not only willing to do monotonous work but who was also sufficiently self-organized and self-aware to reflect on how they would manage the boredom inherent in such jobs.

> The selection interview requires both bureaucratically processible talk and a vivid social performance, subtly blended together to produce a credible and persuasive self which aligns with the ideal worker in the new capitalist workplace. Small interactional differences and difficulties feed into larger scale judgements and institutional orders which, in turn, press down on individual decision making.[13]

The production of such a hybrid discourse is not easily practiced, particularly for those who are unemployed or employed in an ethnic job market. While the applicant's competence and personality is assessed on the basis of how they talk, the linguistic and cultural nature of the assessment remains, in fact, unacknowledged and invisible.

MULTIPLE VULNERABILITIES

As long ago as 1992, a group of British linguists argued that there is 'a linguistic dimension to discrimination. But language continues to be one of the least visible, least measurable and least understood aspects of discrimination which can easily be squeezed out by a proper and understandable focus on structural and institutional racism.'[14] The previous section's exploration of language in the job interview has demonstrated that linguistic disadvantage operates independently of race and ethnicity. However, in the section on ethnic names on CVs we saw that a name, as a linguistic indicator of ethnicity, disadvantages different groups differently:.while fictitious applicants with Chinese and Middle Eastern names experienced disadvantage, those with Italian names did not. This means that linguistic barriers to employment and linguistic discrimination at work do not operate in isolation. Rather, language intersects with other forms of disadvantage or privilege. As we saw in Chapters Two and Three, linguistic diversity can be conceived of as a differentially valued pyramid and the value of a particular linguistic repertoire cannot be determined in isolation from the value accorded in society to the speaker of that repertoire. Consequently, the linguistic repertoires of those disadvantaged in other ways—think, for example, race, ethnicity, country of origin, gender, education—will constitute an additional disadvantage and compound their vulnerabilities at work.[15]

In labor market policies, the identities of workers are usually overlooked in favor of an assumption of rational human capital allocation. Many migrant destination countries have a points system that attempts to objectively measure the human capital a prospective migrant will bring. In this system, skilled visas are allocated on the basis of a score for educational qualifications, work experience, English proficiency, and age. Despite the persistence of migrant un- and underemployment (see next section), the story of a rational labor market where different outcomes are due to objective differences in human capital continues to be told. What continues to lend credence to the idea of the rational labor market despite the obvious disadvantage and exclusion of certain groups is the perpetual imponderable of English language proficiency. The assumption is that excluded groups are being held back by their lack of proficiency in the national language, and that, once they have achieved an adequate level of proficiency, they will be competing on a level playing field.

That this is not necessarily the case and that some 'non-English-speaking backgrounds' are more equal than other 'non-English-speaking backgrounds' is demonstrated in research by the sociologist Val Colic-Peisker.[16] On the basis of Australian Bureau of Statistics data the researcher compared the labor market outcomes of long-term migrants from different origin groups. The sample included Australian residents who met the following criteria. First, participants had been born overseas in one of the following eight countries: Chile, China, Croatia, Germany, India, Philippines, Russia, and Somalia. Second, participants were long-term migrants with at least ten years of residency in Australia. Third, they had vocational or tertiary qualifications and were employed at the time of the 2006 census. Fourth, they self-assessed their language proficiency as 'speaking English very well' in the 2006 census.[17] The labor market outcomes of Australian residents who met these criteria were then compared to each other and to two other groups: the Australia-born and the UK-born.

If the Australian labor market were indeed rational and the result of nothing more than objective human capital assessments, then a similar portion of people in each origin group should be working at a similar level: most people with vocational training would be expected to work in medium-skilled or paraprofessional jobs and most tertiary-educated people would be expected to work in paraprofessional or professional jobs. Granting a 'native speaker bonus,' as the researcher does in her hypothesis, one could assume that the Australia-born and the UK-born fare somewhat better than all the other groups. However, as all the other members of the sample speak English 'very well,' that difference should be minor and there should be no differences between those other groups.

It did not quite turn out that way.

Employment success for each group was measured as a single quantity, namely, the average of occupational level where '1' equals 'manual and semiskilled,' '2' equals 'medium skilled,' '3' equals 'paraprofessional,' and '4' equals 'professional.' For a group to be adequately placed in the job market according to the human capital approach, those with vocational qualifications should average 2.5 and those with a tertiary degree should average 3.5.

Among the vocationally qualified, expected scores between 2.4 and 2.5 were achieved by those born in Russia, UK, Germany, China, and Australia (in that order). Among the tertiary-educated, expected scores between 3.3 and 3.5 were achieved by those born in Australia, UK, Germany, Russia, and Chile. This means that the rational human capital approach works for these groups. That the order of the country-of-origin groups is different for the vocationally skilled and the tertiary-qualified is indicative of the fact that language is more important in the professions. The higher someone is qualified, the closer to the imagined standard language their linguistic repertoire is expected to be.

In sum, the labor market operates rationally, working in accordance with human capital criteria for the Europeans, and for the Chinese in the case of the vocationally trained. Those born in Germany and Russia, in particular, fare equally well as those born in Australia and the UK.

Now let's consider the other end of the spectrum, those for whom the labor market does not operate rationally. The researcher found particularly low scores for those from the Philippines (2.19 for the vocationally trained and 2.73 for the tertiary-educated) and Somalia (2.18 for the vocationally trained and 2.87 for the tertiary-educated), which means that these groups are employed significantly below their educational level.

There may be many reasons for this: Somalis as a group are relatively recent arrivals to multicultural Australia and so are likely to be perceived as more culturally distant than members of migrant groups who have been around for longer. As a group, they may also suffer from the combined stigmas of being African, being refugees, and being Muslim.

The fact that employment outcomes are worst for migrants from the Philippines may be the most surprising result of the study. The 'obvious' prejudices that may operate in the case of the Somalis do not apply to this group. The likely explanation for the underemployment of the Philippines-born has less to do with ethnic discrimination than with gender and occupational field: most migrants from the Philippines in Australia are women, who may have put their careers on hold to raise families and, upon re-entry into the workforce, ended up in jobs they are overqualified for, as is a common female experience irrespective of country of origin. Furthermore, many Philippines-born tertiary-educated migrants work in the medical field, a field where the recognition of prior qualifications is much harder to achieve than in most other fields.

What this research demonstrates is that 'language has a color.'[18] It also has a gender. For groups who are discriminated against on the job market, their linguistic difference from the imagined standard language ideal constitutes an additional vulnerability. Conversely, moving closer to the imagined standard language ideal carries greater rewards for those who are not subject to racial discrimination, such as the Germany- and Russia-born in the sample, and fewer rewards for those who are additionally facing racial and gender barriers, as the Philippines- and Somalia-born do.

SURVIVAL EMPLOYMENT AND DESKILLING

Most adults have to work in order to be financially independent. Consequently, groups that are excluded from employment consistent with their qualifications will seek work below the level they are qualified for. For instance, in the study discussed in the previous section, 73% of Philippines-born with vocational training and 65% of Philippines-born with tertiary qualifications were working below their level; in other words, they were underemployed. Taking a job below one's level of qualifications is often an economic necessity for new migrants, hence the term 'survival employment.' At the same time, survival employment is widely assumed to be temporary. It is assumed that, once a migrant has a foot in the employment market, they will be able to quickly regain their social position and find work consistent with their qualifications. And they will also have the opportunity to practice their English and thus gain valuable language learning opportunities in addition to work experience in the new country. Or so the theory goes. That it is not that simple is already obvious from the research discussed in the previous section: the sample included only residents who had been in Australia for at least ten years, which means that any underemployment would have become entrenched by then. It also included only residents who spoke English 'very well.'

In this section we will explore the consequences of group-specific barriers, including language barriers, to the job market. The focus here is on structural consequences that serve to further entrench the disadvantage and exclusion experienced by particular groups. In the following section we will focus on the linguistic consequences of underemployment and examine the language learning opportunities offered by survival employment.

In Australia, the overqualified migrant taxi driver has become a stock character of literature. However, the deskilling of skilled migrants is not unique to Australia and is also a feature of Canada's skilled migration program. An interview study with migrants from sub-Saharan Africa in Vancouver by the sociologist Gillian Creese looks beyond the statistics to examine the experience of long-term underemployment.[19] The focus of the interviews was on the experience of re-entering the labor market post-migration. Most of the interviewees were tertiary-educated, most of them came from Anglophone countries and had been educated in English, and most of them had pre-migration professional experience. And they had one more thing in common: post-migration, they were mostly long-term underemployed:

> Their educational credentials and experience in Africa went unrecognized; their 'African-English' accents posed additional barriers to many types of employment; and their additional Canadian education often failed to translate into the expected occupational rewards.[20]

Deskilling plays out differently for men and women because the labor market is not only racialized but also gendered. Men do not have their qualifications and experience recognized but there are still jobs for them in the production sector and other blue collar work. Women's qualifications and experiences are not recognized, either, but, unlike their male counterparts, they do not even have access to blue collar work. At the same time, they do not have access to the lower rungs of the feminized Canadian labor market such as retail and service work, either, because they do not 'look and sound right' for customer service. All that is left to the women is cleaning work and some light manufacturing. Consequently, they invested more heavily into continuing education, usually at a lower level than warranted by existing credentials and experience, and following the gendered advice of settlement agencies, which pushed them into care work.

In effect, for Vancouver's Africans, the labor market worked to transform people who entered the country as 'skilled migrants' into 'uneducated Africans' once they had become landed immigrants. One of the interviewees, Lwanzo from Zimbabwe, summed up her experience of education and migration like this:

> When you are coming here, they say they cannot accept people who are not educated. They are accepting people who are educated, and when they come here, they treat them like uneducated people. What's the use? Why not take people who are not educated then, if what you want are janitors, you know. Bring people who are janitors then, who'll do that job gladly. Because I know people from home wouldn't go to school if they came here to work as janitors. Janitors would do that job very gladly. But I'll not do that happily. I will not do it happily. I'll complain, you know.[21]

Entrenched underemployment meant that the interviewees lost not only economically in terms of low wages, insecurity, and unemployment but also in terms of their dignity and respect.

Vancouver's skilled African migrants were vulnerable to deskilling for a number of reasons: not only did their English have a color, but in the absence of useful social networks in the new country they were dependent on employment agencies to help them find work. The latter did little to help them bridge any gaps that may have existed between their pre-migration qualifications and the Canadian equivalent of those qualifications. Stereotyping African women in particular as 'domestic' and 'caring,' such agencies in fact often gave negative and inappropriate advice, seeing Africans predominantly through the lens of 'cheap labor.' Additionally, neoliberal employment agencies have a clear incentive to channel migrants into immediate jobs rather than helping them develop a long-term career strategy:

> As neo-liberal restructuring proceeded in the 1990s, the focus of immigrant employment programmes was further narrowed in accordance with new government directives. Accountability was measured by the number employed at the end of a programme, regardless of the type of job, and programmes provided for immigrants were reduced to 'job clubs and resume services' while funding for more complex skills-based bridging programmes for skilled immigrants disappeared [. . .]. Thus employment programmes offered by settlement agencies are both limited in scope and actively push immigrants into low wage employment, raising questions about the nature of the government's role in facilitating economic integration.[22]

An Australian politician expressed the push for new migrants to enter the workplace as quickly as possible without consideration for the long-term consequences with the slogan, 'We want to see a seamless transition for new arrivals from the airport to the workplace.'[23] In addition to the short-term strategy of prioritizing immediate savings in welfare spending over long-term investment into human capital and social integration, there is yet another reason why policy makers and contemporary settlement agencies favor immediate job entry at whatever level. That reason is the assumption that the workplace is the best place for new migrants to improve their linguistic proficiencies. We will now examine that assumption in more detail.

LANGUAGE LEARNING ON THE JOB

One of the most famous research subjects ever to have participated in second-language learning research is a man known in the literature as Alberto.[24] In 1973 Alberto participated in a ten-month longitudinal study of his learning of various English syntactic structures, particularly questions, negations, and use of auxiliaries. At the time, Alberto was thirty-three years old and had moved to Cambridge, Massachusetts, from his native Costa Rica four months earlier. The reason Alberto is famous in the field of second-language learning is because during the ten months of the research project he hardly made any progress at all in producing the syntactic structures under investigation. The theory of 'fossilization'—that adult language learning plateaus at a state that is different from full mastery—is to a significant degree based on the empirical research with Alberto. Alberto is the poster boy of failure in second-language learning, if you will.

For our discussion here, Alberto's failure to make much progress in his English is noteworthy because it occurred while Alberto held not only one but two jobs, and worked both night and day. That Alberto would not make progress without formal instruction was not surprising to John H. Schumann, the researcher who conducted research with Alberto. As it was, Schumann considered the fact that Alberto 'chose to work at night as well as in the day, rather than attend English classes' as evidence that Alberto was not keen to learn English.[25]

Alberto is not unique. A large cross-national European study conducted in the 1980s investigated the 'naturalistic acquisition' (i.e., immersion language learning without formal instruction) of

Dutch, English, French, German, and Swedish by work migrants with six different first languages (Arabic, Finnish, Italian, Punjabi, Spanish, and Turkish) and came to similar conclusions: the task of learning a language while communicating in that language is an immensely challenging one. The learner 'has simultaneously to learn and communicate whilst achieving other communicative and non-communicative goals, in relation to target language speakers who can be more or less understanding, friendly, helpful or dominant.'[26]

The second-language learning research with Alberto and migrant workers in Europe was not primarily interested in language learning at work. The focus of that research was on linguistic and cognitive aspects of second-language learning by adults who had little or no prior knowledge of the target language, had low levels of formal education and were blue collar work migrants, or, in the parlance of the time, 'guest workers.' It just happened to be the case that these research participants spent a lot of their time at work and work was of central importance in their lives. And the research findings for this group are unambiguous: in the absence of formal language instruction, language learning at work has poor outcomes.

Since the research with Alberto and migrant workers in Europe in the 1970s and 1980s, international work migration has increased significantly, as have so-called '3D-jobs' where migrant workers are concentrated. '3D' stands for 'dirty, dangerous, and difficult,' although the third 'D' is sometimes also taken to stand for 'demeaning,' 'dull,' or 'demanding.' '3D' is a translation of the Japanese term '3K,' which stands for *kitanai, kitsui, kiken* (汚い, きつい, 危険; 'dirty,' 'difficult,' 'dangerous'). Internationally, 3D jobs are associated with migrant labor. In 2013, about one-third of all international migrants were unskilled or low-skilled.[27] Furthermore, the number of international migrants in 3D jobs is higher than the number of low-skilled migrants because a substantial portion of medium- and high-skilled migrants experience deskilling and become stuck in survival employment, as we saw in the previous section.

For this population, entering the workforce does not in itself constitute an opportunity to practice English, as Australian research with meat workers from the Philippines demonstrates.[28] Since the mid-1990s the Australian meat processing industry has increasingly relied on migrants to fill labor shortages as employment conditions in the industry have deteriorated. Large meat processing enterprises hire meat workers in bulk from countries such as Brazil, China, and the Philippines. The meat processing plant in a rural town in Queensland where the research took place hired almost exclusively from the Philippines. On the job, opportunities to practice English were exceedingly rare: to begin with, work was organized in a conveyor-belt system where any communication carried the danger of holding up the line. Communication was thus detrimental to work and in conflict with workplace goals. With communication during work extremely limited by the nature of the work, communication opportunities were restricted to break times. However, because most workers at the plant were from the Philippines, most communication during break times took place in Tagalog. Many workers felt too exhausted to say much—in any language—during break time, as one interviewee explained: 'When it is our break time we eat and then have some rest. Sometimes I want to be by myself and rest my back against a tree.'[29]

With communication opportunities—and thus English language learning opportunities—severely limited during regular work and break times, there remained only one context in the workplace where language was involved and that was during staff meetings and other communication scenarios with management. These occasions were extremely rare and when they did occur, management had installed a Filipino go-between who was asked to interpret.

In sum, for these migrant workers language learning opportunities at work were virtually nonexistent. In fact, the challenge of multitasking that second-language learning researchers have noted—the challenge of learning a new language while communicating in that language and of communicating in a new language while learning that language—largely did not even present itself to these workers because communication simply is not part of butchering and meat-packing work.

The same is true of many 3D jobs: the nature of the work is such that very few opportunities for any kind of language use exist. As a way to overcome this obstacle and provide migrants with language learning opportunities at work, factories with many migrants used to provide language training at work, particularly in Australia or Canada.[30] While most postwar migrants found themselves in relatively secure production work, the structure of work has changed significantly. To begin with, the production sector in many migration destinations has shrunk. Where it still exists, production work, too, is now often casualized and outsourced. Research with Polish metalworkers in Finland, for instance, found that the metalworkers were employed by a recruitment agency and then 'rented out' to metalworking plants, as the need arose.[31] Consequently, job insecurity and regular moves from one workplace to another were a normal part of the experience of these workers. Neither the recruitment agency nor the actual workplaces considered the provision of Finnish language training as part of their responsibilities.

While the production sector has shrunk and the organization of production workplaces has been transformed, the growth of migrant employment has been predominantly in the service sector of the 'new economy.' The provision of on-the-job language training seems virtually nonexistent in this sector. For instance, research examining how English language proficiency structures work in the hospitality sector in Sydney remarks precisely on the absence of on-the-job language training programs. Lack of English language proficiency presented a significant problem both for workers and for management. However, the provision of on-the-job language training was not even contemplated:

> Finally, the question arises as to why hotels did not seek to improve and reinforce the English language skills of their staff as they did with other required competencies. [. . .] This contrasted with management's approach to the other 'soft skills' and attributes that the hotels nurtured among their staff—such as grooming, customer service skills and even

trustworthiness—where considerable on and off the job training was used to reinforce desired qualities.[32]

Where on-the-job language training exists, the workplace can indeed provide ideal language learning opportunities, as German research has found.[33] Designed in consultation with stakeholders in a particular workplace, German language training courses were offered on the job to low-skilled migrants working in cleaning, hospitality, construction, and care work. The program evaluation found high satisfaction levels on the part of workers and employers as language learners experienced a close fit between their communicative needs and the language instruction they received. They were delighted with the tangible progress they made as they could immediately practice newly learned linguistic elements in real life.

In sum, the workplace is usually not the ideal language learning context it is often imagined to be. Naturalistic language learning presents a significant challenge as language learning and communicative goals have to be achieved simultaneously. Furthermore, the conditions in workplaces where migrant workers are clustered are often not conducive to language learning, as 3D conditions can make language learning a low priority and speaking may even be considered an obstacle to satisfactory workplace performance. If work is not conducive to language learning, immediate entry into such work constitutes a further factor in the permanent deskilling of migrants, as it may permanently lock them into low-skilled, manual, short-term work. Limited proficiency in the dominant language upon entering the workforce jeopardizes social inclusion in the long term and may permanently disadvantage migrant workers. On-the-job language training programs constitute a potential way out of this trap. However, as we have seen, such programs are relatively rare and are possibly decreasing under neoliberal employment conditions in the 'new economy.' While contemporary employers seem reluctant to support language learning at work, there is another aspect of linguistic diversity at work that is often closely managed, and that is the use of languages other than the dominant language.

SUPPRESSING LINGUISTIC DIVERSITY

While the Sydney hotels in the research mentioned above did not have an English language learning policy, they had a policy against the use of any language other than English in the workplace because it was considered as damaging to the 'the look and feel of the hotel' if guests were to observe workers speaking in another language. 'It's not professional, it's not a good look,' as the executive housekeeper of a five-star hotel explained.[34]

Sydney hotels are by no means unique in imposing workplace policies against the use of non-dominant languages. In July 2010, a hospital in Baltimore, Maryland, for instance, made headlines when it fired four nurses because they were accused of speaking Tagalog instead of English during their lunch break.[35] The hospital has an English-Only policy as part of its 'Emergency Department Expectations,' which make English the only language allowed for on-duty nurses in the emergency room. The four nurses, however, had not violated the on-duty English-Only policy but used Tagalog during their own time during lunch break. In fact, from the media reports it was not even clear whether they conducted an entire conversation in Tagalog or whether their English was mixed with some Tagalog words. Indeed, when the four nurses filed a discrimination and unfair dismissal complaint, their lawyer argued that the lack of guidelines in the hospital's English-Only rule made it impossible to abide by: 'All it takes is just one word. That can be a greeting, a remark or even the name of a Filipino dish. Based on this rule, you could say *bagoong* (a fish sauce) and lose your job.'[36] According to the lawyer, the hospital actually could not even cite specific instances where or when the alleged violations of their English-Only rule had taken place. The US Equal Employment Opportunity Commission eventually found that the dismissal was discriminatory and awarded damages to the four women. In the statement of determination, the Equal Employment Opportunity Commission argued that English-Only policies for which no 'business necessity' exists are discriminatory because they have 'a significant disparate impact on persons of non-U.S. national origins whose first languages are not English.'[37]

In this case the law was on the side of the plaintiffs and English-Only rules at work were found to constitute unlawful discrimination. However, this is a relatively unusual outcome. If they are brought at all, discrimination suits based on language choice in the workplace are likely to be unsuccessful.[38]

The sociolinguist Deborah Cameron noted in 1995 that 'linguistic bigotry is among the last publicly expressible prejudices left to members of the Western intelligentsia.'[39] In the same vein, one could argue that linguistic discrimination is among the last legal forms of discrimination left to Western employers, and we will now examine an unsuccessful discrimination case brought by a cleaner in Germany.[40]

It was not use of a language other than German in the workplace that was at the heart of this case but the level of German language proficiency required to do the job. The case was brought by Ms. K., a woman born in 1951 in what was then Yugoslavia and whose first language was Croatian. Ms. K. had been a resident of Germany since the early 1980s and since 1985 she had worked as a cleaner in the aquatic center of a small city in northern Germany. As part of her employment duties, she occasionally also had to staff the reception and sell tickets for entry into the center. From 2006 onward she was repeatedly told by her supervisor that her German was inadequate. She was also asked to undertake a German language course, during her own time and at her own expense, in order to improve her German. Over the following two years she was on various occasions—both orally and in writing—blamed for 'repeated communication problems with colleagues, supervisors and customers' and asked to present evidence that she had enrolled in a German language class. In a letter to her lawyer, the employer alleged that Ms. K., 'simply needed to give up her resistance against the language of the country in which she has been residing for more than twenty-five years.'[41]

Ms. K. felt insulted by these reprimands and requests.

When her German language proficiency was raised again and she was issued a formal warning about her German language proficiency in 2008 after returning to work from an extended period of sick leave, Ms. K. brought an ethnic-harassment case against her employer. She alleged that repeated requests by her employer to improve her German and to attend German language classes constituted a form of harassment on the basis of her national origin. Both the court of first and second appeal found against her, and argued that it was legitimate for her employer to require her to improve her German.

At a general level, the court's ruling that an employer's request for an employee to learn the national language does not constitute unlawful discrimination makes perfect sense. Even if the requirement to learn German disproportionately affects members of non-German ethnic groups, as the courts acknowledged, business and organizational needs of the employer are of overriding importance. The courts therefore held that requiring an employee to learn and/or improve their German language proficiency was legitimate.

While it is obvious that an employee needs to possess the linguistic skills that are required to do their job, the courts did not address the anomaly that Ms. K. had done the exact same job for more than twenty years (from 1985 to 2006) before her German language proficiency first became an issue.

To begin with, the nature of Ms. K.'s work never changed: she was predominantly employed as a cleaner, a role for which German language proficiency is irrelevant. She was also occasionally required to staff the reception and sell tickets. Her German was sufficient to engage in this low-level customer service. However, the employer claimed that when she staffed the ticket booth Ms. K. was unable to do the accounts in the evening independently and needed help from a coworker. Other than that, her German was sufficient to do her job.

Second, from a language learning perspective it would have been much more sensible to require Ms. K. to undertake German language classes when she was first hired into the position: at that time, she would have had age on her side. As we saw above, the ability to learn new languages generally decreases with age. By 2006, when she was fifty-five years old, Ms. K.'s German language proficiency would long have fossilized at a level that allowed her to get on with her job. Language learning is doubtlessly more difficult for an older worker with severe health problems than it would have been for her younger self a quarter of a century earlier. One might also consider that Ms. K. is as likely as any woman to have to work a 'second shift' at home, and she just may not have had any time or energy left to devote to language classes.[42]

Third, neither the employer nor the courts seemed to have had any specific expertise to determine the plaintiff's level of language proficiency, and no such expertise was sought by any of the parties in the court case. As discussed in Chapter Three, assessment of the linguistic proficiency of second-language speakers is often treated as if it were a free-for-all and no particular expertise on the part of dominant language speakers was required to pass judgment on the proficiency of second-language users of that language. In fact, other than the reference to her inability to do the accounts by herself, the only specific instance of Ms. K.'s linguistic incompetence that was cited in the court documents related not to the language requirements of her work but to a complex organizational environment that led her to query whether her workplace still belonged to the public service or had been privatized. The speech act in question ('Is the pool still open service?' instead of 'Does the pool still belong to the public service?') was in fact described as 'simple' in the court ruling.[43]

It is also remarkable that no one seemed to have noticed that Ms. K.'s 'incomprehensible' utterance had obviously been understood. Had it not been understood, a recast into Standard German would not have been possible. When misunderstandings occur in communication, it is rarely only the fault of one person—that is why speakers and listeners usually share the communicative burden. However, we also know from intercultural communication research that dominant speakers of the dominant language oftentimes opt out of sharing the communicative burden in interactions with subordinated speakers of subordinated varieties.[44] Instead, they place the responsibility for ensuring communicative success exclusively on the shoulders of subordinated speakers, who are thus faced with a double handicap: despite having fewer standard language resources at their disposal, the communicative challenges they face are greater as dominant speakers often opt out of cooperating.

In sum, a further injustice related to linguistic diversity arises at work when employers seek to suppress linguistic diversity in the workplace. This can happen through bans on the use of languages other than the dominant language or through attempts to enforce specific ways in which the dominant language is to be used. While the former has sometimes been considered unlawful discrimination when a specific case has been tested in the courts, the latter is more likely to be accepted as 'common sense.' There are many work contexts where specific ways of using language are an intrinsic part of the work that is to be performed. This is most obviously the case for translators and interpreters but a wide range of jobs have a linguistic component. In such cases, language-related job requirements are perfectly legitimate. However, in many employment situations language requirements are not clearly specified and blanket suppressions of linguistic diversity are in place. It is here where injustices are bound to arise, as is the case when a specific language regime is enforced even during break times or when specific language requirements are immaterial to the performance of the job.

ALTERNATIVE LANGUAGE REGIMES

So far, this chapter has demonstrated that migrants face systemic barriers to employment. These barriers are of a linguistic and non-linguistic nature; they also force migrants not only into survival jobs but also into ethnic job markets where alternative language regimes may apply. In this section we will explore the relationship between linguistic diversity and employment justice in sectors of the job market where alternative language regimes apply.

Nail salons constitute one such alternative job market.[45] Globally, nail salons are a Vietnamese-dominated job market. In the USA, for instance, less than 1% of the population is Vietnamese but 80% of nail technicians in California and 43% nationwide are Vietnamese. A *Los Angeles Times* article goes so far as to claim 'it's hard to meet a manicurist who isn't Vietnamese.'[46] Vietnamese nail technicians also dominate the market in the UK and most of continental Europe, in Australia, New Zealand, and other parts of Asia including, of course, Vietnam.

How are the emergence of nail care as a new industry and the transnational domination of that industry by a specific ethnic group related to language?

As we have repeatedly seen by now, migrants often find that lack of proficiency in the dominant language of their destination country is a barrier to workplace entry in their field and/or at the level at which they are qualified. Linguistic barriers to employment are highest in the professions, where usually (part of) the qualifications and training process needs to be redone and/or certifying and registration exams need to be undertaken in the new language. That is why migrant lawyers are rare. Linguistic barriers to employment are lowest for self-employment in areas with little state regulation. That is why migrant-owned corner stores are common.

Within a particular industry, the same rules apply. Let's take the beauty industry: if you are a cosmetic surgeon and move to another country, chances are you will never work as a cosmetic surgeon again. Depending on where you are from and how your previous qualifications are assessed, you face years of retraining, qualifying exams in the new language, and other hurdles to regain your license to practice in the new country. At the other end of the beauty industry, you will find nail technicians: to practice as a nail technician in Australia, for instance, you do not need any formal qualifications whatsoever.[47] Limited proficiency in English thus poses no or only a minor obstacle to workplace entry as a nail technician. However, speaking Vietnamese might confer an advantage, as I will explain now.

In the 1970s, the family of a former commander in the South Vietnamese Navy found that there were few opportunities for them and fellow Vietnamese refugees in California. Like many others in a similar position, they tried their luck in all kinds of ways, eventually opening a beauty school, the Advance Beauty College in Garden Grove, an area of Los Angeles also known as 'Little Saigon.' They taught classes in Vietnamese and after a short course, students could go and start their own nail salon. Many of them did because in addition to the lack of linguistic barriers, the financial investment was low.

At that time, nail salons hardly existed in California (or elsewhere) and manicures and pedicures were a preserve of the rich and famous. However, the emergent supply of Vietnamese nail technicians and nail salons meant that manicures and pedicures suddenly came within the reach of Californian women of lesser means.

> Vietnamese nails-only shops revolutionized manicuring in much the same manner that McDonalds revolutionized inexpensive, fast food service. Like McDonalds, the nails-only shops appealed to busy Americans who wanted quick, dependable service, when convenient to their schedules, and who were content with the provisioning of the service in an impersonal manner.[48]

Vietnamese entrepreneurs thus did not fill an existing market niche but created a new one. Once established, the new nail care market spread through franchises. For instance, Regal Nails, which is located within Walmart, was founded by a first-generation Vietnamese, as was the Australian market leader, Professionails.

Once established, linguistic necessity became a virtue for Vietnamese nail entrepreneurs, as ethnic networks ensured a continuing supply of first-generation workers with few other options. As such, the continuation of the business model depends on continuing emigration from Vietnam because second-generation Vietnamese with better education and bilingualism do not need to rely on their ethnic ties and have many other employment options.

As I have explained, it was the absence of regulation combined with the availability of training in Vietnamese that made California the birthplace of the Vietnamese-dominated nail care industry. Furthermore, when the State of California introduced licensing exams for nail technicians in the 1990s, there was the option to take the certifying exams in Vietnamese. Thus, the Californian state chose, in this instance, not to erect a linguistic barrier to employment for its Vietnamese-speaking citizens.

Once established, and as the nail care industry expanded beyond California across the USA, and later went global, Vietnamese domination had the effect of excluding non-Vietnamese from the industry so that today lack of proficiency in English is rarely a barrier to becoming a nail technician but lack of Vietnamese does constitute such a barrier. As the industry globalized, it moved back to Vietnam and many nail technicians now train there before emigrating and have jobs already lined up before they even leave the country. It is the continued 'Vietnamization' of the supply chain that makes cheap manicures and pedicures possible.

> [. . .] they work in the least skilled, least revenue-generating segment of the beauty industry. Most typically, when Vietnamese entrepreneurs expand their business involvements they do so by opening additional salons of the same sort, not by diversifying their beauty care offerings to include those that are most profitable. Similarly, nail technicians do not invest in additional training to qualify for the better paying jobs in the beauty industry. Vietnamese, accordingly, are creating conditions that work against their own longer-term interests. They are fueling intra-ethnic competition that is likely to drive down their earnings, unless they further increase demand for their services.[49]

The story of the Vietnamese nail care industry is partly a success story where ingenuity in the face of linguistic barriers to mainstream employment led to the creation of a new industry and a valorization of Vietnamese in that industry. At the same time, the dominance of

Vietnamese in the industry may make individual workers vulnerable to exploitation. In fact, the story of ethnically segmented labor markets is often told as one of exploitation of vulnerable workers whose lack of proficiency in the dominant language leaves them at the mercy of unscrupulous co-ethnics. In Australia, for example, instances of the exploitation of migrant workers without English are regularly reported by the media. Forced labor and illegal and underpaid employment of foreign workers are predominantly found in the sex industry but also in agriculture, construction, hospitality, manufacturing, and nursing.[50] At the time of writing in early 2015, the most recent case to have been publicized involved Chinese construction workers who were subcontracted onto an Australian construction site by a Taiwanese company.[51] A factor in the exploitation of these workers, who were paid significantly below award rates and housed in substandard accommodation and who had their travel documents confiscated by their employer, was their lack of English language proficiency. As a union investigator stated, 'the Chinese workers seem to have no English at all.'

Obvious as the role of language in the exploitation of workers such as these Chinese construction workers may seem, it is complicated by their precarious legal status. Their temporary visa was employer-sponsored and tied to that particular employment. It is also complicated by global income inequalities: while an annual take-home pay of AUD7,000 after deductions for construction work with overtime is outrageously low in Australia, where the average annual take-home wage of a construction worker is AUD40,737, it is still significantly above the average annual salary of USD4,755 in China.[52]

These complexities of language proficiency, legal status, and economic inequality are unraveled in an ethnographic inquiry into the language practices in a *locutorio*, a call shop, in Barcelona, Spain.[53] A *locutorio* offers all kinds of telecommunication services such as billed calls in booths, the sale of top-ups for mobiles, fax services, Internet access, and international money transfers. Most customers in *locutorios* are migrants as are most employees, and they thus serve as meeting points for working-class Spaniards and migrants, both documented and undocumented, from a variety of countries of origin. Beyond the sale of telecommunication services, a *locutorio* also provides access to information and a place to hang out. The *locutorio* under study even served as the 'public' toilet for homeless people in the neighborhood, mostly undocumented men from West Africa.

The *locutorio* in question was part of a chain of similar call shops owned by a Pakistani venture capitalist whose aim was to make a profit rather than provide social services for Barcelona's marginalized. It was his employee Naeem, who was in charge of running the *locutorio*, who ended up caught between more than one rock and more than one hard place. Naeem was a fellow Pakistani hired by the owner in Pakistan two years before the fieldwork began. Naeem's position was legal as a temporary resident but in order to achieve permanent residency in Spain he needed another two years of proven work, which left him vulnerable to exploitation by the owner. He worked twelve hours per day, seven days a week, for a meager salary of less than Euro 800 per month. Naeem's job consisted of opening the *locutorio* in the morning and closing it at night. He would start by booting up the computers and making sure all the equipment was running. During the day, his duties consisted of assisting and charging customers, and making various phone calls (to his boss, to call card distributors, to the money transfer agency, etc.). Additionally, he was in charge of maintaining the premises, including sweeping the floors, removing garbage, and cleaning the toilets.

Much of this work is obviously language work and Naeem had to operate in a complex sociolinguistic environment. In addition to a range of varieties of Spanish—from Standard Peninsular Spanish via various Latin American varieties to a range of second-language varieties—this included Catalan, English, Urdu, Punjabi, and Moroccan Arabic in various spoken and written constellations and used by clients with variable levels of proficiencies, including proficiencies in the use of telecommunication services. In this highly diverse environment, communication was rigidly regimented by the meters on the machines where communication was paid for by the minute.

Unsurprisingly, misunderstandings and communication break-downs were common. On top of all this, Naeem had to deal with customers who tried to cheat him (the balance of each financial irregularity was deducted from his meager salary) and who abused and insulted him. Working in a highly constrained yet highly diverse environment left little room for personal autonomy and, only in his late twenties, Naeem was suffering from eating disorders, chronic fatigue, and anxiety attacks and was a compulsive smoker.

Like the nail care industry, *locutorios* are characterized by a new language regime where inclusion is no longer simply predicated on proficiency in the dominant language. In contrast to the nail care industry, it is not one particular language that is substituted for the dominant language in *locutorios*. Rather, it is multilingual repertoires that are valuable in *locutorio* work. However, despite the value that Naem's multilingual repertoires added to his work, he was far from being adequately remunerated for his (language) work. Under the legal and material conditions in which he found himself, it was impossible to convert his 'multilingual capital' into fair remuneration. Naeem faced various forms of exploitation in his work, including linguistic exploitation. As the researcher concludes, *locutorio* language workers constitute 'a voiceless army of multilingual mediators.'[54]

SUMMARY

Linguistic diversity undergirds a range of injustices in the world of paid work and employment. We began this chapter with the injustice of obfuscation that arises where 'insufficient language proficiency' is used as a blanket explanation for the exclusion of migrants from paid employment or for their underemployment. Actual linguistic barriers to employment are constituted by linguistic stereotyping on the basis of ethnic names in written application documents as well as differences in pragmatic norms related to conducting a relaxed job interview or telling a good story. Linguistic stereotyping does not operate in isolation from other forms of disadvantage and constitutes but one of many facets of multiple vulnerabilities. Lack of proficiency in the dominant language is most damaging to those who are also disadvantaged in other ways while the rewards of linguistic proficiency are greatest for those who are also privileged in other ways.

Those particularly vulnerable to the penalties of limited proficiency in the dominant language often find themselves permanently excluded from adequate work. Where long-term incorporation into the labor market takes the form of 'survival employment,' migrants may not only experience deskilling but also find that their opportunities to improve their proficiency in the dominant language may be limited. Naturalistic language learning in workplace contexts has been shown to have poor results for a number of reasons. First, the pressure of having to learn a new language and having to communicate in that language at the same time can be substantial. Second, in prototypical migrant work such as 3D jobs there is often a conflict between getting the work done and talking. Third, the availability of structured language training on the job has become exceedingly rare in contemporary employment arrangements, characterized as they are by outsourcing, casualization, and part-time work.

A further language-related injustice at work is constituted by the suppression of linguistic diversity at work. This may be enacted through prohibitions against speaking non-dominant languages at work or language proficiency requirements that exceed those required by the nature of the work. In the same way that job descriptions in some jurisdictions are required to have clear descriptions of the skills required to perform the job, it would be useful to have clear descriptions of the linguistic skills required to perform a particular job.

The persistent exclusion of migrants from dominant job markets has resulted in a range of alternative language regimes at work. Alternative language regimes may lock individuals into particular market segments, often ethnically segmented labor markets but increasingly also highly diverse and highly multilingual 'migrant segments' of the labor market. Here, lack of proficiency in the dominant language is often perceived to be the key factor that lays bare individuals to exploitation, particularly by unscrupulous co-ethnics. However, this narrative lets the dominant group off the hook too easily: it is only against the backdrop of profound legal and economic inequalities that 'lack of dominant language proficiency' can assume the power that it has in the lives of far too many people.

Chapter 5

Linguistic Diversity in Education

From the previous chapter's discussion of language-related injustices faced by adult migrants, this chapter will now move on to an exploration of children's and youths' experiences with linguistic diversity. First-generation migrants often accept the hardships of migration as a sacrifice they have to make in order to improve the opportunities of the next generation. Schools play a key role in facilitating—or blocking—these dreams and aspirations. Where schools fail linguistically diverse populations, migrant disadvantage can easily become entrenched in the next generation and lock out some groups in the long term, as has been the case with indigenous populations.

Formal education has long been a key terrain where struggles for equality and justice play out. Today more children than ever before enroll in formal education, and language as a barrier to access is not a burning issue, in the same way it presents a barrier to employment. Instead, the central social justice concern related to schooling is the quality of education. Educational quality in many contexts is so poor that the UNESCO global monitoring reports on the 'Education for All' goals have repeatedly spoken of a global 'learning crisis.' The most recent report at the time of writing notes that almost 40% of primary school children—or around 250 million out of a total of 650 million—leave school without having learned the basics of reading and mathematics. Almost half of children in sub-Saharan Africa, India, and Pakistan leave school without having achieved minimum standards. In North America and Western Europe, that figure stands at around 4%. The global figures 'conceal large disparities within countries' where 'poverty, gender, location, language, ethnicity, disability, and other factors mean some children are likely to get less support from schools to improve their learning.'[1]

Consequently, our focus here will be on the ways in which language undergirds disparities in educational outcomes. As before, it is worth keeping in mind throughout that language rarely operates alone and may constitute but one factor in a bundle of disadvantages. As discussed, this is particularly true of ethnicity, for which language often serves as a proxy. Our focus will again be on international migration where linguistic diversity in schools is the result of parental mobility, but we will also examine the role of language in the educational disadvantage of indigenous populations.

THE MONOLINGUAL HABITUS
OF MULTILINGUAL SCHOOLS

Most sociologists agree that the education system does not merely serve the obvious purpose of teaching the next generation and instilling knowledge in the young. Additionally, schools have a 'hidden curriculum' of social reproduction: to maintain and perpetuate the socioeconomic order. Since the advent of universal schooling in the nineteenth century the 'hidden curriculum' has largely been defined by the needs of the state and industry for faithful patriots, obedient soldiers, or docile workers. The nationalist agenda of schooling included the suppression of linguistic diversity and the inculcation of the standard variety of the dominant language as the only legitimate form of linguistic expression. The sociolinguist

Dell Hymes described the language-related hidden curriculum of schools as follows:

> A latent function of the educational system is to instill linguistic insecurity, to discriminate linguistically, to channel children in ways that have an integral linguistic component, while appearing open and fair to all.[2]

The monolingual habitus of formal education has always flown in the face of linguistic diversity and has often had the express aim of eradicating subordinate indigenous languages. This traditional agenda to suppress linguistic diversity is the baggage that formal schooling has brought to the education of the 'new' multilingual school populations of the late twentieth and early twenty-first centuries. Essentially, schools have maintained their traditional monolingual institutional habitus in the face of students' (and, increasingly, teachers') multilingualism.[3]

We will now examine what it means for schooling to bring its monolingual habitus to bear on the education of a multilingual population with a case study of schooling in Székely Land.[4]

Székely Land is a region comprising the three counties of Harghita, Covasna, and Mureş in Transylvania in Romania. Also known as *Székelyföld* in Hungarian, *Ţinutul Secuiesc* in Romanian, *Szeklerland* in German, and *Terra Siculorum* in Latin, its many names are indicative of the region's complex history. Since medieval times, Székely Land has been settled by Székely Hungarians and formed an autonomous region within the Hungarian Kingdom until the middle of the nineteenth century. While Székely Land lost its autonomy in the Austro-Hungarian Empire, it continued to form part of Hungary until it was awarded to Romania after World War I in the Treaty of Trianon. In the 1940s, Székely Land became again part of Hungary for another five years. Since 1946 Székely Land has been part of Romania. For most of the 1950s and 1960s, Székely Land was administered as Hungarian Autonomous Province within Socialist Romania. The Hungarian Autonomous

Province was dissolved in 1968, one year after Ceauşescu became head of state. For the next twenty years, the Romanian authorities pursued a policy of 'Rumanization,' which involved the mass resettlement of ethnic Romanians in Székely Land and the resettlement of Székely Hungarians with higher education outside of Székely Land in other parts of Romania.

According to the most recent Romanian census data from 2011, the contemporary population of Székely Land is 1,071,890, and 609,033 of these, or almost 60%, identify as Székely Hungarians. Proportionally, this is a significant decline from the 2002 census, when the total population of Székely Land was 809,000, and 612,043 of these, or just over 75%, identified as Hungarian. Within Székely Land there are significant differences between the three counties: in Harghita, Székely Hungarians account for 82.9% of the total population, in Covasna 71.6%, and in Mureş 36.5%.

In post-Communist Romania, the minority rights of Székely Hungarians are protected by the constitution. Protection of minority rights was a key requirement for Romania's 2007 ascension to the European Union and is regularly monitored. Furthermore, Hungarians constitute the most vocal and best-organized minority group in contemporary Romania. The position of Székely Hungarians in Romania is often considered exemplary in contemporary Eastern Europe.

So, how does this 'model minority' fare when it comes to education?

Székely Hungarians enjoy a constitutional right to bilingual education. Because this constitutional right has been achieved only relatively recently and because it is implemented in an education system with a history of suppressing Hungarian, education in Székely Land can be considered paradigmatic of the experience of multilingual schooling in schools with a monolingual habitus. The key finding is that this kind of schooling does not produce good outcomes and that students in this context underachieve both in Hungarian and in Romanian. Underperformance in each language is clearly tied to monolingual ideologies that shortchange young

Székely Hungarians. These operate in different ways for each language; I will now describe the teaching of each language in turn.

The home language, Székely Hungarian, has been severely damaged by decades of more or less active anti-Hungarian policies. Thus, contemporary Hungarian-medium education suffers from a lack of qualified teachers, appropriate teaching materials, and specialized dictionaries. Even if Székely Hungarian is their first language, vocational teachers may not be competent to teach vocational subjects in Hungarian because they lack specialized technical vocabulary in the language. Since the end of communism, many advanced textbooks have been translated into Székely Hungarian but this has been done in an ad hoc manner and there is a lack of standardization, as textbook translations are not moderated and translators are not necessarily technically competent.

These problems of Hungarian teaching could be easily solved because Hungarian is not only a minority language in Romania but also the national language of neighboring Hungary, a fellow member state of the European Union. In Hungary, a fully functional national educational system through the medium of Hungarian exists. Therefore, the problems of teaching Hungarian in schools in Székely Land could be solved by providing professional development for Székely Hungarian teachers through teacher training institutions in Hungary, by importing teaching materials from Hungary, and by standardizing local textbooks with reference to norms operating in Hungary. However, this seemingly straightforward solution is not an option because the Romanian state insists on its educational sovereignty and prohibits such measures.

In sum, despite constitutional language rights, Székely Hungarians in practice largely lack the opportunity to extend their mother tongue into the domains of vocational and higher education and thus find themselves excluded from pursuing vocational and higher education through the medium of Hungarian.

What about Romanian then? Can the Székely Hungarians not pursue vocational and higher studies through the medium of Romanian?

Unfortunately, Romanian language education in Székely Land is lacking in quality, too, particularly in Harghita and Covasna where Hungarians continue to constitute more than three-quarters of the population. Lacking the opportunity to practice Romanian in everyday life, Székely Hungarians there rely on the school to learn Romanian. Romanian is indeed a compulsory subject throughout the entire education system and some subjects such as Romanian history have to be taught through the medium of Romanian even in Hungarian-medium schools. Even so, the Romanian proficiency of many students is so poorly developed that they fail final school examinations at the end of Year Eight. Even those who make it to the end of Year Twelve often do not speak Romanian correctly and fluently.

The reasons for these unsatisfactory outcomes are related to teaching methods. Despite the fact that Székely Hungarian children start school without knowing Romanian and are not exposed to Romanian in their daily lives, Romanian is not taught as a foreign language. Instead, it is taught as if it were the children's mother tongue, including a heavy emphasis on literary analysis. Consequently, students' comprehension may be severely limited. A teacher of Romanian Language and Literature in a Székely Land high school explained the situation as follows:

> Competence in Romanian doesn't develop even in twelve years' time. Naturally, this can be explained by the fact that the textbook that we use was written for Romanian students, and they do not expect that students will possibly have any difficulties with them, and none of the textbooks concentrate on communicative language use. So, our students learn by heart everything they have to know for the exams.[5]

Again, it would seem that there is a straightforward solution for this problem, namely, to employ foreign language teaching methods rather than mother-tongue teaching methods. However, the term 'foreign language' with reference to Romanian in Romania is so ideologically laden that curriculum change is unthinkable and it is impossible to implement adequate teaching methods.

Székely Hungarians aspire to high levels of bilingualism as a resource for socioeconomic participation in Romania and Europe. Despite constitutional guarantees, however, the ways in which Hungarian and Romanian are used in the education system present a barrier to their full participation. Nationalist language ideologies present an obstacle to pragmatic solutions to local problems and serve to exclude Hungarians from receiving a quality education.

In contrast to the vast majority of children in the world who start school with linguistic repertoires that differ from those valued and endorsed by the school, Székely Hungarians enjoy constitutional rights to have their language used in school as a medium of education. Even so, educational outcomes are poor for this group, as we have seen. So how do minority children without such constitutional protections fare?

SUBMERSION EDUCATION

In Chapter Four, we examined the paradoxical situation of adult language learners in the workplace: they have to learn a new language by communicating in that language and they have to achieve communicative goals while learning the new language. Young language learners in schools face exactly the same paradox: they have to learn a new language by learning content in that language and they have to learn new content while learning the language in which the content is delivered. If these children are taught in the same ways as those whose linguistic repertoire is very similar to the language of the school, an obviously unfair situation arises: the latter can concentrate on learning content, while the former, who are learning language and content at the same time, will always be playing catch-up.

This unjust educational approach which places a double burden on minority children is known as 'submersion education.' 'Submersion education' refers to a situation where students are made to study exclusively through the medium of a language that they have not yet fully mastered. They are learning a new language *and* curriculum content at the same time. And they usually do so in the presence of peers who are native speakers of the language of instruction and in the absence of any structured language learning support.

It is beyond doubt that this type of education produces poor results, both in regards to language outcomes and in regards to content learning. In a key textbook about bilingual education, *Foundations of Bilingual Education and Bilingualism*, the educationist Colin Baker lists the negative consequences of submersion education:

> Listening to a new language demands high concentration. It is tiring, with a constant pressure to think about the form of the language and less time to think about curriculum content. A child has to take in information from different curriculum areas and learn a language at the same time. Stress, lack of self-confidence, 'opting-out', disaffection and alienation may occur.[6]

As early as 1974 the US Supreme Court ruled in a famous court case, *Lau v. Nichols*, that submersion education constituted a violation of civil rights:

> [. . .] there is no equality of treatment merely by providing students with the same facilities, textbooks, teachers, and curriculum; for students who do not understand English are effectively foreclosed from any meaningful education.[7]

Despite the obvious injustice of submersion education, submersion education continues to be the predominant mode of educating minority children around the world. While some 'traditional' minorities, such as the Székely Hungarians discussed above, may no longer find themselves subjected to submersion education, most 'new' minorities do. Furthermore, where submersion education has given way to bilingual education, it has mostly been on the primary level and, to a smaller degree, on the secondary level. At the tertiary level, submersion education continues to be by far the predominant mode of operation.

Even at the tertiary level, submersion education disadvantages minority students, as recent New Zealand research demonstrates.[8] Most research into submersion education has been conducted with students who do not speak the language of instruction at all. However, in higher education a certain proficiency level in the language of instruction is typically an admission requirement. Even so, students who meet the language-related admission requirements but do so at a relatively low level of proficiency are still disadvantaged by the combined weight of having to improve their linguistic proficiency and having to learn complex academic content at the same time.

The study analyzed the performance data of 297 pharmacy students in a four-year degree at the University of Otago in Dunedin on New Zealand's South Island. Participating students entered the program in three consecutive years and the study examined whether performance in the program could be predicted on the basis of student variables such as English language proficiency, ethnicity, and residency status. Two hundred sixty-five of the total of 297 pharmacy students graduated in the end. Of those who graduated twenty-eight had to repeat a year, and 105 failed at least one paper at some point during their studies. That means the degree was relatively plain sailing for 132 students; 133 students experienced varying degrees of difficulties ranging from failing a paper to failing a year; and thirty-two students failed completely.

It is an admission requirement into the program where the study took place to sit an English diagnostic test. Those who fail the English diagnostic test may still enter the program but will be required to pass a remedial English paper in the first year. The number of students who were admitted despite failing the English diagnostic test was forty-eight and these were coded as having 'weak English.' The number of students who should be considered English language learners was probably higher but the study did not use further measures of English language proficiency. The data were coded for ethnicity, though (ninety-four students were European or Maori; 186 Asian; and seventeen 'other'), and one might assume that the 'non-local ethnicity' students (Asian and 'other') included some more language learners even if their English might have been good enough to pass the diagnostic test.

The strongest predictor of success in the program (graduating within four years; not having to repeat a year; not failing a paper) was, unsurprisingly, academic performance on entry. The predictors of low performance (not graduating; having to repeat a year; failing one or more papers) were more complex, and included 'having weak English, being of non-local ethnicities, being male, and having lower grades at entry.'

In his discussion, the researcher sums up the language problem as one of submersion education in higher education:

> Within our own university, the students reported on in this study that are identified as having lower English proficiency in the [admission] screening test are enrolled in a remedial programme that they are required to pass. All students are then re-screened in the second year of our programme, but none of those identified in the first year excel, and 77% of them fail a subsequent screening test in second year, and are then directed to further remedial help and further rescreening. That the students who are initially identified in the first year continue to have academic difficulties, even at the end of the programme, in spite of having to seek remedial help, and being further retested suggests two possibilities. The first is that the remedial help is ineffective, but the second, and in my opinion more likely, possibility, is that students who start with weaker English will be improving their English skills over time during the course, but are unable to make up enough ground.[9]

Submersion education is a 'sink-or-swim' approach. It disadvantages linguistic minority students because they face a double challenge that jeopardizes their academic performance.

COMPOUNDING DISADVANTAGE

Not all minority students fare equally poorly under conditions of submersion education. A meta-study of North American research found that in subjects such as reading, social studies, and the sciences, minority students in submersion contexts on average caught up to national norms within five to seven years.[10] Some students were faster and some never caught up. In mathematics, the average was two years and, again, the variation was significant. In a more recent Israeli study, immigrant students from Russia were found to take on average nine to eleven years to catch up to fifth-grade-level norms in mathematics and five to seven years to catch up to ninth-grade-level norms.[11] The same study found that the average immigrant student from Ethiopia never caught up to grade-level norms. These studies demonstrate that, in addition to the large achievement gap in mathematics between native-born and immigrant students under submersion education conditions, there are also substantial differences within immigrant students. This variation is more than can be explained by differences in academic ability alone. The differences in mathematical performance between Hebrew language learners from Ethiopia and Russia demonstrate that, yet again, the injustice of submersion education works as a compound product.

In order to understand those compounding factors we will now examine the educational pathways of the children of Brazilian migrants in Japan.[12]

The Japanese education system consists of nine years of compulsory schooling, comprised of six years of elementary school and three years of middle school. These are followed by three optional years of high school. Despite the fact that it is not compulsory, almost all Japanese children attend high school. However, among the children of migrants, the high school enrollment rate is only 71%. It is thus obvious that migrant children are educationally disadvantaged vis-à-vis their non-migrant peers.

The researchers, Hirohisa Takenoshita, Yoshimi Chitose, Shigehiro Ikegami, and Eunice Akemi Ishikawa, investigated the family characteristics and characteristics of the local context that distinguish migrant children who were enrolled in high school from those who were not in a sample of 203 adolescent and young adult second-generation residents in Shizuoka prefecture. They considered parental education and employment, gender, race, age at migration, transnationalism, local context of reception, and parental Japanese language proficiency. We will now review their findings of the educational success of the sample group relative to each of these factors.

It is well known that parental level of education is a key determinant of children's educational achievement. This is true of both migrant and non-migrant populations. However, the researchers found that the correlation between Brazilian parents' educational level and their children's high school enrollment was much more modest than is generally the case. That means that parental educational level gets devalued in the process of migration. The devaluation of the educational credentials of first-generation migrants in the labor market is not uncommon, as we know from Chapter Four. What is surprising is the devaluation of migrants' educational credentials also with regard to parental ability to transmit their educational achievements to their children.

The relative unimportance of parental education for the academic success of their children in this context can be explained by the way Brazilian migrants are incorporated into the Japanese labor market. Irrespective of their educational level and other characteristics, Brazilian migrants are incorporated into the irregular labor market working unskilled or low-skilled jobs. The regular Japanese labor market, from which Brazilian migrants are largely excluded, has traditionally been characterized by strong company-based labor unions, lifetime employment, seniority earnings, and, overall, a high level of labor protection and stability. However, in Japan, as elsewhere, globalization has involved a concerted assault on labor and the regular labor market has been shrinking fast while irregular jobs have been mushrooming. And that is where Brazilian migrants find themselves. They are typically employed through agencies in temporary, unstable, and poorly paid jobs without benefits.

Ninety percent of Brazilian migrants work unskilled or low-skilled jobs under irregular conditions. By contrast, only 30% of all Japanese workers are employed in such jobs and, at only 12%, that figure is even lower for male Japanese workers. As a result of their precarious employment status, migrants work longer hours than their native-born counterparts. This is significant because more time spent at work means less time spent with children—a fact that disadvantages the children of the working poor from birth and plays a significant role in the intergenerational transmission of disadvantage.[13]

Overall, parental employment turned out to be the most significant factor distinguishing migrant children who were enrolled in high school from those who were not. Having a father employed in standard work was the most significant factor that correlated positively with migrant children's high school enrollment.

Gender was also highly significant, with boys being more likely to be enrolled in high school than girls. The researchers explain this gender difference with persistent gender discrimination in Japan: it is more rational for migrants to invest what limited resources they may have into the education of their sons because girls, by comparison, are not likely to get very far in education and employment anyway. Additionally, when parents both have to work long and irregular hours, girls are often deployed to look after siblings and the household.

Race presented another surprise: it was not correlated with high school enrollment. On the basis of other studies that had shown that non-Western non-Japanese children are often bullied in Japanese schools, the researchers had hypothesized that race might influence high school enrollment, too. Therefore, they distinguished between *nikkei* and non-*nikkei* migrant children. The former are born to two parents of Japanese descent and would thus look phenotypically similar to native-born Japanese children, while the latter are born to at least one parent who is not of Japanese descent. It turned out that race played no role in high school enrollment and that *nikkei* migrant children had no advantage vis-à-vis non-*nikkei* migrant children. In fact, both groups were equally disadvantaged vis-à-vis their non-migrant Japanese peers. The researchers explain this finding with regard to Japan's myth as a homogeneous nation and the collective denial that Japan has become an immigration country.

As regards age at migration and transnationalism, the authors found that the so-called '1.5 generation' is the most educationally disadvantaged: those who had migrated between the ages of ten and fourteen, the maximum age for inclusion in the study, were least likely to have gone on to high school. By contrast, the high school enrollment rates of those who were four years or younger at the time of migration and those who were born in Japan were almost as high as those of their non-migrant Japanese peers. When it comes to the educational success of migrant children, younger is clearly better as these children had more exposure not only to the Japanese language but also to the Japanese education system.

By the same token, children whose parents moved frequently back and forth between Japan and Brazil found their exposure to the Japanese language and the Japanese education system frequently interrupted and these interruptions significantly reduced their likelihood of high school enrollment. Children of parents who had no history of re-migration to Brazil were four times more likely to be enrolled in high school than those who moved back to Brazil for an extended period one or more times.

That transnationalism should be so disadvantageous is related to the socioeconomic circumstances under which it takes place. Where migrants are incorporated into the lower and temporary segments of the labor market, as Brazilian migrants are in Japan, their transnationalism is usually related to the vagaries of their employment. Their involuntary transnationalism means a lack of stability for their children and therefore constitutes an obstacle to educational achievement.

The researchers also explored the local context of reception as a factor in migrant children's educational outcomes. Throughout Shizuoka prefecture, migrants find themselves in highly diverse circumstances as regards the targeted services available to them. The largest concentration of Brazilians in Shizuoka lives in Hamamatsu, an industrial city. Hamamatsu municipal government has provided a variety of special education programs targeting migrant children since the 1990s, including the provision of Portuguese-, Spanish-, and Chinese-speaking tutors to provide Japanese language support. Additionally, Hamamatsu municipal government subsidizes private ethnic schools and organizations devoted to the education of migrant children. Therefore, it is reasonable to assume that migrant children in Hamamatsu would be more likely to be enrolled in high school than their counterparts living elsewhere in Shizuoka. This is indeed what the researchers found: residency in Hamamatsu with its targeted services that ameliorate submersion education was favorably associated with high school enrollment.

Finally, the effect of parental proficiency in Japanese turned out to be relatively small. Unsurprisingly, there is a positive correlation between higher levels of self-reported parental Japanese proficiency and children's high school enrollment but it is one of the smallest correlations examined by the researchers.

In sum, the most important positive factors are the regular employment of the father and residence in Hamamatsu. The most important negative factors are female gender, having been aged 10 or older at the time of migration, and having experienced multiple migrations between Brazil and Japan. As the researchers explain, 'the family's economic resources facilitate their children's enrollment in high school. In other words, Brazilian children's schooling is impeded by employment instability among their parents.'[14]

While submersion education disadvantages all migrant children, this effect is compounded by various factors, principally for the children of parents who experience significant disadvantage at work. Conversely, the disadvantage of submersion education is less of an insurmountable obstacle for those who are being raised in stable socioeconomic conditions. The disadvantage of submersion may also be offset through the provision of targeted bilingual services, and we will now examine attempts to ameliorate submersion education through the provision of such services.

TESTING AGAINST LINGUISTIC DIVERSITY

Recognition of the fact that submersion education is unjust is not new. As mentioned above, as early as 1974 the US Supreme Court ruled that submersion education was discriminatory. Since then, many attempts have been made to overcome or ameliorate the submersion model. Such attempts include the provision of bilingual education, particularly for 'traditional' minorities, as we saw in the example of Hungarian-Romanian schooling in Székely Land. Attempts to provide bilingual schooling to 'new' minorities have been rarer and have usually been subject to the proviso 'where numbers warrant.' Well-known large-scale attempts to educate migrant children bilingually are related to English-Spanish bilingual education in some US states. On a smaller scale, individual schools may pursue bilingual education models. In Sydney, for instance, individual schools run bilingual programs in Arabic, Armenian, French, German, Italian, and Japanese. In addition to attempts to substitute bilingual education for submersion education, there have also been many attempts to ameliorate submersion education through the provision of targeted language tuition in the dominant language (e.g., English as a Second Language provisions in Anglophone countries), through the provision of heritage language classes, and through the provision of bilingual teaching assistants. The specifics of these programs are immensely varied and subject to frequent modifications as the political climate changes.[15]

The fact that efforts to overcome submersion education continue to be a political football subject to all kinds of local and national vagaries, almost half a century after submersion education was first recognized to constitute a form of discrimination, is in itself evidence of the persistence of the monolingual habitus of schooling and the exclusions this produces.

Even where schools have attempted to overcome the monolingual habitus and submersion education, this progress has been undermined by another educational development which, on the face of it, seems to have little to do with linguistic diversity: the trend toward an ever-increasing focus on standardized assessment, year-group performance targets, and league tables. Contemporary educational policies often celebrate diversity and may well support bilingual learning. However, standardized assessment, year-group performance targets, and league tables undermine diversity and bilingual learning and can be highly damaging to the academic achievement of minority students.

The British Statutory Framework for learning in the early years offers a case in point.[16] The Statutory Framework is mandatory for all British education providers catering to children up to the age of five. In its Introduction, the Statutory Framework espouses four foundational principles, three of which highlight the diversity of children: 'every child is a unique child'; 'children learn and develop well in enabling environments, in which their experiences respond to their individual needs'; and 'children develop and learn in different ways and at different rates.'

Before you read on, take a moment to reflect what 'the individual needs' of 'the unique child' might be in a linguistically diverse society. Are you thinking that all children should get the opportunity to experience different languages in early education? Are you thinking that children with a home language other than English should get the opportunity to develop both English and the home language? Are you thinking that a childcare provider should have measures in place that value all languages and promote linguistic diversity?

The Statutory Framework states that 'providers must take reasonable steps to provide opportunities for children to develop and use their home language in play and learning, supporting their language development at home'[17] but offers no guidance as to what such 'reasonable steps' might be. However, even this limited vision of linguistic diversity in the early years is undermined by the assessment requirements. In fact, there is a fundamental contradiction between the recognition of children's diversity and the requirement for the continuous assessment of child performance against learning targets. This contradiction is particularly explicit in the field of 'communication and language,' a designated prime learning area.

In this area, only English is recognized in determining adequate performance:

> When assessing communication, language and literacy skills, practitioners must assess children's skills in English. If a child does not have a strong grasp of English language, practitioners must explore the child's skills in the home language with parents and/or carers, to establish whether there is cause for concern about language delay.[18]

This assessment requirement equates 'communication and language' with English, and with English only. The assessment requirement effectively devalues all other languages, associating them with language delay and a deficit view.

What do these assessment requirements mean in practice in actual childcare centers? The education researchers Leena H. Robertson, Rose Drury, and Carrie Cable discovered, unsurprisingly, that these assessment requirements undermine any form of bi- or multilingual provision in early childhood education. They found British childcare centers—including those that have multilingual teachers and staff—to be monolingual spaces where languages other than English are silenced. For children who have a home language other than English this means that, rather than their individual needs being recognized and supported as those of 'the unique child,' they are streamlined into monolingual children. For all children, irrespective of their home language, the silencing of languages other than English in this first institutional space they are likely to encounter in their lives is a lost opportunity.

The overall result is that the Statutory Framework creates the illusion that linguistic diversity is valued in early childhood education while simultaneously rendering languages other than English illegitimate and worthless forms of 'communication and language' for young children.

Not only do standardized assessment, year-group performance targets, and league tables create an educational environment where linguistic diversity is silenced and languages other than the dominant language are undermined; they also create the failure of individual children who are unfamiliar with the dominant language. I will illustrate the ways in which standardized assessment and year-group performance targets create the academic failure of minority children first with an anecdote about the reading performance of a refugee child in a US school and then with systematic research into the literacy and numeracy performance of indigenous children in Australia.

The anecdote is about Oscar, a Grade Five student in a school in Vermont.[19] Like about half the school's children, Oscar is the son of refugees who were recently resettled in the school's catchment area from a refugee camp in Africa. Despite the fact that he was new to the country, new to English, and new to formal schooling, Oscar had to take the same nationally standardized Grade Five reading test as all the other kids his age around the country who had grown up in the USA and spoken English all their lives:

> Oscar needed 20 minutes to read a passage on Neil Armstrong landing his Eagle spacecraft on the moon; it should have taken 5 minutes [. . .] but Oscar was determined, reading out loud to himself.

The first test question asked whether the passage was fact or fiction. Oscar explained his reasoning to his teacher: 'Oh, Mrs. Irvine, man don't go on the moon, man don't go on the back of eagles, this is not true.'

From the explanation it is obvious that Oscar had understood the text. It is also obvious that he had understood the difference between factual and fictional writing. However, his lack of exposure to (American) media meant that he did not have the required cultural knowledge to interpret the passage correctly. Oscar got the first question wrong. In fact, he got all the other five questions wrong, too, because they were based on having identified that the text was factual.

Oscar failed because his knowledge of the world was quite different from that of the middle-class native-born 'standard' child the test designers seem to have had in mind. Cultural bias has been a concern for assessment researchers and practitioners since the emergence of IQ tests in the first half of the twentieth century. Standardized assessment disadvantages not only migrant children but all children whose cultural and linguistic repertoires differ from those valued by the middle class.[20]

The newspaper article from which I learned about Oscar's story does not tell us what happened to Oscar in the long term. A likely scenario is that he became demotivated by failing a test into which he had put his best efforts and which he felt he understood. Maybe he came to believe that he was not good at reading and that school was not his thing. Maybe he dropped out of school early and ended up as just another small number in the large statistic of the academic underachievement of African refugee children.[21] I hope this scenario is not what happened and that it all turned out differently for Oscar.

It is not uncommon that the test results of children like Oscar, who are forced to take unsuitable tests, end up stigmatizing not only the individual but the whole group. Another injustice resulting from the standardized testing of linguistically diverse populations is thus the way in which collective underperformance on such tests is seen not as evidence of the failure of policy makers and test designers, but as evidence that casts aspersions on the academic abilities of disadvantaged groups.

Like African refugee children, Australia's indigenous students are another case in point. Each year since a standardized national testing regime was first introduced in Australia in 2008, students in the Northern Territory, where most indigenous students live, have been found to underperform dramatically on the so-called 'NAPLAN' test. 'NAPLAN' stands for 'National Assessment Program—Literacy and Numeracy.' In 2012, for instance, more than 30% of Year Three students in the Northern Territory were found to perform below the national minimum standard in Reading, Writing, Spelling, and

Numeracy. For Grammar and Punctuation, the number of Northern Territory Year Three students performing below the national minimum standard was close to 40%. Across Australia as a whole, the figures for not meeting national minimum standards were between 5% and 7%.[22]

Around 40% of students enrolled in Northern Territory schools are indigenous. Across Australia as a whole, their number is 4%. The dramatic underperformance of Northern Territory students in national standardized testing coupled with the fact that this underperformance is obviously related to the high proportion of indigenous students in the Northern Territory has regularly resulted in highly politicized debates about indigenous academic underachievement. Conservatives blame 'underperforming schools' and progressives blame 'systemic socioeconomic disadvantage' for the persistent achievement gap. After much soul-searching when the annual NAPLAN results are published, the failure of indigenous education in Australia is usually shelved in the too-hard basket for yet another year.

. Unfortunately, few commentators, educators, and policy makers stop to consider that NAPLAN does not actually tell us anything about literacy and numeracy achievements in remote Northern Territory schools because NAPLAN is a test designed and standardized for first language speakers of English. However, English is a second language across remote Northern Territory locations. This situation leads to a number of specific linguistic challenges that Northern Territory students face when undergoing NAPLAN testing.

. In remote indigenous communities English is exclusive to the school. English is not the language of wider communication and children are rarely exposed to English outside school settings. Even so, it is not always recognized that English is, for all intents and purposes, a foreign language in remote communities. This is due to the fact that the majority of indigenous people in remote locations speak an English-based creole. While most people are prepared to accept that there are problems associated with having to perform on an English-language literacy and numeracy test if the test takers speak a clearly distinct language as their main language, this is not always the case when it comes to creole speakers. Creole speakers are often not even recognized as speaking a language that is distinct from English. They are simply considered to speak 'bad English.'[23]

Creoles spoken in Australia differ widely but most have English as the lexifier language and are structurally based on an indigenous language. Australian creoles thus often sound like English but may, for example, not have subject-verb agreement nor distinguish singular and plural. When examining Year Three NAPLAN sample tests, linguists Gillian Wigglesworth, Jane Simpson, and Deborah Loakes identified many linguistic problems that would have made the test misleading to a creole speaker.

As an example they examine the spelling test item: 'We jumpt on the trampoline.' In the test, test takers have to correct the underlined item to 'jumped.' Leaving aside the fact that presenting an incorrect item to a learner is highly problematic in itself, test takers need to identify that 'jumpt' is in the past tense and that the final [t] sound is therefore graphically represented as <ed>. However, past tense in Australian creoles would usually be realized as 'bin jamp.' For creole speakers this spelling test item is thus not actually testing spelling. It is testing grammatical knowledge that creole speakers are unlikely to have.

The problem is compounded by the fact that final stops such as [t] are extremely difficult to hear for people with high frequency hearing loss. This is relevant because ear infections are extremely high in remote indigenous communities and about 70% of all children there are affected by some form of hearing loss.

Just like Oscar in Vermont, students in remote Northern Territory locations are further disadvantaged by the fact that the reading passages in the NAPLAN test are littered with cultural concepts quite alien to the experience of children in remote Australia. The sample tests examined by the researchers were populated with 'cinemas,' 'paperboys,' 'picket fences,' 'letter boxes,' and 'parking meters'—none of which exist in remote communities.

In sum, the NAPLAN test is linguistically and culturally problematic for creole-speaking children in remote communities because a standardized test designed for first-language speakers of English will always fail second-language speakers, particularly if they are not even recognized as such.

Global diagnoses such as 'underperforming schools' or 'systemic socioeconomic disadvantages' ultimately mean that, as a society, we can collectively throw up our hands in despair and decide that indigenous education is a problem that is too big and intractable to fix. Because there is nothing we can do, we might just as well ignore the problem. However, this is adding insult to injury. The global diagnoses miss the clear language side of the academic failure of indigenous children. And there are obvious, realistic, and doable solutions to the problem: bilingual education with the use of the mother tongue as medium of instruction in the early years of schooling; simultaneous systematic instruction in English as an additional language; and, of course, tests designed for the actual population of test takers rather than an imagined monolingual mother tongue speaker of Standard English.

MISDIAGNOSING LANGUAGE PROFICIENCY

NAPLAN test results in Australia throw up a further anomaly. As part of the personal data collected about test takers, each test paper has a tick box for 'Language Background Other Than English.' Abbreviated as 'LBOTE,' this category is to be ticked if 'either the student or a parent/guardian speaks a language other than English at home.' You do not have to be a social scientist or a linguist to see that this is a pointless category to have: a test taker who is considered 'LBOTE' could be someone who is a monolingual speaker of Standard English (with a parent who speaks another language), a bi- or multilingual speaker whose repertoire includes Standard English or some other form of English, or, finally, a monolingual speaker of a language other than English who has no proficiency in English whatsoever. In short, having 'LBOTE' status does not say anything about the proficiency of the test taker in Standard Australian English, the language in which the test is administered.[24]

Because 'LBOTE' is a meaningless category, it is not surprising that it results in 'strange' correlations: across Australia, there is little difference in the test results of 'LBOTE' and 'non-LBOTE' groups, although 'LBOTE' students in fact slightly outperform 'non-LBOTE' students. This situation is different only in the Northern Territory, where 'LBOTE' students perform significantly lower than 'non-LBOTE.' This is obviously nonsensical. But what does it mean for social justice?

To begin with, linguists Sally Dixon and Denise Angelo found in a survey of eighty-six schools in Queensland that only two out of these eighty-six schools felt reasonably confident that the language data they held about their students were accurate. In addition to the 'LBOTE' status of NAPLAN test takers, schools also recorded a 'main language other than English' on enrollment in forms that were variously filled in by parents or administrators as they saw fit. If 'main language other than English' was left blank on the enrollment form, 'English' was sometimes entered on transfer into the database instead of a null response. Some students also received 'English as an additional language or dialect' status. This category was variously assessed by teachers if and when students seemed to have problems and funding for additional English language support was available.

These three categories were internally incoherent and did not match across categories in eighty-four out of eighty-six surveyed schools. This shocking finding is related to the fact that language-related categories are poorly defined, as we saw in the example of 'LBOTE.' It is also related to a general language blindness in schools, further evidence of the monolingual habitus of multilingual schools. Furthermore, schools were particularly 'language-blind' when it came to indigenous children: as in the Northern Territory, creoles and contact varieties were not necessarily recognized as anything other than 'English.' By the same token, some students with clear ethnic affiliations were categorized as speakers of that language irrespective of their proficiency in that language.

The overall consequence of all these 'dodgy data' floating around in relation to language is that educators come to see language as meaningless because it does not really distinguish between one group and another. Overall, 'LBOTEs' and 'non-LBOTEs' seem to perform more or less the same (except for the Northern Territory, where there is that 'intractable' indigenous problem, as discussed above), and the same seems to be true of 'MLOTEs' ('main language other than English,' in case you have lost track), 'non-MLOTEs,' 'EAL/Ds' ('English as an additional language or dialect'), and 'non-EAL/Ds.' However, it is not language that is meaningless as a factor in student performance. It is dodgy data that creates this illusion. The very fact of proliferating data categories more or less referring to the same status will inevitably leave people confused and unwilling or unable to take 'language' seriously.

In Chapter Four, we noted that, by and large, the general public is not particularly good at making everyday judgments about language proficiency. However, that the same is true of teachers, school administrators, and other educators is outrageous. There is currently no compulsory language-related training or qualification requirement in Australia's teacher training. As we have seen, this short-changes students who come to school with linguistic repertoires that do not include Standard Australian English: 'the racial inequality that is in danger of being "locked in," is whether language learning is recognised as such, is supported as such and is lauded as such.'[25]

In addition to creole speakers, there is another group of language learners who are often not recognized as such. These are students from minority language backgrounds who have high levels of oracy in the dominant language but low levels of (academic) literacy. Often these are students who entered submersion schooling in the dominant language at a relatively young age. Their accents and oral proficiencies for social purposes make them indistinguishable from their peers who are monolingual in the dominant language. However, because they were never recognized as language learners and received no language learning support, their literacy in the dominant language lags behind and they are several grade levels below their peers in reading and writing. On account of their oral proficiency, their difficulties in reading and writing are not recognized as a language learning problem but are misdiagnosed as academic underachievement.

This group of students comprises a substantial segment of students with migrant backgrounds in the world's school systems. In New York City, for instance, formally defined 'long-term English language learners' account for about one-third of high school students requiring English language learning support. Students are considered 'long-term-English language learners' if they have attended school in the USA for seven or more years and are still requiring language learning support.[26]

Despite the fact that the numbers of long-term English language learners in New York City schools are substantial, they do not receive any specialized services, and the services they receive are mismatched. For English language learning support they are usually placed in the same class as new arrivals with limited or no oral proficiency in English. As a consequence, this support is way below their level, they get bored, and they disengage.

Because of their high levels of oral proficiency, these students are often misdiagnosed and their need for reading and writing support is overlooked. Furthermore, their low literacy in English results in poor academic performance. The high school average of a sample of long-term English language learners studied by linguists Kate Menken and Tatyana Kleyn was a D+. Almost 20% of the sample had an F average. Failure breeds failure and many long-term English language learners drop out of school altogether.

Long-term English language learners have been failed on numerous occasions. To begin with, submersion education has denied them the English language learning support they would have needed to acquire adequate English language proficiency and learn adequate academic content. From there, the fact that these students were English language learners simply got forgotten and they ended up being nothing more than poor students. From there, the students were on a slippery slope to becoming school dropouts, one of the most powerful predictors of lifelong exclusion from socioeconomic security. Long-term English language learners have also been failed in yet another way: they have missed out on the opportunity to develop high-level language proficiencies in their home language and have thus been denied the benefits of high-level bilingual proficiencies.

DENYING THE BENEFITS OF MULTILINGUALISM

Not only does submersion education lead to poor academic outcomes. As we have seen, it is also a far from ideal way to learn the dominant language and leaves some young people as long-term language learners. However, submersion education not only limits dominant language learning but also stunts the development of the home language. Submersion education is also known as 'subtractive language learning,' where 'learning a second language means losing the first.'[27] Stunting development of the home language by switching exclusively to the dominant language has negative effects not only on language learning but overall cognitive development and academic achievement. By contrast, extending the home language while learning the dominant language and acquiring high-level oral and written language proficiencies in two or more languages has a number of benefits, which are being denied through submersion education. In addition to linguistic and academic disadvantages, stunting the home language also has negative behavioral and economic consequences, as we will now discuss.

Proficiency in the home language is important for the mental health of minority children and youths, as a study tracking the development of anxiety disorders and behavioral problems among Asian-American children from kindergarten to Grade Five discovered.[28] Problem behaviors increased for all children during that period but they increased least in those who were balanced bilinguals and in those who were dominant in the language other than English. Those who were monolingual in English or English-dominant experienced a faster growth rate in mental health problems and those who were monolingual in a language other than English experienced the highest growth rate.

The fact that lacking English language proficiency in the USA is not good for personal well-being is obvious and requires little explanation. However, the fact that bilinguals fare better than monolingual English speakers flies in the face of current educational practice, which, as we have seen, is to mainstream migrant children into English as quickly as possible. At the same time, we should not be surprised: bilingual children get the best of both worlds and in addition to building relationships through school, they also have access to additional social and cultural resources in their community. These may include being able to communicate with parents and grandparents as opposed to being shut out from such family conversations if the child does not speak the home language. Linguistic inability to develop meaningful intergenerational relationships in migration contexts is not as unusual as it may sound. The ethnographer Sandra Kouritzin documented situations in migrant families in Canada where parents could never have a conversation about difficult topics with their adolescent children because the children's proficiency in the home language was not up to such conversations and the parents' proficiency in English was inadequate.[29]

Stunting the home language may not only exacerbate behavioral and mental health problems but also diminish the economic opportunities of minority youths, as another US study of the earnings of second-generation migrants relative to their level of bilingual proficiency has revealed.[30] Re-examining data from two large-scale longitudinal studies conducted between 1988 and 2003 in the USA, the researcher, Orhan Agirdag, analyzed the linguistic proficiency and earnings of 3,553 individuals. These individuals were either born to at least one migrant parent or came to the USA at a young age. In the early 2000s, they were in their mid-twenties.

On the basis of participants' self-reported proficiency data, the researcher distinguished three language groups: high-level bilinguals, who had high levels of proficiency, crucially including the ability to read and write, in both English and their home language;

low-level bilinguals, who had low levels of proficiency in both English and their home language; and English-dominant, who had high levels of proficiency in English but no or low levels of proficiency in their home language.

Based on our discussion so far, it is to be expected that the English-dominant would constitute the largest group. This was indeed the case and more than half of those surveyed were English-dominant. Low-level bilinguals accounted for slightly more than 20% of those surveyed. These are the long-term language English language learners we encountered above as young adults. The number of high-level bilinguals in the sample was very similar to that of low-level bilinguals and also stood at slightly above 20%. The high-level bilinguals are the lucky ones who either lived within the catchment area of a school with a bilingual immersion program when they were children or whose parents put in the effort of teaching them how to read and write the home language after school and on weekends.

Parental investment into high-level bilingualism pays off for this group. High-level bilingualism was robustly associated with a higher earnings differential of around USD3,000 per year, and the effect held even if other variables that are known to influence earnings were controlled for (e.g., gender, parental socioeconomic status, educational achievement). The effect also held across language groups, even if some languages were more valuable than others (e.g., Chinese-Americans were found to earn more than other migrant groups but within the group of Chinese-Americans those with high-level bilingual proficiencies earned more than those who were English-dominant or those who had low-level bilingual proficiencies). Interestingly, when other variables were controlled, there was no earnings difference between those who were English-dominant and those who were low-level bilinguals.

A higher earnings differential of USD3,000 per year when everything else is kept constant is a sizable effect, particularly considering that the sample consisted of people in their twenties who might not yet have reached their full earning potential. Additionally, the actual financial advantage of high-level bilingualism is likely to be greater due to indirect effects which are obscured by keeping other variables constant such as the link between high-level bilingualism and educational achievement (i.e., high-level bilinguals are more likely to achieve high levels of education and thus they have a compounded earnings advantage).

Mainstreaming migrant children into the dominant language is bad for them educationally, cognitively, and socio-psychologically. As this research demonstrates, it is also bad for them economically. Beyond the economic disadvantage suffered by individuals who have been forced into linguistic assimilation, their linguistic assimilation through the education system is bad for the economy and thus for everyone: decreasing the earning potential of second-generation migrants through linguistic assimilation will, inter alia, lower the tax base and increase the demand for social services. Conversely, those who earn more spend more.

SUMMARY

Linguistic diversity in education raises specific social justice concerns based on the entrenched mismatch between schools as institutions with a monolingual habitus serving linguistically diverse societies. This mismatch jeopardizes the quality of education received by students from both 'traditional' and 'new' minority backgrounds. Even where 'traditional' minorities have constitutional rights to education in the mother tongue and to bilingual education, the quality of their education is often undermined by nationalist and monolingual ideologies that make pragmatic solutions to language-related problems of teacher qualifications, teaching methods, or teaching materials impossible. These problems are exacerbated for minority students in submersion education.

Submersion education militates against the academic achievement of minority youths. This is the case because of the double challenge of having to learn curriculum content through a new language and having to learn a new language while studying curriculum content in that language. Furthermore, the trend toward standardized assessment, year-group performance targets, and league tables has undermined many improvements that have been made to minority education in the past decades because standardized assessment is always conducted in a particular language. By designating literacy and numeracy performance in a particular language as simply 'literacy and numeracy performance,' the fact that academic performance is always demonstrated in a particular language is obscured. This turns literacy and numeracy tests into literacy-and-numeracy-cum-language tests for learners of the dominant language and undermines both their academic and linguistic achievement.

In addition to jeopardizing academic achievement, submersion education has poor language learning outcomes and may permanently damage linguistic development in the dominant language. Misrecognition of language learner status presents a continuing obstacle to academic achievement and locks some minority students into a vicious cycle where limited proficiency in the school language and poor academic outcomes continuously reinforce each other.

Submersion education breeds academic failure and linguistic failure in the dominant language. Furthermore, it has poor language proficiency outcomes in the home language. Where minority youths fail to achieve high levels of linguistic proficiency in both home and school language, they are locked out of significant mental health protections and economic opportunities that bilingualism can confer.

In the early twenty-first century, many societies have experienced considerable angst over the long-term alienation of some second- and third-generation youths with migrant backgrounds. In response many societies have started to re-examine the schooling of children with a migrant background focusing on their academic underachievement and prescribing ever-earlier exposure to the dominant language and ever-earlier assessment on standardized tests. As the discussion here has shown, this 'more of the same' approach is likely to be counterproductive.

The evidence is clear· mainstreaming minority children into the dominant language presents a risk factor for poor academic, socioeconomic, behavioral, and emotional outcomes. By contrast, for schools to nurture bi- and multilingualism is an investment for all members of a society to be able to lead healthy and productive lives, and to strengthen the social and economic fabric of our societies. Conversely, failing to nurture bilingualism in minority children tears at the social and economic fabric and affects us all.

Chapter 6

Linguistic Diversity
and Participation

Article 27 of the Universal Declaration of Human Rights enshrines
the right 'freely to participate in the cultural life of the community,
to enjoy the arts and to share in scientific advancement and its benefits.' The worlds of work and education are crucial domains where
community participation takes place, as we have seen, and linguistic
diversity mediates equality of opportunity to participate in employment and education. This chapter will now extend the inquiry to less
clearly circumscribed domains of community life such as social services, health care, civic and political engagement, leisure activities,
and even such intangibles as experiencing a sense of belonging. Because no aspect of community participation exists in isolation, linguistic disadvantage at work and in education will indirectly result
in disadvantage in other areas as well. For instance, those who have
been excluded from adequate employment will also find their opportunities to participate in leisure activities restricted. Similarly,
low academic achievement restricts not only career opportunities
but is also related to crime and substance abuse. While it is obvious
that social justice is multidimensional and disadvantage intersects
across domains, this chapter seeks to isolate linguistic disadvantage
that specifically affects opportunities for participation in the life of
the community outside of work and education. As before, we will

take two distinct perspectives: in the first instance, we will examine language as a barrier to participation before moving on to explore how language affects the quality of participation.

LINGUISTIC BARRIERS TO PARTICIPATION

In a globalized world, there will always be situations where linguistic restrictions to participation exist. The language proficiencies of even the most talented multilingual are necessarily limited, and in a highly mobile world the limits to the linguistic proficiencies of individuals usually constitute barriers to their participation in community activities where those linguistic proficiencies are required. Lack of proficiency in the language of wider communication in a society constitutes an immense barrier to participation and can result in almost complete isolation. We will start our examination of language as a barrier by exploring in some detail the case of a young woman whose linguistic isolation had fatal consequences.[1]

In November 2007, in a fit of rage, Soltan Azizi strangled his wife of fourteen years, Marzieh Rahimi, to death in their home in Melbourne. At the time, Marzieh was thirty-three years old. She had been born to Afghan parents in a refugee camp in Pakistan, where she spent the first nineteen years of her life until her arranged marriage to her cousin, who was ten years her senior. For the first four years of their marriage, the couple lived in Afghanistan before they had to flee that country again, this time to Iran. They spent the next seven years of their lives in refugee camps in Iran waiting for permanent resettlement in a safe country. In 2005, the family was granted a humanitarian entrance visa for resettlement in Australia. It is difficult to reconstruct Marzieh's educational history but it is certain that she hardly spoke any English when she arrived in Australia and that during her two-and-a-half years in the country she had little opportunity to learn or practice English. In addition to having to look after three young children, who had been born in Iran, she gave birth to two more children in Australia. While her husband attended a government-sponsored English language learning program, she did not. It needs little imagination to see that caring for an increasing number of young children in the absence of the support of an extended family network would have left little time for learning English. If time constraints are not enough to explain her failure to learn English, it also needs to be borne in mind that the traumatic experiences of her life as a refugee—she had seen her first-born child killed by gunmen in Afghanistan when that little girl was three years old—almost certainly made language learning even more difficult for her.

During her husband's murder trial it emerged that, for an extended period of time prior to her death, the marriage had been fraught; that Marzieh had seriously contemplated getting a divorce; and that she had been scared of her husband. In such circumstances, the best course of action would be to seek assistance, either informally within one's wider social network or formally through domestic violence support services. It is well known that, in cases of domestic violence, abusers often seek to preclude precisely that course of action by keeping their victims isolated. In Marzieh's case it would not have taken much to keep her isolated as neither informal nor formal avenues of support were open to her in any meaningful way. Access to informal support networks was limited by the size of her home-language community and access to formal support services was limited by her proficiency in English.

Marzieh's home language was Dari. Usually classified as a dialect of Persian spoken in Afghanistan, Dari is considered an emergent community language in Australia, where Dari speakers began to settle in significant numbers only during the first decade of the twenty-first century. The treatment of Dari as a category in Australian census data over the years demonstrates the language's emergent status[2]: the 1991 Census had no category for Persian or Dari, and both varieties were classified as 'Asian Languages, not elsewhere included.' Reflecting growing immigration from Iran, by the next census in 1996 'Persian' had its own category, and the census recorded 19,048 speakers resident in Australia (0.1% of the total population). In 2001, the category remained as 'Persian' and the total number of speakers had increased slightly to 25,238 but their percentage of the total population remained virtually unchanged. The 2006 Census saw a significant change both to the category and to the numbers: the category was now labeled 'Iranic languages' with three distinct subcategories: 'Persian (excluding Dari),' 'Dari,' and 'Other.' 'Other' includes languages such as Kurdish, Pashto, and Balochi. The total number of 'Iranic' speakers rose to 43,772 (0.2% of the total population) and included 14,312 Dari speakers, who appear as a separate group for the first time. Dari speakers thus accounted for a minuscule 0.07% of all Australian residents. By the time of the 2011 Census the number of Dari speakers had increased to 20,179 persons (0.09% of the total population).

In the following, I will refer to data from the 2006 Census as these match the community profile during Marzieh's time in Australia between 2005 and 2007 most closely. During that time, Dari speakers accounted for 0.07% of the total population. Assuming that she may have been able to communicate also with speakers of Persian and other 'Iranic' languages, the proportion of people she could potentially have communicated with rises to 0.2% of the general population. Of course, these Dari and Persian speakers are distributed unequally across the Australian continent. Table 1 shows the numbers of Dari and Persian speakers in Australia, metropolitan Melbourne, the local government area of Casey, and the suburb where the family lived, Hampton Park. As these figures show, Marzieh and her family did not live in an ethnic enclave. On the contrary, their chances of meeting other speakers of Dari or related languages were relatively slim.

In addition to the fact that she was a speaker of a small but growing community language, there is another aspect of Marzieh's linguistic profile that is unusual: the fact that she did not speak English. Despite Australia's linguistic diversity and high migrant intake, the vast majority of the population speaks English only or is bilingual or multilingual with their linguistic repertoire including speaking English well or very well.[3] Residents who do not speak English well or not at all constitute a relatively small minority, as Table 2 shows.

Table 1: DARI AND PERSIAN SPEAKERS IN AUSTRALIA, 2006

	Number of residents	Number of Dari speakers		Number of speakers of Dari, Persian, and other 'Iranic' languages combined	
		Total	%	Total	%
Australia	19,855,288	14,312	0.07	43,772	0.22
Metropolitan Melbourne	3,371,889	4,331	0.13	10,842	0.32
Local government area of Casey	214,959	1,577	0.73	2,442	1.40
Suburb of Hampton Park	22,164	152	0.69	209	0.94

(Source: 'Census Home,' 2012)

The importance of multilingual service provision in order to ensure fair and equitable access has been recognized in Australia for a number of decades. As a result, the Commonwealth Government runs a national translating and interpreting service which is intended to facilitate the communication between government agencies and Australians who do not speak English well or at all.[4] The national translating and interpreting service provides for the translation of written and audiovisual public service messages into community languages as well as for mediating spoken interactions between individuals and public service personnel via telephone, face-to-face, or video-conference interpreting. For obvious practical reasons, provisions in emergent community languages are lagging behind those available in established community languages, both quantitatively and qualitatively. The need to engage an interpreter is usually at the discretion of a government official, and occurs

Table 2: AUSTRALIAN RESIDENTS NOT SPEAKING ENGLISH WELL
OR AT ALL, 2006

	Number of residents	Residents not speaking English well or at all	
		Total	%
Australia	19,855,288	443,188	2.23
Metropolitan Melbourne	3,371,889	142,878	4.24
Local government area of Casey	214,959	5,838	2.72
Suburb of Hampton Park	22,164	79	0.36

(Source: 'Census Home,' 2012)

either in response to a direct request for an interpreter by a client or based on the official's ad hoc assessment of the client's English language proficiency.

It is against this background of a small community of Dari speakers in an English-dominant society that Marzieh's isolation needs to be understood. As became clear during her husband's murder trial, Marzieh's only contact with other speakers of her language outside her immediate family was not in her local community at all but with her sister, who lived in the USA, and who she spoke to on the phone every few weeks. With informal support networks largely unavailable, Marzieh's main support was a maternal health care worker, who she met during hospital appointments and with whom she communicated through an on-site interpreter; and a domestic violence support officer, who the maternal health care worker referred her to and who she met with only once, communicating through a telephone interpreter. A few days prior to her death, Marzieh sought further help by making two calls to the national telephone emergency service, Triple Zero. In both cases, she hung up before the operator could bring a telephone interpreter into the conversation. The trial judge was scathing of multilingual service provision in her sentencing:

> Then on 1 November 2007 your wife made two calls to triple 000 in the early hours of the morning seeking police assistance. It is most unfortunate and an indictment on our society that no assistance was forthcoming, as a result of a very disappointing reaction by the telephone operator, to your wife's inability to speak English, in anything other than a broken English manner.[5]

Providing emergency services in linguistically heterogeneous environments is undoubtedly difficult. A study of Spanish-language calls to the US emergency telephone service found that sending a call through to the telephone interpreting service more than doubled the response time and thus was often resisted by the operator because that additional time could make the difference between life and death in an acute emergency.[6] Given the time it takes to reroute an emergency call through the telephone interpreting service, it is perhaps not surprising that Marzieh became impatient or was forced to abandon her call for help before she could actually communicate with the police. What is surprising—indeed incomprehensible—is the fact that no attempt was made to call her back and that no police car was dispatched to her place of residence despite her two aborted attempts to call emergency services.

Domestic violence is a recognized problem in Australia and there is a network of formal support services available to women who find themselves in danger. However, these formal support services operate almost exclusively in English and gaining access in another language remains difficult. As an examination of the barriers faced by migrant women in accessing legal services in the state of New South Wales put it, persons who do not speak English well in Australia are 'a long way from equal.'[7]

Cases like Marzieh's challenge us to rethink linguistic arrangements in linguistically diverse contexts in order to make access to emergency services—and social services in general—more equitable. It may be tempting to think that this is too tall an order and that ensuring equitable access through multilingual service provision is impossible. Let's return to the study of Spanish-language calls in the USA in order to examine this assumption more closely. As pointed out above, transfer of a Spanish-speaking caller to the telephone interpreting service almost doubled the response time and thus was highly inefficient. However, the situation was different in cases where bilingual operators were available in the same call center. In such cases, a Spanish emergency call was immediately transferred to a bilingual operator and the response time remained virtually unaffected. It is therefore clearly possible to provide effective multilingual services by hiring multilingual telephone operators who can handle calls in the dominant language and one or more other languages. However, in the city where the researcher recorded the bulk of his data there was not a single bilingual operator who spoke Spanish on the staff. When one knows the demographic profile of this city, the absence of English-Spanish bilingual emergency telephone operators becomes almost unbelievable: the city where the research took place is located in the USA Southwest and at the time of data collection in 2010 more than 50% of the city's population was of Hispanic origin. This information turns the assumption that monolingual emergency services are natural and normal on its head: exclusively employing monolingual English-speaking emergency telephone operators in such a context almost seems perversely designed to prevent fair and equitable access.

LANGUAGE AND THE GENDER GAP

Even today, not one single country in the world has achieved gender equality. Within societies some groups of women face multiple vulnerabilities. Migrant women are one of the most vulnerable groups and linguistic isolation can constitute one key aspect of their disadvantage, indeed their very survival as we saw in Marzieh's case. The World Economic Forum's annual gender gap reports regularly note that the gender gap is greatest in the areas of economic participation and political empowerment.[8] Therefore, this section will explore gender-specific language barriers to participation, examining how linguistic diversity and gender intersect to produce compound disadvantage.

In 2013 women constituted 49% of the world's 214 million international migrants.[9] It is often assumed that transnational migration is empowering to women, particularly if their destination country is one where women enjoy greater levels of gender equality than they do in their country of origin. Ethnographic research with women migrants to Australia from Asia, Eastern Europe, and Latin America shows that the story is not that simple.[10] For women in the study, migration to Australia, where the gender gap is smaller than it is in each of the women's countries of origin, had the perverse effect of re-establishing more traditional gender roles than they had experienced pre-migration. This cohort of highly educated skilled and business migrants had established themselves as successful professionals or businesswomen pre-migration but were turned into stay-at-home housewives and mothers in Australia. This was primarily due to the way in which visa procedures defined them as secondary to a man—their husband—as well as to barriers to re-entry into the workforce at their level, as discussed in Chapter Four.

The denial of equality to migrant women through bureaucratic procedures is most obviously related to linguistic diversity in some forms of citizenship testing. Language testing for citizenship has in recent years become increasingly formalized in many countries around the world.[11] In Australia, for instance, the English language requirement for becoming a naturalized citizen was changed in October 2007. Prior to that date, a prospective citizen demonstrated English language proficiency in an oral interview with an immigration officer by responding adequately to simple questions such as 'Where do you live?' or 'What are the privileges of Australian citizenship?' The pass rate was well above 95%. The new test is a computerized test consisting of twenty questions related to Australian citizenship. Three out of these twenty questions relate to the privileges of Australian citizenship and these three questions have to be answered correctly; overall, a score of 60% has to be attained. Language testing experts Tim McNamara and Kerry Ryan explain how this change in the format of the English language test has affected different groups of prospective citizens differently:

> [S]ince the test's inception in October 2007 to September 30, 2009, the overall success rate in passing the test on the first or subsequent attempt for the skilled migrant stream has remained stable at 99%, whereas the success rates for the family stream (94% down to 91%) and the humanitarian program clients (84% to 79%) have dropped. More alarmingly however, in the 3-month period from July 1, 2009, to September 30, 2009, the success rate for humanitarian program clients dropped to 70% with less than half (49.1%) passing the test on their first attempt. This compares with 91.5% and 77.9% pass rates for the first attempt for the skilled migrant and family stream clients.[12]

While the new test continues to be nothing more than a mere formality for highly educated test takers, it presents a formidable obstacle for test takers with no or limited schooling who are clustered in the family reunion and humanitarian entrance streams. Within this group the test particularly discriminates against women who had been excluded from educational opportunities in childhood. The school attendance rates of girls in countries such as Afghanistan or Sudan, where a substantial number of Australia's humanitarian entrants in the first decade of the twenty-first century originated, are some of the lowest on the planet. Formal language testing is a particular challenge for those with low levels of formal education, and thus serves to further discriminate post-migration against those who were most disadvantaged pre-migration. As a result, Australia

Day stories about gendered exclusions from Australian citizenship such as this one are becoming familiar:

> [The day after Australia Day] each year is a no-brainer for a newspaper editor with a little space to fill. Like the proud snap of a loving mother with her newborn baby captured a tick or so into the New Year, the late-January photo of a flag-waving new citizen outside a town hall somewhere on Australia Day is part of every summer.
>
> This year, the Age went with a Sudanese family: Dad, Mum and four kids. The accompanying article told a story of more than two decades spent on the run from appalling violence, first in wars and then in refugee camps. Now, after Abraham Biar Koul Biar collected his Australian citizenship certificate with a bullet still in his arm, everyone in the family can proudly and happily call themselves Australian. All except his wife Achol, that is. She had failed the citizenship test. 'I don't know computers well,' she told the Age.[13]

At first blush the key problem in the exclusion of women such as Marzieh and Achol seems to be their low proficiency in English. However, their isolation is also related to the small size of their home language community and limited availability or total lack of services in their home languages. In fact, the language ecology in the settlement destination can make a significant difference to the participation opportunities of women migrants, as we will now examine with reference to Spanish speakers in the USA and Chinese speakers in Australia.

Hispanics are the largest and fastest-growing minority group in the USA. The 2010 census identified 50.5 million Hispanics (excluding four million Puerto Ricans) who accounted for 16.3% of the US population. 'Although Latinos continue to be concentrated in certain US states, the Hispanic presence seems to be ubiquitous, no longer only in major urban areas of such traditional population centers as New York, Texas, California, and Florida, but also in small towns all over the United States.'[14] The broad group of 'Hispanics' includes some of the most disadvantaged groups of recent immigrants, such as significant numbers of undocumented migrants. While most Hispanics in the USA are bilingual in English and Spanish, the latter group in particular also includes large numbers of monolingual speakers of Spanish.[15]

It is against this context that sociologists Joana Dreby and Leah Schmalzbauer examined the experiences of Mexican migrant women relative to the size of the Spanish-speaking community and the availability of Spanish-language services in the settlement location.[16] How do these intersect with the women's experiences of autonomy (or lack thereof) inside and outside the home?

The first research site, an urban neighborhood in New Jersey, was characterized by a high density of Mexican immigrants and the availability of bilingual social services within walking distance or accessible by public transport. The second research site was a suburban location in Ohio, where Mexican migrants live in relative isolation from each other, the availability of social services in Spanish is more limited, and the ability to drive and access to a private vehicle are prerequisites for mobility. Finally, the third research site was in rural Montana, characterized by the inaccessibility of social services in Spanish and by rugged terrain and great distances.

The experiences of the women, all of whom were of low socioeconomic post-migration status, and the relationship between autonomy inside and outside the home, differed significantly across the three sites.

In New Jersey, the women were mobile outside the home, even if they had unsupportive or even abusive husbands. Many of them worked outside the home, and they were actively involved in their children's schooling because communication was always in English and Spanish. Access to a large network of Spanish speakers meant that emotional and practical support was available in case of difficult family situations.

In Ohio, the situation was quite different. There the women were dependent on good relationships with their husbands in order to be autonomous in the public sphere. In the absence of social net-works, public transport, and bilingual services, autonomy outside the home was dependent on autonomy inside the home. Women with unsupportive husbands were stuck. One research participant, for instance, was keen to attend English language classes in order to improve her prospects. However, the round trip from her trailer home to the English language class took four hours on public trans-port. Because she had no access to her husband's car and the trans-port ordeal was difficult to fit into her children's school schedule, she was unable to attend English language classes.

In Montana, Mexican women found themselves in a difficult sit-uation no matter how supportive or otherwise their husbands were. Living in relative isolation, even grocery shopping was a challenge for some. Not only was driving in the rugged terrain more arduous than in urban and suburban environments but Mexicans driving in Montana also attracted police attention. Being pulled over for a traffic check was more than a hassle: it was associated with the omnipresent fear of deportation for those without a legal status. In these precarious conditions, many participants were afraid even to leave the house and anything requiring any kind of external sup-port, such as illness, could quickly degenerate into a major disaster.

In sum, the study demonstrates that linguistic exclusion is a matter of context: while typically assumed to be the result of an individual characteristic ('lack of proficiency in the dominant lan-guage'), it is, in fact, social organization that turns linguistic dif-ference into an obstacle or otherwise. 'Ethnic enclaves' are much maligned in immigration debates as encouraging segregation, but linguistic concentration may in fact provide the very environment for migrant women's empowerment, as we will now examine with reference to postnatal depression.

The combination of two deep human experiences, migration and motherhood, poses a major settlement and mental health challenge. In Western countries, the majority of new mothers experience some form of 'baby blues' and around 20% are estimated to be affected by postnatal depression. It is widely assumed that these figures are higher in migrant mothers, particularly if they lack proficiency in the dominant language. However, in the same way that lack of English language proficiency is not an obstacle to personal autonomy in urban New Jersey with its bilingual services, it may also have differential mental health outcomes in new mothers, as research with different groups of Chinese-speaking mothers in Brisbane, Queensland, demonstrates.[17]

To begin with, cross-cultural comparative studies have shown that postnatal depression is virtually unknown in China, including Hong Kong and Taiwan. New mothers get special treatment during the postpartum month known as *zuo yuezi* (坐月子; 'sitting the month; month-long confinement'). They are expected to stay in bed for a month, they are given special strengthening foods to eat, and they are relieved of all household chores. The idea is for them to regain their health but also to be pampered for the effort of producing a child.

However, while postnatal depression is virtually nonexistent in Chinese mothers in China, its incidence in Chinese migrant mothers in Australia is higher than in the general population. Health researcher Cordia Chu argues that the occurrence of postnatal depression in Chinese migrant mothers is related to the quality of their support networks and feelings of isolation as well as employment issues and financial problems. In an interview study with three different groups of Chinese migrant mothers who had had babies in the past three years in Brisbane, she demonstrates that the key variable affecting their mental health was their country of origin.

Whether the women originated from the People's Republic of China, from Hong Kong, or from Taiwan was related to a number of additional differences, since the migration circumstances of each group differ. As a group, the Chinese in Australia are highly educated and have mostly been admitted as skilled or business migrants. However, while most migrants from China came initially as tertiary students or skilled migrants, most migrants from Hong Kong and Taiwan were admitted as professionals and business owners. That means that, in addition to their human capital, they usually also brought financial capital to Australia. Furthermore, the majority of migrants from Hong Kong arrived in the 1980s and 1990s, while immigration from China is more recent, with the largest cohort of China-born recorded in the 2011 census having arrived in the decade between 2000 and 2009. Chinese languages are the most widely spoken languages other than English in Brisbane. In the 2011 census, 50,852 Brisbane residents (2.5% of the total population) claimed Mandarin, Cantonese, or another Chinese language as their home language.

All three groups were more likely to be unemployed or underemployed than the general population, but migrants from mainland China experienced the greatest downward occupational mobility. Despite the fact that migrants from China were the most highly educated group of the three, they were most likely to work in unskilled or semiskilled jobs.

Another difference between the three groups was that Hong Kong- and Taiwan-related community organizations were abundant in Brisbane: of twenty-one Chinese religious and voluntary associations operating at the time of the study, nine serviced Taiwanese only, five Hong Kong-born only, five were open to all Chinese (including those from South-East Asia), and only one catered exclusively to migrants from the People's Republic of China. As a result, less social support was available to migrants from China, and they had less access to information, services, networks, and recreational activities than their counterparts from Taiwan and Hong Kong.

Overall, eleven out of thirty interviewees (ten in each origin group) reported experiencing symptoms of postnatal depression. Six of these originated from mainland China. Ten of these cited lack of social support as their main problem, a problem that the women who did not experience symptoms of postnatal depression were able to circumvent by bringing their mothers out to Australia during the postpartum period or by going back home to give birth. Both these options of securing family support were costly and thus open only to the financially secure participants, mostly from Hong Kong and Taiwan.

Whether new mothers had the choice to become housewives after the birth of their child or not was also related to financial security. Six each of the women from Hong Kong and Taiwan chose to become stay-at-home moms and not to return to paid work. None of these reported symptoms of postnatal depression. By contrast, becoming a housewife was not an option for any of the women from mainland China, who said they needed to be in paid employment in order to survive. Unsurprisingly, all of them reported various degrees of stress and fatigue as a result of being in paid employment while also caring for a young baby.

Despite the fact that they were in paid employment, which as we have seen is often assumed to be closely linked to higher levels of English proficiency, the China-born women, and also those from Taiwan, reported that they were not confident enough in their English to use it in health communication. Consequently, they had to seek out Chinese-speaking doctors and clinics to obtain care for themselves and their babies. Given the limited availability of Chinese-speaking surgeries, this meant long travel and waiting times and was thus another source of stress.

Finally, the women who reported symptoms of postnatal depression were also less likely to be aware of support services available to them and thus failed to access mainstream services such as antenatal classes or mother-and-baby groups.

In sum, the link between language and postnatal depression in migrant women is not direct but mediated by other—and usually less conspicuous—factors such as financial security and community networks. For financially secure women from Hong Kong and Taiwan who could bring their mothers to Queensland to help them, who had the choice to become stay-at-home moms and who had access to intra-ethnic networks for support and information, English language proficiency did not matter. By contrast, for China-born women who were struggling financially and did not have a wide community network, their lack of English language proficiency—or their lack of confidence in their English language proficiency—became another source of stress and anxiety.

LINGUISTICALLY MOTIVATED VIOLENCE

The linguistic barriers to equal participation that we have discussed so far result from an extreme mismatch between the linguistic repertoire of an individual and community norms. Usually, the difference between individual linguistic repertoires and community norms is smaller and affects the quality of participation rather than constituting an absolute barrier to participation. Language discrimination is one form of linguistic subordination that denies subordinate speakers the opportunity to participate on equal terms in the life of the community. Language discrimination is not rare, as a 2008 US study found: 12% of surveyed Asian-Americans reported having experienced discrimination on the basis of language in a service encounter in the previous two years.[18] This was more than those who reported that they had experienced discrimination on the basis of race. The researchers also found that there was a statistically significant correlation between having experienced language discrimination and health: those who had experienced language discrimination were more likely to suffer from chronic conditions than those who did not have that experience.

Language discrimination can take many forms. We will first discuss language-related violence before moving on to microaggressions in the next section.

Colonial Australia provides a fertile source for anecdotes of interpersonal violence between speakers of different languages. An example comes from bushranger lore about a gang of three men operating in early-nineteenth-century Tasmania: the bushranger gang consisted of two Irishmen, Scanlan and Brown, and an Englishman, Richard Lemon.[19]

Lemon did not like Brown and Scanlan talking in Gaelic, of which he understood not a word. One morning when Brown was out hunting [kanga]roos, Lemon crept up on Scanlan at the campfire, put a pistol to the back of his head and pulled the trigger. He then strung up the corpse by the heels on a gum tree, as if he were hanging a 'boomer' (big kangaroo) for skinning. 'Now, Brown,' he laconically observed when his partner returned, 'as there are only two of us, we shall understand one another better for the future.'[20]

Those were violent times, and Scanlan, Brown, and Lemon were psychopathic criminals and outlaws. Even so, the killing of a gang member for merely linguistic reasons seems excessively paranoid. However, in colonial Australia, paranoid fear of the linguistic other was not restricted to gang violence but also sanctioned by the state. As the historian Robert Hughes explains in his book *The Fatal Shore*, in the very first years of the colony a division emerged between English-speaking Protestants and Gaelic-speaking Catholics, and simply having a conversation in Gaelic could become a punishable offense. In 1793, for instance, just five years after the beginning of the European occupation of Australia, two Irishmen, Maurice Fitzgerald and Paddy Galvin, were sentenced to 300 lashes each for nothing more than 'walking about together and talking very earnestly in Irish.'[21]

Many of the Irish convicts shipped out to Australia in the late eighteenth and early nineteenth centuries would not have spoken any language other than Gaelic. As Catholic rebels against the British colonization of Ireland, they were under blanket suspicion in Australia, too. The chief Anglican clergyman of New South Wales at the turn of the nineteenth century, Samuel Marsden, offered this assessment of Catholics:

> Their minds being destitute of every principle of religion and morality render them capable of perpetrating the most nefarious acts in cold blood. As they never appear to reflect upon consequences but to be always alive to rebellion and mischief, they are very dangerous members of society.[22]

Today, Catholics have of course entered the Australian mainstream but religious and linguistic paranoia have not disappeared.

The similarity between the paranoid fear of Catholics in the early colony and the contemporary paranoia about Muslims should give us pause to reflect. In early 2015, for instance, the New South Wales Attorney General, Brad Hazzard, issued a ban for prison inmates to speak in Arabic during visits or on the phone, or to write or receive letters in Arabic.[23]

Just as criminal and state-sanctioned violence against Gaelic speakers were interconnected in colonial Australia, abuse of speakers of languages other than English today occurs within a larger climate of the denigration of speakers of other languages. We will now discuss a contemporary example of violent aggression triggered by the public use of a language other than English.

In November 2012, Fanny Desaintjores, a 22-year-old tourist from France, and two of her friends caught a late-night bus in Melbourne.[24] Sitting at the rear of the bus and in a party mood, they started singing a French song. However, their playful mood was not appreciated by other passengers. An Australian woman at the front of the bus began to shout the sporting chant 'Aussie, Aussie, Aussie,' which is supposed to draw the response 'oi, oi, oi.' Initially, the French tourists took this to be an attempt to join them in a chorus or singing match and raised their voices further. In response, another bus passenger told them to 'Speak English or die!' From around that point, yet another bus passenger started to record the scene on his mobile phone. The video shows a quickly escalating ugly scene dominated by a middle-aged white Australian male with a baby in a pram and a bewildered four- or five-year-old kid in tow: the man is ranting abuse at the French women, including grotesque violent threats. After he gets off the bus, the window closest to the French women is smashed, presumably by something he throws.

The video of the incident went viral on YouTube within days of its publication and the media began to pay attention to the episode, which was variously described as 'racist abuse,' 'racist bus attack,' 'racist rant,' or 'racist violent bus abuse.' Two of the perpetrators, Hayden Stirling Stewart and David Robert Graham, were subsequently charged with racial abuse and sentenced in January 2014.

During the court hearing, it also emerged that Graham had lost his job as a builder's laborer and had been evicted from his apartment as a result of the notoriety he gained from his behavior. From the media reports and comments on social networking sites as well as the social isolation and the jail term that the abusers received, it is clear that the public evaluated the incident as racist abuse.

The story is further complicated by the fact that everyone initially involved in the incident—the French singers as well as their Australian abusers—were white. Therefore speaking a language other than English on a Melbourne bus marked Fanny Desaintjores racially. This may seem strange and one might want to dismiss it as the alcohol-fueled fantasy of her attackers. However, they are obviously not alone in equating speaking a language other than English with racial inferiority, as an examination of the video of the incident and the subsequent media reports reveals.

Once the abusive rant was underway, most of the swearwords uttered were sexist insults (the c-word figures prominently on the video, as does 'bitch') and most of the threats of violence were also specifically of sexist violence such as the threat to cut off the women's breasts. The only explicitly racist label used by the main agitator, Hayden Stewart, was 'ding,' a derogatory Australian term for migrants from southern and central Europe, particularly Italians, Greeks, and Yugoslavs.[25] Even so, racism became an important part of the event when another white middle-aged male bus passenger, David Graham, took his cue from Stewart and started to rant against black people. His tirade was not addressed at the French women— who, as mentioned above, were all white—but the person who took the video on his mobile phone: that person, Mike Nayna, is a young Australian man whose parents are from the Maldives and the Netherlands and who describes himself as 'brown.' In a media interview he said, 'Pretty much all the French girls were white, and there was just me who was brown and another dark guy on the bus.'[26] The target of the rant against black people—the actual racial abuse—is Nayna rather than Desaintjores. The latter was targeted because of her linguistic difference and her vilification took mostly the form of sexist insults. In this highly volatile context the expression of linguistic and sexist abuse against Desaintjores then licensed the expression of racial insults to Nayna in a bigoted mélange where various prejudices fed off each other. Even so, the media consistently referred to Desaintjores as the target of the racial abuse, too, and no one seemed to find it surprising that her skin color should have been referred to as 'black' or that references to slavery should have been made. Obviously, the abusers' confused association of speaking a language other than English in public in Australia with 'blackness' was not surprising to commentators and made sense to them: they did not object to the association between language and race but to the invocation of racial hierarchies.

The fact that the language that triggered all this was French is highly unusual: French is a European high-prestige language that is generally more likely to attract admiration than vilification. What is not unusual is that speaking a language other than English in public attracts disapproval and negative reactions in Australia. While not all such cases make it into the media, some do. In 2013 a similar case was reported where a 21-year-old Anglo-Australian woman on a bus in Hobart, Tasmania, became so enraged by the fact that a 15-year-old refugee from Afghanistan spoke Persian that she swore at him and hit him about the head.[27] In order to avoid negative reactions, many speakers of languages other than English exert caution and avoid speaking their languages other than English in public. Widespread disapproval of the public use of a language ideologically coded as foreign is not unique to Australia, as a large-scale survey of young Swiss men demonstrates.[28] In response to the question of how they felt about hearing foreign languages in public spaces, such as on the street or on public transport, about half of more than 43,000 young adult men surveyed said that they felt annoyed by hearing foreign languages in public spaces.

Intolerance of deviations from linguistic social norms is widespread, as this book has copiously demonstrated so far. Violence as a means of enforcing linguistic norms is rare and constitutes a criminal offence. However, in the same way that fear of sexual or racial violence restricts the freedom of women and people of color, the danger of linguistically motivated violence presents the most extreme aspect of linguistic domination.

MICRO-AGGRESSIONS

Aggression toward speakers of subordinate languages rarely takes the blunt and violent forms of abuse discussed in the previous section. Critical race theorists have argued that a far more insidious instrument of the continuous construction and reconstruction of racial hierarchies is effected by everyday put-downs. Each of these put-downs may in itself seem innocuous but their cumulative weight can constitute a crushing burden placed on people of color and exclude them, covertly but effectively, from equal participation. Termed 'micro-aggression,' the concept was first introduced by psychiatrist Chester Pierce in the 1960s to describe 'brief and commonplace daily verbal, behavioral, or environmental indignities, whether intentional or unintentional, that communicate hostile, derogatory, or negative racial slights and insults toward people of color.'[29]

Micro-aggressions consist of micro-assaults, micro-insults, and micro-invalidations. Examples of micro-assaults include the use of racially derogatory terms. Micro-insults include communications that convey rudeness and demean the target's racial identity. Micro-invalidations are 'characterized by communications that exclude, negate, or nullify the psychological thoughts, feelings, or experiential reality of a person of color.'[30] In itself any act of micro-aggression may seem harmless but their cumulative effect over time can be deleterious: it causes stress, takes time and energy, and leads to an erosion of confidence and self-image. Because micro-aggressions are often subtle the target may frequently experience uncertainty about the accuracy of their perceptions of exclusion. This kind of ambiguity has been associated with anxiety and depression.[31]

Although the construct of 'micro-aggressions' has mostly been used to explore racial discrimination, it has recently been extended to explore other forms of discrimination such as gender discrimination and discrimination on the basis of sexual orientation.[32] In the same way, it can also be profitably extended to the analysis of linguistic subordination, as I will now demonstrate with reference to the exclusion of international students in contemporary international education.

A persistent theme in research with international students in Australia is the tension between dreams of inclusion pre-departure and the experience of exclusion once in the country. In ethnographic studies of the experiences of international students from Japan and Taiwan, for instance, participants often spoke about how their decision to study abroad was partly motivated by dreams of being part of a multicultural inclusive student body.[33] Participants described elaborate fantasies of how they had imagined themselves being part of an 'Australian' or 'international' (which pre-departure had meant 'non-Japanese' or 'non-Chinese') group of friends, hanging out in a cool café in Sydney and chatting away in their fluent English. Indeed, marketing materials for study abroad abound with images of groups of diverse students jointly engaging in study or leisure activities. Inclusiveness in such images is typically signaled by images of people who look phenotypically different from each other.

Unfortunately, in real life such scenarios hardly ever happened for the research participants. Making friends, joining study groups, and collaborating in groups all turned out to be extraordinarily difficult. A student from Taiwan, for example, described his experience as follows:

> Sometimes in group discussion everyone was talking and giving opinions. They don't notice you. They ignore your opinion. They would stop when you are talking, but after you finish they go back to their own discussion. You feel bad about it. I had doubts about my English being good enough. Later I found, nah, other international students told me they all felt it. They felt the same. So it was not only my problem. I thought it may be a bit racist.[34]

Being ignored, left out of conversations, and made to feel bad about themselves is not unique to the Japanese and Taiwanese participants in these two studies but comes up again and again in research with international students: locals stick to themselves and international students stick to their co-ethnics. The campus advertising images of happily collaborating diverse student groups only seem to happen for the camera and fostering an inclusive culture on campus remains a vexing problem for universities. Already in 2003, higher education researchers noted that 'it is one thing to have a culturally diverse student population and yet another to have those students engaged in positive interaction.'[35] While there is a large body of advice aimed at individual international students ('Don't be shy!'; 'Show confidence!'), the actual daily exclusion of international students from positive interactions with local students remains poorly understood.

US research with Hispanic students at US elite universities goes some way toward explaining micro-aggressions on campus.[36] As with international students at Australian universities, Hispanic students at US universities often experience exclusion and isolation. In focus group interviews, students spoke about their experiences of interpersonal relationships on campus. Everyone had a story to tell about subtle and not-so-subtle exclusions. The net result of many trivial interactions was a sense of non-belonging and a lack of feeling comfortable on campus, as one student explained:

> I'm not really comfortable just being in the classrooms. Just going to class I feel the fact that I know that I'm different and I'm reminded of it every day . . . There's me, a Black male and a Black female, and everybody else is White in my classroom. And me and those two Black individuals tend to sit together every session, every class session, whereas everybody else would just kind of tend to sit away from us. So as I put my book bag on the table, I would notice that the rest of the chairs would be empty while the other table would get crowded. It would be sixty people sitting at one table pushing each other off whereas

I would be by myself sitting at my own table. [. . .] The professor
is talking and the whole time you're thinking . . . Why doesn't
anybody sit here?[37]

Experiences such as these made campus a stressful and exhaust-
ing place for Hispanic students in the study. They responded by
withdrawing and by creating safe spaces with co-ethnics. The latter
often led to accusations of self-segregation and so was an ambiva-
lent strategy, too, even as it helped to ameliorate the acute sense of
exclusion they experienced in the wider campus community.

In the 1960s, Chester Pierce had argued that the best defense
against micro-aggression was the ability to recognize it and to
defend promptly so as to reduce the cost of accumulation. That
seems true of the Hispanic students in the study, too: their ability
to recognize micro-aggressions as racist gave them the chance to
create counter-spaces and, at the very least, to recognize that their
exclusion was not their individual personal problem.

As regards international students, the racism inherent in micro-
aggressions is often obscured by linguistic proficiency and the assumption that they are being excluded because their 'English isn't
good enough.' Making micro-aggressions visible is thus a key task
in order to create a more inclusive campus experience and to work
toward the equal participation of subordinate speakers.

LINGUISTIC ALIENATION

Experiencing linguistic barriers to participation, fearing linguistically motivated violence, and being subject to micro-aggressions
can result in a deep sense of isolation and exclusion, even while it
is impossible to separate linguistic isolation and exclusion from
gender and racial discrimination. So far, this chapter has attempted
to analytically isolate linguistic barriers and linguistic discrimination but also explore intersections with gender in regards to access
to participation. This section will now take up an intersectional

perspective again by examining quality of participation holistically. We focus on the continuum of belonging and alienation, which can be conceived as one specific quality-of-participation indicator. Linguistic subordination can constitute a central facet of social alienation but it rarely operates in isolation. This section is designed to explore the experience of linguistic alienation as it intersects with class, embodiment, and media use with reference to the experience of three diverse groups of Londoners: recent settlers from Poland, long-term settlers from Pakistan, and sojourners from East Asia.

Let's begin with a recent network study of the ways in which newcomers go about establishing networks in a new place.[38] The newcomers in this study are Poles, who have settled in the United Kingdom since Poland's ascension to the European Union in 2004. Between 2004 and 2011 more than half a million Poles settled in the United Kingdom, and Polish became the most widely spoken home language after English during that period. Sociologist Louise Ryan employed a network study to examine how these new settlers decided where to live, how they found jobs, and how they participated in their new society. Readers meet people such as Marek, a single university graduate in his twenties. Through a Polish network, he had accommodation and a job lined up when he arrived in London. So his ethnic network allowed him to get a foot in the door. However, Marek soon realized that that was the end of the potential of his Polish network: living and working with other Poles, he had no opportunities to improve his English and the job opportunities that particular network had access to only extended to low-skilled, low-paid jobs, offering no avenue into a career or work consistent with his qualifications. Marek decided that improving his English language proficiency was a priority and a precondition for seeking alternative employment. Therefore, he moved out and moved into share accommodation with Australian and New Zealander backpackers on a gap year. They got on like a house on fire; Marek's English improved and he acquired an ever-widening circle of mates from Down Under.

However, Marek's success in perfecting his English and making English-speaking friends did not translate into other social benefits such as career advancement that are usually expected to flow from improved language skills and improved social networks. In a sense, Marek backed the wrong horse: his English-speaking friends were newcomers like himself but, in contrast to him, they had no desire to 'make it' in London: they were there to fill a gap year, to see the world, and to party. Marek reflected on the fact that his English language learning success and friendship networks had not provided him with a way in:

> I didn't have here in London people, if I had a problem, for example . . . to sort out at an institution, to go somewhere, sort something out . . . I never had a person, who I could ask, who could tell me: you'll do it like that and everything will be OK. No . . . all the people, I was surrounded by, didn't have a clue about anything.[39]

Another group who found that acquiring English and English-speaking friends did not necessarily translate into social capital in their new environments were mothers. Migrant mothers of young children often find it relatively easy to access local networks through school, and the Polish women with children in the study were no exception. Practically, such mothering networks translated into play dates for the children and some childcare support. However, mothering networks did not translate into desirable ways into British society, either, because migration had changed the women's class position. Two of the Polish mothers featured in detail were university-educated and would have been considered middle-class in Poland. However, in London they lived in a working-class and underprivileged neighborhood. While they made friends with other mothers in their local area, they found that they did not actually have much in common with them. Like Marek's Australian backpacker friends, local mothers did not have a clue, either, how to gain access to the professional worlds the migrant women aspired to.

In sum, Polish newcomers experienced a mismatch between their pre- and post-migration class positions. While they were well-educated, spoke English competently or learned it quickly, and were highly motivated to integrate and fully participate in British society, their class dislocation severely affected the quality of their participation. The Polish participants in this study were relative newcomers to London and it is possible that the quality of their participation might have improved over time. However, research with another group of Londoners, long-term settlers from Pakistan, shows the relative permanency of class alienation across the lifespan.

Anthropologist Kaveri Qureshi undertook research with chronically ill working-class men from Pakistan to understand the ways in which social participation is related to actual bodies on the move.[40] The researcher starts with the observation that, according to the literature, Pakistanis in Britain have

> developed a 'transnational ethnic world' that is continually reproduced through long distance phone calls, frequent return visits and holidays, the consumption of circulating goods and media products, exchanges of gifts, philanthropic investments in schools, hospitals and humanitarian projects in Pakistan and so forth.[41]

Descriptions of a British-Pakistani transnational world such as these are based on normalized assumptions of healthy, materially secure migrants whose first priority is their cultural and ethnic identity. The chronically ill men the researcher encountered in East London told a different story, a story where their ailing bodies tied them to London.

The postwar manufacturing boom in Britain was to a considerable degree made possible by the labor of commonwealth migrants. After fifteen to twenty years of hard 'back-breaking' manual labor, many of these workers found their health deteriorating at exactly the time when the manufacturing base started to disappear in the 1980s. With their bodies no longer able to do hard manual labor and their education insufficient for 'light' office jobs, many of them have been unemployed ever since.

Benefits-dependent, these men have for more than two decades been made to feel superfluous and useless. The fact that their work migration has cost them their health has ironically meant that they are neither here nor there. Their lack of financial resources has tied them to London and has made practices of transnationalism difficult: for instance, 'cheap' airfares were not 'cheap' to them but involved years of budgeting ahead and borrowing; their disability coupled with the fact that Pakistanis back home see them as 'rich' and expect bribes and presents at every turn, made movement in Pakistan difficult and unpleasant for them; and phone cards, the so-called 'social glue' of transnationalism, had to be carefully rationed.

Not only did these men find it difficult to maintain transnational ties with Pakistan. Sometimes, actually severing those ties was their only way to stay afloat: for many of them, selling ancestral land titles in Pakistan or houses they might have built there during better times was their way of coping with unexpected larger expenses such as home renovations.

Qureshi's interlocutors were predictably bitter about their experiences. They felt they had given their youth and health to Britain, and that Britain had aged them prematurely but did not allow them to age well. One man said:

> I used to keep very well you know, I was doing a good job. You can't even imagine. I have a younger brother here, he was younger than me by 13 years but when we sat together, people used to think I was the younger one. Before I came to this country, from '75 to '90 I never used to go to the doctor, never ever to the hospital. But now I'm just a big mareez [patient].[42]

It was not only their failing health and financial precariousness that they were bitter about but also the ways in which they had been treated by 'the system': the legal-medical apparatus through which they continually had to prove their disability and ill health in order to be entitled to benefits while simultaneously finding that the same system had been slow to attend to their medical needs and had often exacerbated their condition through long waiting times or malpractice.

The men did not attribute the low quality of their participation in British society, and specifically of their encounters with medical practitioners, to 'miscommunication' due to language difficulties or cultural differences. Rather, there was no doubt in their minds that their exclusion was the result of racial and class discrimination. They saw doctors as taking sides with the state and with employers rather than with patients and it was their view that doctors' priorities often were to save money rather than to heal.

In sum, the people we meet in Qureshi's research are not cool transnationals belonging to two places but bitter patients who are alienated from two places. The advent of new means of communication—phone cards, satellite TV, instant messaging, the Internet—has done little to ameliorate their alienation. Their socioeconomic position meant that these new means of international communication were not as easily accessible to them as they have come to be seen by many. However, for Londoners in a quite different class position, privileged young women from China, Japan, and Korea, home-country media became a way to deal with their alienation from London.

Media researcher Youna Kim interviewed young women from China, Japan, and South Korea sojourning in London about their media consumption and daily routines in order to understand their participation in their origin and destination societies.[43] All the women in the study were well-educated and came from relatively privileged backgrounds. One of their key motivations to move to London had been to further their education and to free themselves from the traditional constraints imposed on women back home, including the imperative to marry. When they spoke about the motivations for their move to London, they frequently mentioned the Western media, which they had perused and enjoyed back home. In many cases, these media had instilled a hope for self-transformation in them and had been one of the key drivers in their pursuit of an international education.

However, once they had left home and moved to London, the women's patterns of media consumption changed drastically. They lost interest in the Western media that had motivated them in the first place and had been so appealing back home. Instead, they started to turn to home-country and home-language media. The reason for that change was not nostalgia, as one might expect, but rather an acute sense of exclusion, as expressed in quotes such as these:

> In the first year I watched television to know this society. Now [after three years] don't watch. The more I watch, the more I feel alienated . . . There's no connection. It's too British. I liked the British accent before because it sounded posh, but now that accent feels alienating too. (Korean woman in London)
>
> No quality food, no caring for others' feelings . . . I stop fighting because it was my choice to move here, because my English is not good enough. I cannot even express frustration to outsiders as they say, 'You live in attractive London!' My friend depressed in Paris hears the same, 'You live in beautiful Paris!' (Japanese woman in London)
>
> I feel like a woman warrior of China. I feel the wall, whether that is racism, invisible hostility, coldness, or superiority in culture . . . I am becoming more Chinese while living abroad. This feeling grows. (Chinese woman in London)[44]

One of the reasons for the boom in international education in general and for language study abroad in particular is that study abroad and the proficiency in English it is supposed to confer are frequently touted as the high road to social inclusion in the imagined West. However, as these women discovered, this imagined form of aspirational social inclusion comes at the cost of being socially excluded in a mundane, everyday sense. Like many transnational migrants, they lost their connections with home or saw real connections transformed into virtual connections. At the same time, they did not find a way into the host society, either:

these young women spoke about domestic discomforts ('no quality food'), their overall disappointment with what they considered surprisingly low levels of quality of life, and their sense of marginalization at not being able to share a joke. Above all, they traced their sense of exclusion back to everyday interactions: routine encounters became daily reminders that they are different and that they do not belong.

In sum, privileged class positions, youth and good health, and access to a wide range of communication media do not guarantee a good quality of participation for people on the move, either. For these women, not feeling comfortable in mundane everyday interactions was enough to create a deep sense of alienation. The research is evidence of a perpetual dialectic that is at the heart of the intersection between language and social inclusion: while language learning and international education hold the promise of social inclusion as economic advancement, in everyday life they may actually serve to marginalize and exclude even relatively privileged transnational migrants from a sense of home.

SUMMARY

Language is central to the ability to fully participate in the life of the community. However, the ability to deploy language for effective participation is unequally distributed. As Bourdieu reminds us:

> The competence adequate to produce sentences that are likely to be understood may be quite inadequate to produce sentences that are likely to be listened to, likely to be recognized as acceptable in all the situations in which there is occasion to speak. Here again, social acceptability is not reducible to mere grammaticality. Speakers lacking the legitimate competence are de facto excluded from the social domains in which this competence is required, or are condemned to silence.[45]

Not being listened to in social domains that are central to full community participation is yet another aspect of linguistic injustice. We started this chapter with an exploration of linguistic barriers to being heard. Where people are not being listened to in social domains that are crucial to full participation—such as emergency service provision—their basic human rights are under attack. Social arrangements where a domestic violence victim is not being listened to when calling emergency services are obviously unjust and place us under a moral obligation to reconsider such arrangements. The analysis highlighted the need for multilingual service provision to tear down barriers to equal participation. However, linguistic justice is more than that: recognizing the practical limits to multilingual service provision, linguistic justice is also about broadening our linguistic imagination to acknowledge that everyone has the right to be heard and to be listened to. While it may have been impossible to provide Dari-language emergency services to Marzieh Rahimi, it would have been possible to dispatch a police car to her residence—had she been considered worth listening to.

Those who we condemn to silence and who are excluded from full community participation are rarely excluded on the basis of language alone. Linguistic injustice works hand in glove with the injustices of gender, class, and race. Out of all these, linguistic injustice remains the only one where victim blaming is still widely considered acceptable. Disadvantaged speakers are typically seen as the agents of their own exclusion and it is assumed that the barriers they face are due to inadequate proficiency in the dominant language. However, it is social arrangements that exacerbate linguistic disadvantage or, alternatively, enable participation as we saw when comparing the experiences of Spanish-speaking women in New Jersey, Ohio, and Montana. Bilingual services together with a dense ethnic network and public transport in New Jersey allowed residents there high levels of autonomy and participation in contrast to their counterparts in Montana, who were virtually confined to the home. Similarly, lack of confidence in their English language proficiency was connected to postnatal depression in Chinese migrant mothers in Brisbane only in the absence of targeted community services, personal networks, and financial security.

Just as sexist, classist, or racist structures undergird gender, class, and race injustice, linguistic injustice is actively produced and reproduced through processes of linguistic discrimination. Linguistic discrimination may take the blunt form of linguistically motivated violence and abuse. While relatively rare, fear of linguistically motivated violence and abuse restricts the freedom of subordinated speakers and enforces linguistic domination. A more subtle but ubiquitous and hence more damaging form of linguistic discrimination is constituted by micro-aggressions. Micro-aggressions invalidate the contributions of subordinate speakers and undermine their everyday mundane participation in interactions with extensive negative consequences for their ability to participate fully in the life of the community.

Linguistic discrimination, too, intersects with gender, class, and race discrimination to produce social alienation, as I showed with reference to the experiences of three different groups of Londoners. From Polish newcomers who were unable to fully participate in the life of the community due to class displacement, via Pakistani old timers who were excluded once they were no longer able to labor, to East Asian sojourners who felt reminded daily of their nonbelonging, they all share the experience of social alienation resulting from linguistic, gender, class, and race subordination.

Exclusion from full participation in the life of the community is closely tied to the perils of long-term social alienation. As long as we fail to recognize the injustices of language, let alone correct them, the fragmentation that comes with alienation threatens the well-being of us all.

Chapter 7

Linguistic Diversity
and Global Justice

The preceding three chapters explored the relationship between language and social justice within liberal-democratic nation-states. This focus on the national level is due to the fact that social justice is usually conceptualized with reference to the state. However, while the state remains the almost exclusive reference point for research into and discussions of social justice, economic globalization has largely eroded the capacity of the nation-state to be an effective agent of economic development and hence social justice. Some states in the global south never developed the capacity to be effective agents of social justice in the first place. However, inequality within states is undergirded by global inequality between states. This chapter will therefore change perspective and explore the relationship between linguistic diversity and global social justice.

Internal and external social justice are closely connected and need to be brought together for a range of reasons. To begin with, the vast majority of the world's disadvantaged live in the global south so it is important to understand the articulation of linguistic diversity and social justice in global terms, rather than by reference to only a relatively small group, namely, those disadvantaged internally in the countries of the global north. Second, the exclusion of communities, nations, and even the whole continent of Africa from economic well-being, education, and healthcare is a key factor in international migration and often a precondition for the internal disadvantage faced by migrants in the cities of the global north. Finally, the countries of the global north achieved their relatively high levels of social inclusion internally in large part through maximizing external inequality through colonialism and neo-colonialism.[1]

Many of the linguistic injustices we have examined so far with reference to the nation-state operate globally, too. Linguistic diversity is stratified and a global language hierarchy overlays the national and local language hierarchies we have discussed. Globalization has placed an extra layer of disadvantage on subordinate speakers of subordinate languages as their subordination is extended beyond their relationship with locally dominant languages to their relationship with globally dominant English. Therefore this chapter is designed to examine the discourse and practice of the global spread of English from a global justice perspective. The central argument is that, as appealing as the notion of a global lingua franca and 'English for everyone' may be, in reality, discourses and practices related to the global spread of English have become a key mechanism to entrench global inequalities. We will begin by examining how English is conceived relative to development and then focus on the ways in which English structures access to education, to knowledge, and to economic goods. Finally, we will examine the ways in which global English entrenches injustices of representation.

LANGUAGE AND DEVELOPMENT

Linguistic diversity has long been perceived as an obstacle to development. During the period of political decolonization in the middle of the twentieth century, development policies typically associated development with linguistic assimilation toward national monolingualism. With a few exceptions such as Bahasa Indonesia, it was the language of the former colonial master that became the dominant national language in the newly independent former colonies. Consequently, the English-speaking world has often been conceived of as consisting of a set of concentric circles with the United Kingdom and its settler societies Australia, Canada, Ireland, New Zealand, South Africa, and the United States as 'the center.' This Anglophone center is conceived of as surrounded by an 'outer circle' of former colonies that have accorded English official status and where English plays a significant role in national life such as Ghana, India, or Jamaica. The rest of the world is imagined to surround these two circles in an 'expanding circle' of countries where English is widely taught in the education system and where it has some functions in sectors such as the tourism industry or international communication.[2]

The lines between the various circles are, of course, far from clear-cut. But the circles model can be seen as a metaphor for the linguistic hierarchies implicit in global English, with 'center English' dominating 'outer' and 'expanding' varieties of English. The focus in the following will be predominantly on societies in the 'expanding circle' where the spread of English and the social justice issues it raises have been most pronounced in recent decades. Before we begin, let's briefly return to the idea that a newly independent state needs to overcome its linguistic diversity and adopt one single language in order to decolonize and to develop.

A dataset on 'ethnolinguistic fractionalization' compiled by US political scientists Charles Taylor and Michael Hudson has often been used to demonstrate a correlation between a high level of linguistic diversity and underdevelopment: correlating linguistic diversity in a country and gross domestic product, these authors found a negative correlation between the number of sizable language groups in a country and the size of the country's GDP; in other words, the greater a country's linguistic diversity, the greater its poverty.[3] Data such as these were then used to argue for the promotion of linguistic assimilation as a way to grow the national economy and to alleviate poverty.

Another political scientist, Jonathan Pool, has offered an incisive analysis of the flawed reasoning behind the assumption that linguistic assimilation will further development and alleviate poverty.[4] The reasoning in all these cases goes something like this: members of a nation's dominant ethnolinguistic group are better educated, find jobs more easily, have a longer life expectancy, and so on, than members of subordinate groups. Similarly, an observation can be made that monolingual countries are more often economically and technically advanced and less likely to experience civil unrest than multilingual countries. On the basis of these facts, many observers have concluded that promoting the linguistic assimilation of minority members in a national unit will be beneficial for the individuals concerned and the nation as a whole. The problem with this kind of reasoning is that it is a correlational fallacy based on static data. The fact that high levels of linguistic diversity and disadvantage co-occur does not mean that there is a causal relationship between the two nor does it mean that changing the language variable toward linguistic assimilation will have the desired development outcomes.

Nonetheless, the correlational fallacy that associates a dominant language with socioeconomic development continues to be immensely powerful. In particular, a discourse has emerged that promotes the English language as a vehicle of development. As a consequence, an ever-larger number of English-language teaching programs, projects, and initiatives have emerged in the late twentieth and early twenty-first centuries.[5]

Critical sociolinguists have argued that, rather than support development, the promotion of global English serves to perpetuate global inequality. This line of argument is most notably associated with the concept of 'linguistic imperialism' coined by linguist Robert Phillipson. Phillipson defines 'linguistic imperialism' by saying that 'the dominance of English is asserted and maintained by the establishment and continuous reconstitution of structural and cultural inequalities between English and other languages.'[6]

How this process might work can be observed in the promotion of English language learning as part of development aid offered to Cambodia over the past few decades.[7]

Financial assistance with English language teaching has constituted an important component of the development aid Cambodia has received. In the mid-1990s, for instance, one British and two Australian aid agencies alone devoted around twelve million US dollars to provide English language teaching aid for Cambodia so as to enable Cambodians to learn English. During the same period the funds devoted by all external aid agencies combined to support basic literacy in Cambodia were only five million US dollars. This difference in spending priorities must be understood against the fact that Cambodia remains one of the poorest countries in the world. In 2013, around 75% of Cambodians lived in the impoverished countryside and lacked basic educational and productive skills. The main export industries in Cambodia are garment production and tourism. Two-thirds of the adult Cambodian population remains functionally illiterate.

Around 90% of the population of Cambodia are ethnic Khmer and speak Khmer as their native language. The remaining 10% are Vietnamese, Chinese, and twenty smaller groups with their own languages. Cambodia was a French colony until 1953. During the colonial period all formal education had been through the medium of French. After a short period of relative stability during which Khmer became the medium of education alongside French, Cambodia was plunged into a devastating civil war, which ended only in the early 1990s. Today, in addition to the national language Khmer, English is the most widely taught language but Chinese, French, and Vietnamese also play a role.

Against this background, aid spending that prioritizes English language teaching aid over basic literacy education is difficult to understand. Sociologist Stephen Clayton argues that the demand for English in Cambodia has been constructed by international aid agencies, including those operating in refugee camps and the United Nations Transitional Authority. All these bodies set up English as a way to lead Cambodia out of international isolation, as a way to access international aid, and thus the means for reconstruction and development. The need for English in Cambodia has therefore been largely constructed by external agencies and is based on an external orientation to development. The external orientation to aid, tourism, and globalization inscribed into English benefits only a tiny Cambodian elite. Those with proficiency in English can access external aid agencies and the model of externally driven development becomes entrenched.

At the same time, the external development model has been failing the rural and urban poor, who constitute the majority of Cambodians. English is out of their reach. For instance, in the export trade, on an average garment worker's wage of forty-five US dollars per month, even English lessons at two cents per hour as provided by some aid agencies are unaffordable. Not to mention that these workers probably have little time and energy left for English study. The vast majority of Cambodians are mired in poverty to such a degree that learning English is not a feasible choice for them—an impossible dream perhaps. What is more, the development model of neoliberal global markets into which English is inscribed has actually removed another choice from the reach of most of Cambodians: the choice to become literate in their own language.

Choice is a marker of privilege. The choice of English in Cambodia was structured on the basis of external and internal socioeconomic inequalities in the first place and the privileging of English within the neoliberal market model further widens those inequalities as an effect of the restructuring of local labor markets.

The ways in which the promotion of English is tied to an external orientation to development can also be seen in another example, which seemingly could not be further removed from the dire poverty of Cambodia. The United Arab Emirates have also relied heavily on English to achieve development, a form of development that is based on oil extraction, that is extremely capital-intensive, and that ultimately serves only the interests of global and local elites. The global English teaching industry is part and parcel of this mode of development, as sociolinguist Soheil Karmani argues.[8]

The United Arab Emirates, or Trucial Oman, as it was then known, became independent from their semi-colonial relationship with Britain in December 1971 and the country has since experienced some dramatic changes: its population has increased more than thirty-fold from 180,226 at the time of the 1968 census to 5,671,112 in 2009; and the country has grown fabulously rich from its oil exports, which began in 1969.

During this period, the United Arab Emirates has also undergone widespread language shift and the predominant public language today is English. English is the medium of instruction in most of the country's private primary and secondary schools and in all of the country's universities. Widespread societal language shift from Arabic to English is surprising given the country's oil wealth. While Cambodians may have little choice but to accept whatever international aid agencies may decree is good for them, surely oil-rich Emiratis are in a position to keep their own counsel and choose their own language?

Sohail Karmani explores the nexus between an oil-based rentier state[9] and the burgeoning English language teaching industry in the United Arab Emirates and other countries of the Gulf Cooperation Council (GCC), which also includes Bahrain, Kuwait, Oman, Qatar, and Saudi Arabia. According to the *Arab Human Development Report* oil has been more of a bane than a boon for the region as it has been subjected to the well-known paradox of the 'resource curse.' The 'resource curse' refers to the fact that countries with plentiful natural resources often have worse development outcomes than those with less because overreliance on primary exports damages a nation's productive sector and the flow-on benefits that come from industry.

Despite the well-known economic and sociopolitical dangers of overreliance on the extraction of primary resources, the overreliance on oil revenues in GCC countries continues for three reasons: first, the rentier economy serves to buy political consensus; second, oil wealth has led to a capital-intensive mode of development instead of a labor-intensive one; and third, soaring international demand creates strong pressure to continue current high levels of extraction and the attendant rentier mode of social organization.

These three reasons for the continued overreliance on oil are directly related to language policy in GCC countries. To begin with, while the rentier state is conducive to political consensus, it is not conducive to political participation in the way a tax-dependent state is. Consequently, state-society links in rentier states are usually weak and underdeveloped. State policies, including language policy, do not need to take the needs, desires, or practices of the Arabic-speaking citizenry into account.

Second, a capital-intensive mode of development encourages reliance on large numbers of international advisors and experts, who, by the very nature of their backgrounds and expertise, not to mention self-interest, favor English. Finally, international demand and pressure for continued high levels of oil extraction also indirectly favor English through their support for the rentier mode rather than mass industrialization and mass education.

Karmani compares the operation of the English language teaching industry in GCC countries to the operations of a cartel, an agreement between competitors to control a market: in this account, the English language teaching industry largely controls language policy and, more crucially, language practices in education, and the profits of the enterprise flow back to Western English-speaking countries. Indeed, despite the huge investments into English that GCC countries have made over the past decades, there is a consensus that overall levels of English proficiency in the region remain low. This lack of 'success' in English language learning is partly an in-built feature of language teaching in a context where language is a commodity, as language proficiency becomes subject to inflationary pressure. However, it is also a feature of the modus operandi of a cartel which lacks accountability and transparency.

In sum, the promotion of English is today deeply implicated in discourses and practices of development. However, English is tied to specific forms of development that are characterized by an external orientation to development without regard to the specifics of the local context. By touting English as a cure-all, the global community is placing a double burden on its weakest members: they have to acquire productive skills and they have to learn English. For most, this is an entirely unrealistic burden, leaving 'development' in the hands of international 'experts.' Furthermore, educational policies such as 'English for all' are by and large designed without reference to industrial policies and fail to create economic activities where English could be used productively. As the economist Erik Reinert explains:

> By emphasizing the importance of education without simultaneously allowing for an industrial policy that creates demand for educated people—as Europe has over the last 500 years—[global development policies] are just adding to the financial burdens of poor countries by letting them finance the education of people who will eventually find employment only in the wealthy countries.[10]

INJUSTICES OF ENGLISH LANGUAGE EDUCATION

How could English language teaching constitute an injustice and serve to entrench disadvantage? We are so used to the assumption that education is a good thing no matter what, that you are likely finding yourself scoffing at the heading 'injustices of English language education.' So, let's consider the evidence. In order to explore how English language teaching could be an imposition that serves to entrench inequalities within a society we will start with a case study, and meet Wei Ru, a young woman from China.[11]

In 2004, Wei Ru was in her final year of senior high school in a rural area of Heilongjiang province in northern China and preparing for the *gaokao* (高考; China's national university entrance exam). Wei Ru is a member of an ethnic group called Nanai. The Nanai are an indigenous people of Siberia and have traditionally lived along the middle reaches of the Amur River Valley. Today, this area of the Amur River constitutes the border between China and

Russia. Consequently, the Nanai, who are also known as Goldi and, in China, as Hezhe or Hezhen, have been divided between these two countries and today constitute a very small minority in both countries: in 2000, there were about 12,000 Nanai in Russia and 4,500 in China. Of these, only around 5,000 speakers of the Nanai language remained in Russia in the first decade of the twenty-first century, and only twenty in China. All twenty were elderly, and Wei Ru was not one of them.

Wei Ru has spoken Chinese all her life and has been educated through the medium of Chinese. Additionally, Wei Ru has spent many years learning Russian both formally and informally. Throughout her childhood and youth there were many Russian language learning opportunities available in Wei Ru's hometown: a brisk cross-border trade means that Russian visitors to the town are a frequent sight, and visits to the Russian side of the border are a regular occurrence. In school, Russian was an important part of the curriculum. Russian teachers were highly qualified and the students enjoyed learning Russian because it was well-taught and was of obvious relevance to their lives. Furthermore, for Wei Ru, who is passionate about her Nanai heritage, Russian carried additional significance as the language that allowed her to connect with the Nanai on the other side of the border. To her, it is almost as if Russian had become the ethnic language of the Nanai.

Throughout her schooling, Wei Ru had been an outstanding student: she ranked top of her class in most subjects and expected to gain university admission into a prestigious university and in her preferred major. However, when China became a member of the World Trade Organization in 2001 and won its bid to host the 2008 Beijing Olympics the same year, university admission regulations in China changed dramatically. The English language component of the *gaokao* became much more important than it had previously been and the value of test scores in other languages, including Russian, decreased dramatically. Furthermore, English became an entry requirement for the most desirable majors, such as business, law, science and technology.

The 2004 cohort of high school graduates in Wei Ru's area was hit particularly hard: they had invested many years into studying Russian but English language instruction had not been available to them. As Wei Ru said wistfully:

[Learning Russian] has become such a disadvantage. An absolute disadvantage! We could have scored 130 or 140 [out of the full mark of 150] on the Russian test in the *gaokao*. Actually, 120 was only an average score for us. But in English we would only be able to get a score of 50. That is the fact.[12]

Given these odds, many of Wei Ru's classmates decided to repeat the final year of high school in order to catch up on English. Wei Ru and her family felt that repeating a year just to learn English was not worth it, particularly as the quality of English language teaching in Wei Ru's hometown was low: when the high school curriculum changed from Russian to English, the only way to meet staffing levels was to deploy Russian teachers as English teachers. In the process, highly qualified Russian teachers in a well-resourced Russian language program were turned into poorly qualified English teachers in a poorly resourced English language program.

As an outstanding student and given a bonus rating for ethnic minority students, Wei Ru still managed to secure admission to a *minzu* (民族; 'ethnic') university, i.e., a university specifically dedicated to the educational advancement of ethnic minority students. However, majors for which English language proficiency had become an entry requirement were not available to her and she enrolled in an anthropology degree. When she spoke to the sociolinguist Jenny Zhang in 2008 about her experiences of learning and using English in China, Wei Ru was still bitter about the way her lack of English proficiency had shaped her educational trajectory. Furthermore, as she pondered her future, English continued to loom large: English was an important part of her studies as many textbooks were in English and some of her classes were taught in English by foreign teachers. So doing well in her studies depended on improving her

English, an effort she considered an arbitrary imposition and consequently resented. Despite her best efforts it was almost impossible to catch up to the English level of her classmates, who had studied English throughout junior and senior high school.

After graduation, Wei Ru was hoping to return to her hometown and enter the public service. It is obvious that proficiency in Russian would be highly useful to a public servant in the Russian-Chinese border area. However, in order to achieve her ambition Wei Ru would have to sit yet another English test, as English—in contrast to Russian—is also a test subject on the public service entrance exam.

Wei Ru's disadvantage was the result of a lack of equal access to English. The injustice of her disadvantage is compounded by the fact that the universal imposition of an English language requirement is entirely arbitrary and comes at the expense of Russian, which in Wei Ru's circumstances has 'real-life' value.

English does have 'real-life' value in many other parts of China, particularly the industrial and urban southeast, as we saw when we visited Guangzhou's Africa Town in Chapter Three. However, that does not mean that access to practice opportunities is any less stratified there, as journalist Leslie T. Chang shows in her book *Factory Girls*, which depicts the lives of young Chinese women migrating from their rural homes for the job opportunities in the export factories of eastern China.[13]

As was the case for Wei Ru, having grown up in a rural area their educational opportunities had been limited, constituting a significant educational disadvantage. Unlike their urban peers, rural young women have had little education when they leave their villages to seek a better life in the city. Nonetheless, they are part of China's English fever and recognize English language proficiency as a way to become upwardly mobile. Some of the women Chang met in Dongguan set aside time on top of eleven-hour working days to study English in private language schools. It was never enough, though, and the practice opportunities necessary to improve eluded them. Practice opportunities were available to office workers who had dealings with foreign businesses, to tour guides, and to hostesses. However, none of these jobs were available to small women.

You have read correctly: height does indeed mediate access to English language practice opportunities in this context. Height is an important and ubiquitous class discriminator in China. In a society that experienced famine within living memory, nothing shows more clearly whether someone is of peasant stock than height. For example, in the factories, women who are taller than 1.6 meters might be considered for clerical work but women who are smaller than 1.6 meters are stuck on the production floor.

Chang, herself Chinese-American, records this poignant conversation, in which one of the women who tries to make it in Dongguan asks her how to improve her English. Chang suggests finding a job in the travel industry.

> She placed her palm flat against the top of her head. 'Look at me. I don't meet the minimum height requirement. Tour guides must be at least 1.6 meters tall.' Right—another dumb suggestion. I had forgotten all the ways in which height could affect the utility of English in a place like Dongguan.[14]

The educational disadvantage of minority students and students from rural areas is widely discussed in China today, as it is internationally. Chinese educational authorities have, in fact, announced that from 2017 onwards the English component of compulsory testing will be reduced or removed.[15] The imposition of universal English language teaching and English language proficiency requirements in order to access higher education and public service jobs serves to entrench ethnic minority and rural disadvantage instead of offering any development benefits. As the sociolinguist Gareth Price concludes in his analysis of the ways in which English language teaching serves to maintain socioeconomic stratification:

> While 'English for all' policies and discourses are framed as opportunities, there is little actual choice to acquire the cultural capital of English when it so fundamentally functions as a gatekeeper in and to education and employment markets. Regions,

schools, and individuals are forced to compete with each other on anything but a level playing field given uneven resource allocation in the public education sector between rural and urban areas.[16]

Even if the opportunities to access quality English language teaching were equal in the school system, the benefits that can be expected to flow from education are still unequally distributed, as an Indonesian farmer explains:

Why should I be bothered sending my children to university and spend a lot of money? A lot of graduates are unemployed. When someone finishes university, s/he only wants a white-collar job and would prefer being unemployed to working in a garden. I do not have anyone who can help my children find work in a government office, and I do not have enough money to bribe them.[17]

To conclude the discussion about the injustices of English language education, I will now summarize an examination of China's compulsory English language learning as a public policy by educational linguists Guangwei Hu and Lubna Alsagoff.[18] Hu and Alsagoff identify four key considerations in evaluating language policy: moral justice, practical feasibility, allocative efficiency, and distributive justice.

From an idealistic position of moral justice universal English language teaching is obviously a public good. Access to English can be considered a form of instrumental language right: everyone has a right to learn the global power code. However, in the same way that students have a right to learn the global power code, they also have an expressive language right to the full development of their mother tongue, and they also have the right to acquire other kinds of useful knowledge. The moral justice argument for English is thus limited to the degree that learning English does not interfere with learning the mother tongue or other subject knowledge.[19]

When it comes to practical feasibility, universal English teaching in China, as elsewhere, is subject to some intractable and incapacitating constraints, some of which we discussed above. These include a severe shortage of qualified teachers, a lack of appropriate instructional materials, and the absence of a sociolinguistic environment in which English is meaningful.

It could be argued that a language policy should not be criticized on the basis of implementation problems because these might straighten themselves out over time. On the other hand, they might not; and if policy makers have failed to come up with an implementation plan together with the policy, there is no reason to believe in magical transformation in the future.

The verdict on universal English teaching becomes even more negative when it comes to allocative effectiveness. The costs of teacher training, of hiring expatriate teachers, of developing suitable materials, and of creating the necessary infrastructure to teach English are high. At the same time, the available evidence suggests that, to date, English language teaching in China, as elsewhere, has not been particularly effective.

Finally, addressing the problem of costly and ineffective English language instruction may have made other subjects more costly and less effective (as we saw in the case of Russian above), raising the question of distributive justice. In fact, the promotion of English has benefited only a relatively small number of students in well-resourced urban schools at the expense of the majority of students. Universal English thus benefits an elite group while disadvantaging everyone else:

> Because of their privileged position, [Chinese elites] are also consuming resources that might otherwise have been allocated to policy options that could benefit the majority, who are not compensated for the losses they suffer as a result of the diversion of these resources. As a consequence, the English medium instruction initiative has not only perpetuated the unequal distribution of power and access but is also creating new forms of inequality.[20]

If moral justice, practical feasibility, allocative efficiency, and distributive justice are taken into account, the verdict on the universal English language learning initiative in China is thus unambiguously negative. The researchers go on to assess the English instruction policy not only for the Han majority but also for ethnic minority students and in that context their verdict is even more dire—'an outlandish extravagance' as they call it.

If universal English instruction is indeed a wrongheaded policy for China's majority and minorities alike, as the authors conclude, what policy alternatives are there? The researchers suggest the provision of English as an enrichment subject rather than as a compulsory subject and the removal of English from high-stakes assessment. Similar conclusions have been reached with reference to English language education in other developing countries.[21]

INJUSTICES OF ENGLISH AS GLOBAL ACADEMIC LANGUAGE

While researchers examining language policy and language rights activists make a case for limiting the role of English in global education, most national education systems around the world are actually expanding the role of English in education. In many non-Anglophone countries, English is fast moving from being a curriculum subject to becoming an important medium of instruction. In fact, the lines between English as a language teaching subject and English as medium of instruction are not necessarily clear-cut, as we saw in Wei Ru's struggle with following English medium lectures at her *minzu* university. The introduction of English as medium of instruction has been most pronounced at the tertiary level, where the term 'Englishization' has been used to refer to the spread of English as medium of instruction in institutions of higher education in non-Anglophone countries.[22]

The key driver behind the spread of English as medium of instruction is the same correlational fallacy that we observed with reference to the universalization of English language teaching. Year after year global university rankings find the world's most prestigious universities located predominantly in Anglophone center countries. In the 2015 *Times Higher Education World Reputation Rankings*, for instance, fifty-eight out of the world's top one hundred universities were based in just three countries, namely, the USA, the UK, and Australia.[23] Consequently, English has come to be associated with academic excellence and the correlational fallacy leads policy makers worldwide to misrecognize English as the cause of academic excellence.[24]

English medium education entrenches social inequalities in a society in the same way that universal English language education does: English medium education further privileges the privileged and further disadvantages the disadvantaged by creating an additional barrier to higher education, as we examined in the previous section. Here we will focus on another form of injustice tied to English medium education, namely, transformations of knowledge. As English becomes equated with academic excellence, knowledge produced and available in other languages becomes devalued.

The spread of English medium education in higher education is inextricably linked to the spread of English as the global language of science and research.[25] Two consequences of this development have been widely discussed. First, the dominance of English as global language of science and research means that other languages lose the capacity to express academic concepts. In other words, they lose or fail to develop the registers necessary to formulate and express scientific knowledge. Second, the dominance of English means that academics who are native speakers of English or who are affiliated with universities in Anglophone center countries are advantaged when it comes to disseminating and publishing their research. Nonnative speakers of English, by contrast, particularly if they are affiliated with universities in peripheral countries, are at a disadvantage when seeking to disseminate and publish their work because the pressure to publish in international journals translates into the pressure to publish in English.[26]

However, there is more to the story: the global spread of English has naturalized English as the medium of academic excellence, and disrupts the production of locally informed and locally meaningful knowledge. We will now explore each of these injustices in turn.

The education scholar Po King Choi explains the fallacy inherent in the naturalization of English as the medium of academic excellence with a metaphor: in the same way that water does not start to flow if all you do is install a tap without having the plumbing in place, you do not get excellence by simply switching the language of instruction.[27] Even so, the equation between 'English' and 'excellence' has become so naturalized that no one seems to think about 'putting the plumbing in place.'

But why would universities, institutes of higher learning, 'forget the plumbing' and be content to accept the simplistic equation that 'English is academic excellence?' For an explanation we must return to academic competition and university rankings. Over the past decade, university rankings have become incredibly influential. Inside and outside the academy, university rankings undergird policy frameworks and funding allocations. Even if people disagree about this or that form of measurement, the idea that university performance should be measured and ranked is now firmly entrenched. The result is universalized academic competition and the belief that university rankings are meaningful and should guide educational, social, and economic policies.

English has become one of the central terrains where competition plays out. Rankings quantify academic performance on the basis of four criteria, which are differently measured and weighted in different rankings: research and publications, learning environment, reputation, and internationalization. Except for learning environment, each of these criteria serves to promote English in covert ways despite the fact that each criterion is ostensibly language-neutral.[28]

Research and publications usually privilege English because English-language journals and publishers are more highly ranked, more prestigious, and 'more international,' as we will see below. Accepting that achieving global impact is the most meaningful form of knowledge production means publishing in English.

Reputation is the most controversial criterion and measured in different ways but obviously linked to all kinds of assumptions. If it is measured, as in one Korean ranking, by asking the human resources departments of multinational corporations from which Korean universities they would like to hire graduates, the link with English is not particularly subtle. Graduates who are planning to pursue careers in local or national organizations are not even considered as potential bearers of 'reputation.'

Finally, the internationalization criterion strongly favors universities where English is the medium of instruction. It puts pressure on non-English-speaking universities to switch to English as a medium of instruction in order to improve their standing in the rankings. Furthermore, other indices of internationalization such as the percentage of international faculty or international students all act as drivers toward increasing the number of classes taught through the medium of English.

In sum, it is obvious that university rankings operate in a way that privileges English and—implicitly—creates a connection between English and excellence. To accept university rankings as drivers of policy is to accept that English means excellence.

University rankings are often touted as a means to hold universities accountable to the public: an institution's standing in the rankings is perceived as a clear indicator of what they are doing with their funding and how they are returning the investment, or so the reasoning goes. By contrast, the purveyors of rankings—multinational media corporations such as Quacquarelli Symonds, TES Global, or Shanghai Ranking Consultancy—are not accountable to anyone. And no consensus as to whether English should be considered as a measurement of academic excellence has ever been sought or emerged. In fact, the equation continues to be hidden precisely because no such consensus exists and is unlikely to be forthcoming.

Instead, university rankings institutionalize the equation between English and excellence de facto. The sociologist Max Weber compared modern institutional practices of bookkeeping, accounting, and performance statistics—of which university rankings are a prime example—to an 'iron cage,' which leaves no option but to submit to its logic.[29] Submission limits the realms of democracy and ethics and makes alternatives disappear. Indeed, the question presents itself as to what the meaning of 'excellence' is if it does not involve service to the common good.

The other side of the equation between English and academic excellence is the devaluation of knowledge researched and disseminated in languages other than English. The dominance of US- and UK-based journals among the most highly ranked journals constitutes not only pressure to publish in English but also pressure to conduct particular types of research, as communications scholar Myungkoo Kang has found.[30]

In the name of globalization and international competitiveness, South Korean academics, just as their colleagues elsewhere, are under pressure to publish in 'high-quality' international journals. The 'quality' of a journal is measured by indexation in the 'Science Citation Index' (SCI), the 'Social Sciences Citation Index' (SSCI), or the 'Arts and Humanities Citation Index' (AHCI), all of which are databases owned by multinational US-headquartered media corporation Thomson Reuters. In South Korean academia, publications in SCI-, SSCI-, and AHCI-indexed journals bring not only prestige but also financial rewards. Furthermore, they have become an important hiring consideration and are indispensable for being awarded tenure.

In 2007, there were 1,865 journals indexed in the SSCI, of which 1,585 (79.62%) originated in only two countries, the United States and the United Kingdom. SSCI-indexed 'international' journals are thus clearly hugely skewed toward those originating in Anglophone center countries. Among Asian countries, seven SSCI-indexed journals (0.38%) originate in Japan, five (0.27%) in China, four (0.21%) in India, three (0.16%) in South Korea, and one each (0.05%) in

Singapore and Taiwan. Even those SSCI-indexed journals published outside the United States and United Kingdom are overwhelmingly English-language publications. So, the fact that pressure to publish in SSCI-indexed journals translates into pressure to publish in English is obvious.

In order to find out whether it is not only the language of publication that changes with the pressure to publish in SSCI-indexed journals but also the research content, Kang analyzed articles published by Asian scholars in the top SSCI-indexed journals in the field of Communication Studies. He found that most such articles 'framed local phenomena with American mainstream theories' or 'appropriated mainstream theories by redefining mainstream theoretical concepts.' By contrast, only a very small number of these articles attempted to formulate research problems from the local context.

The author concludes that South Korea's policy for improving research competitiveness (as expressed in pressure to publish in SSCI-indexed journals) actually jeopardizes local knowledge production and the formulation of research agendas with relevance to the actual needs of local and national societies. In other words, the attempt to foster globally top-ranked social sciences researchers in South Korea constitutes simultaneous encouragement of social sciences researchers to neglect issues within their immediate social contexts.

Many scholars remain committed to the service of their communities through the production and dissemination of locally meaningful knowledge. However, to do so increasingly means to act against their own best career interests and open themselves up to self-doubt about the value of their research, as Hong Kong–based academic Po King Choi explains in a comment on *Language on the Move*:

> [. . .] we dont do research or write merely to get a place in the English-speaking world. We do that because we feel committed to the community or society we are researching on (most likely living in), and we want to communicate with the people with whom we feel a strong sense of allegiance. [. . .] our publications

in Chinese (our first language and language of the majority) dont count—or, they count so little that most of our career-minded colleagues just dont bother to write them. The interesting (and sad) thing is that it affects our psyche so much that we who write in Chinese do sometimes feel that we publish very little, or dont have any publication [. . .]. It is not only unfair on those of us who feel committed to write for their own community, but it also closes the mind of academics not only in our own society, but also in the English-speaking world.[31]

In sum, academic 'internationalization' in effect means the imposition of English-mediated centralized regimes of knowledge. These value knowledge produced and disseminated through the medium of English over knowledge produced and disseminated in any other language. In the process, locally informed, locally engaged, and critical forms of knowledge production and dissemination are being displaced.

PAYING TRIBUTE TO THE ANGLOPHONE CENTER

In May 2013 I was stuck in traffic in Ajman, one of the smaller of the seven emirates that make up the United Arab Emirates, and one that has to do without Abu Dhabi's and Dubai's global glitz. Imagine my surprise when a car painted in the Union Jack came into view![32] The car was not just decorated with a flag sticker, an image of the flag or an actual flag. Rather, it was completely painted as a flag. The status of the little car as an island of Britishness moving in a sea of mundane Middle Eastern traffic was further enhanced by the fact that the car had its steering wheel on the right-hand side: just like in Britain, but unlike every other car in the United Arab Emirates.

The car turned out to be an ad for higher education. Specifically, it was advertising for the University of Bolton and the slogan on its rear window read 'Get a UK degree/At The First British University/ in Ras Al Khaimah, U.A.E.'

The University of Bolton is an institution in the Manchester metropolitan region, and its main claim to fame is that it has consistently ranked last in league tables of British universities. In 2008, the University of Bolton opened a branch campus in Ras Al-Khaimah, the northernmost and least developed emirate. Initially, the university's low ranking at home caused some raised eyebrows but the branch campus now seems to be doing well, with enrollments rising from an initial 100 students to 300 in 2010.

Not favored with oil wealth nor tourist attractions, Ras Al-Khaimah has tried to turn itself into a higher education hub by luring American and British colleges and universities into opening branch campuses in their free trade zone. One of these branch campuses, that of US-based George Mason University, folded spectacularly after only three years in 2009.[33]

Many international branch campuses have ended in a fiasco. In addition to the George Mason University withdrawal from Ras Al-Khaimah, high-profile failures include those of the University of New South Wales in Singapore and the University of Southern Queensland in Dubai. Even so, branch campuses continue to be a popular internationalization strategy, and the number of international branch campuses reached 200 in 2012. This was up from only eighty-two in 2006, representing a remarkable growth figure of around 150% in little more than half a decade.

The largest number of international branch campuses originate from the United Kingdom, and about a quarter of all international branch campuses are located in the United Arab Emirates. However, the scene is fast diversifying. In addition to the United Kingdom, Australia and the USA have long tried to be big players in franchising their higher education institutions overseas. They are now joined by other European countries, particularly France and Germany, as well as emerging source countries such as India, Iran, Malaysia, and Pakistan.

The destination countries of international branch campuses, too, are diversifying away from the Gulf States, with the largest growth now in Asia, particularly China and Thailand. Africa is also starting to attract international branch campuses, with some already set up such as the Iranian Islamic Azad University in Tanzania, and many others, originating particularly from China and Malaysia, in the planning stage.

What drives the extraordinary growth of international branch campuses? Well, you will have guessed that it is not the search for knowledge or the desire to provide more equitable access to higher education. According to sociologists of education Philip Altbach and Jane Knight the primary motivation to establish an international branch campus is the desire to make a profit.[34] This is particularly obvious with for-profit universities and includes a fair number of shady degree mills. But making money is also an increasingly important objective for traditional not-for-profit universities starved of public funding.

You may have been wondering how this account of branch campuses is relevant to our discussion. The relevance to the global spread of English is easy to see: the medium of instruction in international branch campuses is almost universally English and branch campuses are thus part of the Englishization of higher education we explored in the previous section. But what is the connection with global justice?

To begin with, the commercialization of education is a key social justice concern, as the United Nations noted already in 2006:

> There appears to be a strong link between rising inequalities in the distribution of opportunities for a quality education and the recent tendency to commercialize education and treat it as a commodity subject to the rules of an open and competitive market economy. For years, international financial institutions overseeing the implementation of structural adjustment programmes encouraged the Governments of developing countries to charge fees for the delivery of primary education. This reform component was discarded following widespread protests, but there are many other indications that, within the general context of the weakened commitment to public service and reduced

support for universal social programmes, education is increasingly being treated as merchandise and pupils as customers. If nothing is done to address this issue, schools and universities of quality will be accessible only to the privileged classes, while the masses will have to be satisfied with lower-priced and often mediocre institutions.[35]

The subjection of education to the profit motive is objectionable as it entrenches intra-societal disadvantage in ways we have by now discussed at length. Additionally, branch campuses constitute a prime example of the global entrenchment of privilege and disadvantage, as branch campuses in the global south help to subsidize the headquarter institution. Branch campuses thus constitute an example of the neocolonial relationships embedded in the global spread of English: investing in global English means investing in teachers, teacher trainers, materials, and instructional technology originating primarily from Anglophone center countries, constituting in effect a financial flow from the periphery to the center.

We will now examine these English-related financial subsidies from the periphery to the center in some more detail and start by looking at some figures from South Korea as an example.[36] In 2009, roughly 40% of South Korea's public education budget went toward English language education. In absolute figures this means public expenditure on English to the tune of twelve billion US dollars in 2009 alone. Furthermore, private investment into English language education in South Korea is even larger and came to an additional thirteen billion US dollars in 2009. The population of South Korea is less than fifty million. So, these figures mean that South Koreans spend more than five hundred US dollars per person per year on English language learning.

These are the English language learning costs of one single 'expanding circle' country alone; admittedly one that is reputed to spend excessively on English language learning. Even so, it is obvious that, globally, English language learning is a huge industry and means big bucks. And this calculation does not even try to take into account the opportunity cost of investing into English language learning. In other words, the money, time, and effort invested into English is lost to other things that might be equally useful or even more useful.

Given this immense global investment into English, much of which flows directly to educational institutions, publishers, or media corporations in Anglophone center countries, the global spread of English is clearly in the national interest of those same Anglophone center countries. As Robert Phillipson explains:

> Building on research in Switzerland and worldwide, François Grin [. . .] was commissioned by a French educational research institution to investigate the impact of the current dominance of English in education. He calculates quantifiable privileged market effects, communication savings effects, language learning savings effects (i.e., not needing to invest so much in foreign language learning), alternative human capital investment effects (e.g., school time being used for other purposes), and legitimacy and rhetorical effects. The research led Grin to conclude that continental countries are transferring to the United Kingdom and Ireland at least Euro 10 billion per annum, and more probably about Euro 16–17 billion a year. [. . .] Grin [. . .] has also calculated that the U.S. economy saves $19 billion p.a. by not needing to spend time and effort in formal schooling on learning foreign languages.[37]

Global investment into English is obviously immense but these costs are often justified by the gains that will flow from having one common international language. That is why international organizations increasingly opt for the use of English only to conduct their communications. The European Union, with its commitment to multilingual provision through translating and interpreting, is an exception to this trend. The multilingual provision requirements of the European Union are often dismissed as too costly and thus inefficient and unaffordable. However, the dismissal of the

European Union's multilingual language policy as costly and inefficient is wrong, as economists Michelle Gazzola and François Grin demonstrate.[38]

The European Union's language bill for translating and interpreting is 1.1 billion Euros per year. That may seem a lot but amounts to less than 1% of the union's annual budget of 147.2 billion Euros. The expenditure for the European Union's current multilingual language policy is thus 2.2 Euros per person per year; about the price of a cup of coffee.

Despite this small amount, it is true that it would be even cheaper if the European Union abolished all translating and interpreting and adopted an English-only policy. Anyone advancing that argument has to bear in mind that the language costs would not be entirely eliminated because language services to make sure all those documents are well written and legally watertight would still be needed. Cost would shift from translators and interpreters to ghostwriters, copyeditors, and proofreaders.

But the overall cost could still be brought down, right? Well, no, actually not.

Under an English-only regime, most Europeans would be paying much, much more than the equivalent of a cup of coffee for linguistic provision. To begin with, the British and the Irish would not be paying anything at all. Those 7% of continental Europeans who already speak 'very good' English would not be paying, either. That would leave everyone else—around 80% of Europeans—out of pocket for English language learning if they wanted to exercise their democratic right to understand what is going on in the European parliament and to participate in the European project in any other way. The cost for those 80% of Europeans to bring their English up to scratch would be less for some (those who already have 'good' or 'modest' English) and astronomical for those adults who have no English—for all these individuals language costs would be much, much higher than is currently the case. Furthermore, it would no longer be a public expense shared by all, but their own private expense.

Turning language costs from a public expense to personal language learning expenses is unjust. Not only would it make participation in the European project contingent upon an individual's financial capacity to invest in language learning, it would also be unfair for continental Europeans vis-à-vis English native speakers in Ireland and the United Kingdom, who would not have to invest in language learning. Already receiving huge language subsidies by everyone learning their language, as we saw above, they could completely withdraw from sharing the costs of linguistic provision in the European Union. In sum, the evidence is clear: the European Union's multilingual provision is more cost-effective and fairer than an English-only policy could ever be.

PSYCHOLOGICAL DAMAGES OF GLOBAL ENGLISH

So far, we have examined the ways in which the discourses and practices of global English are implicated in inequalities in access to education, in the production and dissemination of knowledge, and in the displacement of language learning costs from the center to the periphery while the center draws a revenue stream from the English language learning efforts of the periphery. This section will change perspective slightly and focus on injustices of cultural representation related to global English. Most theorists of justice agree that at the heart of inequality lies a psychological component. Sociologists consider shame as a key aspect of poverty as it leads poor people to accept that their poverty is their own fault and to accept that the rich deserve to be rich.[39] Similarly, theorists of racial and colonial oppression have long noted a psychological component where those who are subject to racism and colonialism come to accept their oppression as justified because an inferiority complex has been instilled in them.

This section explores the psychological consequences of linguistic subordination. To point out that shame, the colonial cringe or an inferiority complex are a central aspect of linguistic subordination is not new. Mahatma Gandhi argued already in 1908 that 'to give millions a knowledge of English is to enslave us.'[40] Frantz Fanon made a similar point when he argued that colonial languages only offer colonial subject positions to colonial speakers:

> To speak means to be in a position to use a certain syntax, to grasp the morphology of this or that language, but it means above all to assume a culture, to support the weight of a civilization. [. . .] Every colonized people—in other words, every people in whose soul an inferiority complex has been created by the death and burial of its local cultural originality—finds itself face to face with the language of the civilizing nation; that is, the culture of the mother country.[41]

While the colonial inferiority complex may be a thing of the past, the discourses and practices of global English bring with them their own inferiority complexes and are associated with similar psychological deformations as those noted for class and race and, in fact, all social structures of inequality.

I will begin with an anecdote: in 2009, I lived in the United Arab Emirates and was affiliated with a national Emirati university, Zayed University. During that time I had the opportunity to visit a number of universities in other Middle Eastern countries. On one such occasion, I presented a guest lecture about my intercultural communication research. As part of the visit I had to fill in a report form about my person and my visit for the local bureaucracy. In the spot for 'Affiliation' I put down 'Zayed University.' As I did so, the departmental administration officer who was looking over my shoulder said to my academic hosts, 'I thought she was from Australia.' Everyone looked at me and seemed to think I was an impostor. And for a moment I felt like one. Then, one of my hosts kindly asked me to replace 'Zayed University, Abu Dhabi' with 'Macquarie University, Sydney' because that was 'much more prestigious with the higher-ups.' I complied, conscious of the fact that my value as a visiting academic might have been more related to the fact that I was affiliated with a Western institution than to anything I might have to say about my research.

That my experience was not an isolated incident is apparent from research about academic 'self-marginalization' by the discourse analyst Esmat Babaii.[42] In the tradition of postcolonial criticism, the researcher examines how the colonial cringe plays out in academia by examining bio-blurbs published in the conference booklet of an Asian conference related to English language teaching. After discarding the bio-blurbs of keynote speakers and Western academics, the corpus consisted of 512 bio-blurbs of academics from Arab countries, China, India, Indonesia, Iran, Japan, Korea, and Malaysia. The corpus was analyzed for any evidence that the authors downplayed their local credentials and highlighted connections with the West. Such strategies of self-representation were considered to constitute evidence of 'self-marginalization.'

For instance, academics with a PhD from a non-Western university rarely provided the institution where they had obtained their PhD in their bio-blurb, in contrast to presenters who had obtained their PhD from a Western institution. This also worked by association: if presenters were affiliated with or supervised by someone who had a PhD from a Western institution, that information was likely to be shared in the bio-blurb. Some of the bio-blurbs quoted in the paper mention connections to Western institutions so minor and seemingly irrelevant (e.g., having attended a conference in the USA; having attended a short-term study-tour) that they seem almost comical. If a local career of twenty years is mentioned in less detail than having 'once' taught a course in the UK for a semester, as in one example, one cannot help but feel sorry for that academic.

Babaii concludes her study by comparing academics who exercise self-marginalization to strike-breakers:

> Periphery academics who exercise self-marginalization, similar to strike-breakers, slow down, and sometimes, nullify the efforts on the part of those independent scholars who try to resist the 'imposed identities' [. . .] in the world of professionalism dominated by Western ethos.[43]

The self-marginalization of periphery academics is, as always, connected to multiple vulnerabilities: to the disadvantaged material conditions obtaining in periphery institutions, to the subordination of local knowledge we discussed above, and to their status as 'non-native' speakers of English. But is it possible to isolate the language factor more clearly and demonstrate specific linguistic psychological damages?

Let me share another anecdote. In 2001, when I was teaching at the University of Sydney, an overseas student from South Korea who was about to fail a unit I was coordinating left a suicide note under my office door. She described herself as a 'loser' who did not have enough English to cope with her course. She wrote how 'guilty' she felt that her English was not better and how she had 'betrayed' her parents with her poor English, as well as other people who cared for her, including myself as 'a nice lecturer.' I was deeply shocked and tried to help in whatever small way I could. I know that she survived this particular bout of depression, but I do not know what has become of her since because she withdrew from university shortly after and left Australia. I found the experience harrowing and have often thought of her over the years. Her English had, in fact, met the university's admission standards, and so it was not her factual proficiency level in English that was her problem but her belief that her English was not good enough coupled with unrealistically high expectations as to what her English should be like. I hope that she has been able to rid herself of her obsession and found happiness in some walk of life unrelated to English.

Again, the anecdote is not of an isolated case, as research with Korean early study abroad students and their families by Juyoung Song demonstrates.[44] The early years of the twenty-first century saw a 'Korean education exodus' with more and more children leaving South Korea temporarily for *jogi yuhak* ('early study abroad') in the United States and other English-speaking countries. In 2006, 29,511 Korean elementary to high school students pursued education visas, with around half of these being of elementary school age. Furthermore, these numbers do not include children who accompany their parents, i.e., where the reason for the visa is some parental activity. Overall, the researcher estimates that more than 40,000 Korean children were living abroad at the end of the first decade of the twenty-first century in order to pursue an early English education and to acquire 'perfect' English. The typical pattern is for these children to be accompanied by their mothers while the fathers stay behind to provide the financial support for their children's foreign education. So widespread is the pattern that there is a special term for this type of family formation: *kiregi kajok* ('goose family'); like geese, they fly every now and then to see each other.

It is astonishing to think that the allure of English is such that people are willing to trade close family bonds and accept familial separation as the price for English language proficiency. English is put above family and friendship. One of the mothers interviewed by Song, for instance, was upset about the fact that her young daughter's best friend during her study abroad year in the United States was another Korean girl. Because the two girls spoke Korean with each other this mother felt cheated out of her investment into her daughter's English proficiency. Happiness for the mothers was tied to a good return on their investment as measured by their children's English proficiency, and particularly their accent. One mother had this to say:

> English is the place where you can see a close correlation between the money you spend and the improvement of children's learning. The more you spend, the more efficient the learning. Yes, especially when the children are young, the amount of money spent in their English education is visible, which makes me happy.[45]

The quote suggests that investing in learning English is some form of consumption addiction. A language learning market that is more or less saturated, as we saw above, can only continue to grow if addiction is built into the system. How do you become addicted to language learning? Make the goal seem magical and, at the same time, impossible to reach. That is where the other language ideology identified by Song comes in: linguistic self-depreciation. For all their investments into English language teaching and learning, many South Koreans feel that their English is terrible and that English language teaching in the country is hopeless.

Being in thrall to an English language teaching industry that is so rampant that it makes people value proficiency in English more than family relationships and that is geared to instilling a perpetual sense of inferiority is surely a recipe for great profits on the one hand and significant mental health risks on the other. Sadly, the recipe is not restricted to South Korea but—with variations—seems to be working profitably in many places around the world.

For the Korean women in Song's study, learning English meant learning that their English was not good enough. It meant learning to be marginal to the global system of English. Learning English can be deeply alienating as development sociologist Karuna Morarji explains with reference to education in rural India.[46]

In villages in the Aglar River Valley in Uttarakhand in northern India, mass formal education only dates from the 1990s and has been found to constitute a double-edged sword. With universal access to primary and secondary education, everyone there now dreams of achieving a service sector job. Few actually achieve that dream because competition for service sector jobs is fierce and rural children, even with a formal education, cannot really compete with their urban peers who enjoy much better opportunities in the competition for waged office work.

However, while formal education does not really enable these children to join India's urban middle class, it has the additional pernicious effect of closing them off from opportunities to live on the land. School takes children away from being apprenticed into subsistence agriculture or artisan work such as carpentry. Having learned how to read and write instead, they do not know how to do agricultural or other rural labor and, more crucially, they no longer want to engage in manual, non-waged labor. The villagers interviewed by Morarji put forward a similar argument to the

Indonesian farmer quoted above: while education was good if you got a job, without a job an uneducated person was better off than an educated person. Education is thus not only part of the solution to the problem of rural decline in India but it is also, perversely, part of the problem.

Firstly, it is an economic problem, as discussed above. Secondly, it is a psychological problem: as everyone has become conditioned to believe that English proficiency holds many promises, creates opportunities, and opens doors, many learners have to live with the cognitive dissonance that learning English has not opened doors for them. On the contrary, it has simultaneously closed the door of living a meaningful local life:

> Experiences of alienation and disappointment around education illustrate how the dynamics of inclusion and exclusion of a market economy have meant that 'becoming a part of the world has frequently entailed becoming marginal to the world.'[47]

In the accounts of self-marginalization, addictive hyper-consumption, self-blame, and alienation discussed so far the perpetrators of the psychological consequences resulting from global English remain hidden. It is the global 'system' of English-related discourses and practices that produces these deformities. But such an account would let dominant center speakers off the hook too easily. The linguistic inferiority complexes of peripheral speakers we have discussed so far are actively produced in discourses of linguistic shaming. I will here discuss two examples of linguistic shaming: subtitling the speech of peripheral speakers of English for center audiences, and making fun of peripheral English.

Subtitling the speech of peripheral speakers is not uncommon and I will examine one show in detail. The film is called 'How fair is fashion?' and was produced by British educational media producer Pumpkin TV.[48] I do not wish to single out this particular documentary; rather, I have chosen it because it carries an important message about global inequalities and the ways in which consumers in the global north are complicit in the exploitation of garment workers in the global south. Its progressive content notwithstanding, the show's subtitling also serves to render the English-language speech of Bangladeshis as incomprehensible.

'How fair is fashion?' is an excellent resource explaining the circuits of cheap clothes for consumers in the global north, the huge profits of multinational fashion and retail corporations, and the exploitation of textile workers in the global south. The film was shot in Bangladesh and features stories such as those of an 18-year-old woman who has been working in a textile factory in Dhaka for seven years. Working one hundred hours a week, she earns the equivalent of between forty and fifty US dollars per month. Together with her husband she lives in a small room in a slum where they share toilet and water facilities with around ten other families. The mud track leading to their dwelling doubles as an open sewer.

The show ends on an optimistic note by featuring a cooperative in rural Bangladesh producing for fair trade fashion label People Tree.[49] The garment worker interviewed there earns about the same as her Dhaka-based counterpart. However, in contrast to the factory workers in Dhaka, she works fixed hours from nine to five. She has a proper work contract and the cooperative also provides childcare and schooling for her children. Above all, there is dignity in her work since it is more autonomous and diverse. Global English, incidentally, has nothing to do with this developmental success story.

All the workers interviewed for the film speak Bangla while managers, policy makers, and a high-level union official speak English. The language choices in the film are thus reflective of a well-known divide in Bangladesh: that access to English and proficiency in English are markers of privilege.

However, whether they speak Bangla or English, the show treats all Bangladeshi speakers—irrespective of whether they are Bangla-speaking workers or English-speaking elites—as incomprehensible to the British viewer. Both Bangla-speaking and English-speaking Bangladeshis are presented as requiring mediation to become intelligible: Bangla is translated and English is subtitled. To translate

Bangla into English is simply a necessity borne from linguistic difference. It carries no additional symbolic message. The same would be true of subtitling if the purpose of subtitling were to make the show accessible to deaf audiences. However, to subtitle the English speech of Bangladeshis for a hearing English-speaking audience while not subtitling the English speech of British speakers on the show is to render the speech of Bangladeshis incomprehensible and illegitimate. As Bourdieu explains:

> [U]tterances are not only [. . .] signs to be understood and deciphered; they are also signs of wealth, intended to be evaluated and appreciated, and signs of authority, intended to be believed and obeyed.[50]

Subtitled speech is a sign of *lack* of wealth and authority. The elite Bangladeshis featured in this film are all competent speakers of English and I personally found them perfectly comprehensible.[51] Refusing to accept that they are comprehensible and that they can speak for themselves without requiring mediation is to refuse to acknowledge the legitimacy of their speech. It means to shame them into feeling incomprehensible.

Perceiving peripheral speakers as incomprehensible licenses their exclusion from participation in development contexts, just as it does in the contexts we explored in Chapter Six. The literature is full of examples of interactions between international development 'experts' and their local partners where the latter are not being listened to. A Cambodian education expert, Visna, for instance has this story to tell of a work meeting with international educational experts during which an end-of-course exam was discussed:

> Visna and his colleagues had experience of the course (they had all trained on it), the trainees (who came from the same educational context that they had done), and exam writing (they had written exams within that Ministry of Education system). Nevertheless, the expatriate team members decided that they

would write the exam. The completed exam was given to Visna and his colleagues for feedback. They considered the exam inappropriate for the context for three main reasons. First, the time allotted for the exam was too short for the trainees to manage the tasks. Second, the tasks were too difficult: The trainees were being asked to produce a lot of work that was beyond their levels of English and beyond the kinds of skills that they had covered in the training course. Third, the instructions were confusing, and the task was unclear. The original exam writers rejected the feedback, and when the students took the exam, the majority failed.[52]

As the example shows, the value of 'English for development' is severely compromised if English speakers from the global south such as Visna are simply not listened to and ignored.

Another widespread form instilling a sense of inferiority is to make fun of someone's speech.

Imagine the *New York Times* were to ask readers to send in their favorite blonde jokes or to report the funniest thing they have ever seen a person of color do. Now, imagine that once that campaign is underway the blogosphere is full of it and anyone interested in gender or race joins the social media conversation, and even academics in the fields of gender and ethnicity studies get all excited and offer analyses as to how and why blondes or persons of color act in such ridiculous ways. It is not going to happen, of course, because such a thing would be outrageously and obscenely sexist or racist. However, when it comes to language precisely these kinds of jokes are not considered demeaning of subordinate speakers in the same way.[53]

The *New York Times* article I alluded to above was a 2010 article about 'Chinglish,' which ended up being their most e-mailed article for a time. Indeed, it created such a reader response and so much buzz on social media that the newspaper called for readers to send in their own pictures of 'strange signs from abroad.' Even an academic linguistics blog pitched in by offering a series of analyses to illuminate how 'unintentional errors of translation from Chinese result in ludicrous or impenetrable English.' The episode is by no means exceptional and readers will be aware of innumerable websites poking fun at the English of subordinate speakers, particularly of Asian speakers. As is the case with the supposed incomprehensibility of peripheral speakers, these jokes also become interactional resources. One high-profile case was reported in early 2015 when Argentine's president Christina Kirchner mocked a Chinese accent during a state visit to China by replacing 'r' with 'l' in a tweet.[54]

We can be thankful that sexist and racist jokes are no longer widely considered acceptable but it is high time we arrived at a similar understanding with regard to jokes about subordinate ways of speaking. Making fun of someone else's language is just as bigoted as sexist or racist jokes, and can similarly harm the confidence and self-esteem of subordinate speakers.

SUMMARY

The global spread of English is a legacy of colonialism. Today, global English is widely perceived as vital to global development. Hence, English language learning is often expected to contribute to economic growth and to enable the world's disadvantaged to participate more fully in economic and social activities and opportunities. Alternatively, global English is demonized as a 'hydra' or a 'tyrant.'[55] This chapter has examined these assumptions from a global justice perspective and has found them wanting. Assumptions of benefits as well as evil inherent in global English are based on a correlational fallacy that misrecognizes the privileges accruing to dominant speakers as privileges resulting from their speech, and the indignities suffered by the world's poor as resulting from their speech. However, changing the language variable only would mean to change nothing. Global injustice is the product of an unjust neocolonial world order and global English is implicated in entrenching global inequality in complex ways.

As a result of the belief that English is advantageous, many societies around the world have implemented universal English language learning provisions in their school systems. Public English language learning is widely supplemented with private efforts to learn English. Because the quality of English language education depends on the material resources available to a learner or a group of learners, English-for-all policies serve to entrench existing inequalities within a society. Furthermore, universal English language learning detracts resources from learning other content or other languages that might be more locally meaningful.

Generally, the discourses and practices of global English produce an orientation to the global at the expense of the local. With regards to knowledge, that means that knowledge produced and disseminated through the medium of English is regarded more highly than knowledge produced and disseminated through the medium of other languages. The latter become devalued. In the process, the very nature of the problems that get researched changes and local problems become neglected. For a nation's academic institutions to neglect local problems and to concentrate on research that is internationally meaningful ultimately constitutes an act of betrayal as it means slipping out of the obligation to contribute to the common good. As 'international' often in reality means 'American' or 'British,' global 'international' research efforts must also be considered as a form of tribute or subsidy paid to the Anglophone center.

That the discourses and practices of global English constitute a subsidy from the periphery to the center is most apparent when one considers the cost of global English language learning. While the periphery invests heavily in English language learning at great financial and opportunity costs, the Anglophone center is exempt from such costs. The costs of global communication thus have to be shouldered disproportionately by the world's disadvantaged. Furthermore, the expenses associated with global English constitute a significant revenue stream from the periphery to the center, from where much English language education is orchestrated.

Like all subordination, the hegemony of global English also carries psychological costs for the subordinated, as learning English also means to become alive to one's marginality in English and to a perpetual falling short of the imagined ideal of 'perfect' homogeneous English. Much of the psychological damage of English is inflicted through practices of linguistic shaming such as representing peripheral speakers as incomprehensible or as ridiculous impostors.

While English as 'the hyper-central language of globalization'[56] has of necessity been singled out in this chapter, the injustices of English are not inherent to the language per se. They are the injustices of neoliberal empire where 'English' is nothing but yet another commodity through which domination and subordination are enacted; or, as political scientist Peter Ives puts it:

> The 'imposition' of (or supposed 'choice' to learn) any dominant language can be detrimental to subaltern groups because it can further submerge critical consciousness. It can hinder the struggle against oppression and suppression. Learning English, or any dominant language, is not itself inherently detrimental in the abstract, but the context in which it occurs often means that it helps to reinforce psychological, social and cultural fragmentation. Thus, a 'global language' like English can never fulfil the role cosmopolitanism sets for it, that of helping those marginalised and oppressed by 'globalisation' to be heard.[57]

Chapter 8

Linguistic Justice

The answer to Socrates's question, 'What is justice?' can only be this: justice is the overcoming of injustice.[1]

This book has explored language-related injustices. We have seen how the processes of linguistic subordination and linguistic domination operate, and how language is tied to injustices of economic distribution, cultural recognition, and political representation in the areas of employment, education, and community participation at national and international levels. This final chapter changes perspective and asks what the content of linguistic justice might be. Drawing on philosopher Nancy Fraser again, it does so based on the understanding that it is only by contemplating how injustice might be overcome that the abstract concept of justice acquires content.

LINGUISTIC PRIVILEGE

Some readers will have been struck by the absence of any in-depth discussion of language rights and by little reference to discussions about linguistic justice in normative political philosophy in a book entitled *Linguistic Diversity and Social Justice*. As I explained in Chapter One, this has been a deliberate choice based on a pragmatic approach. Following Amartya Sen's argument in *The Idea of Justice*, this approach takes as its starting point the question 'How could linguistic justice be advanced?' rather than 'What would be a perfectly just linguistic order?' Nonetheless, it needs to be considered what a normative approach to linguistic justice can contribute to overcoming the linguistic injustices explored in this book.

Where political theory is concerned with linguistic justice the effort is typically to determine how justice between languages could be achieved, something the philosopher Philippe van Parijs has called 'parity of esteem.'[2] The view of language that undergirds this work is characterized by an almost complete disregard for sociolinguistics. The view of language that is assumed in most language-related work in political philosophy is one where 'language' equals 'a language with a name.' However, most of the injustices documented in this book were in effect 'within one single language,' if you will, and related to the fact that different repertoires of a given 'language with a name' are differently valued; and some are valued so little that they are not even recognized as comprehensible, as we saw in Chapters Four and Seven. Blindness to the fact of linguistic diversity as fundamental to social organization through language is a weakness that severely limits most normative approaches to linguistic justice.[3]

Two broad strands of focus can be distinguished in work related to normative linguistic justice: one is on the inequities between minority languages and national languages, and the other is on the inequities between national languages and global English. Most of this work takes one of two approaches: either, the argument is that linguistic justice between languages is best achieved if the state takes a 'benign neglect' approach and does not interfere in the linguistic choices of citizens. It can easily be argued that the 'benign neglect' approach has severe limitations because state business, particularly education, always has to be conducted in a particular language and the language chosen for that task is favored eo ipso.

Alternatively, a language rights approach is being advanced. In this approach language rights may be conceived as individual rights related to the right to non-discrimination, the right to freedom of speech, or the right to freedom of association. This form of language right is relatively uncontroversial and enshrined in international, national, and sub-national law through its basis in Article Two of the Universal Declaration of Human Rights, which states that human rights and freedoms apply to everyone 'without distinction of any kind, such as race, colour, sex, language, religion, political or other opinion, national or social origin, property, birth or other status.'[4] Proponents of a 'linguistic human rights' approach, however, often conceive of language rights as group rights, such as the right to mother tongue education where numbers warrant. The latter approach has not really received much traction in international law, particularly with regard to 'non-traditional minorities' (see Chapter Three). This is partly because different groups have completely different needs. The right to mother tongue education is a given for nationally dominant groups, and thus mostly irrelevant to them. Immigrant minorities might consider mother tongue education a significant win, in contrast to traditional minorities who might consider mother tongue education a small concession.

As a consequence of all these issues, political philosophers Will Kymlicka and Alan Patten argued in a 2003 article, which has become a classic in the field, that 'political theorists have focused more on criticizing old approaches than on developing new and better ones.'[5]

The philosopher Philippe van Parijs has recently tried to break new ground and go beyond the 'old approaches' of benign neglect and language rights in his 2011 book *Linguistic Justice for Europe and for the World*. Van Parijs is specifically concerned with the 'parity of esteem' between English and other national languages. To begin with, van Parijs argues that the global spread of English is a most welcome development that is likely to advance the cause of global justice because a common language will give everyone access to the global political sphere. In an age where some of humanity's most pressing problems are global problems it is vital for humans to share a common language in which to debate and pursue global solutions to global problems. English is ideally placed to fulfill the role of this common language because it is already being learned and spoken by so many. In the interest of global deliberation, van Parijs in fact argues for a further acceleration of global English language learning.

At the same time, van Parijs is conscious of the fact that the choice of English as the global language obviously privileges native speakers of English and disadvantages other national languages. To solve this problem in a just and equitable manner, van Parijs proposes a two-pronged approach: first, a 'language tax' should be levied on states that have a large proportion of native English speakers. Second, states and territories should put a coercive regime in place to ensure that the territorial language is spoken by everyone, including newcomers who might otherwise prefer to use English. This would maintain the 'esteem' of languages other than English. Overall, van Parijs advances a redistributive approach that attempts to place the costs of language learning on those who enjoy linguistic privileges.

It is easy to dismiss the idea of linguistic redistribution by imposing a language tax on countries with a large proportion of English speakers as unrealistic. However, that would be to miss the point. Van Parijs' focus on the linguistically favored constitutes an important innovation in sociolinguistic thought. To date, examinations of linguistic inequality have been predominantly focused on disadvantage and have, by and large, failed to pay attention to those who are privileged by unjust arrangements. However, in the same way that sexism cannot be understood without paying attention to male privilege and racism cannot be understood without paying attention to white privilege, the cause of linguistic justice cannot be advanced without examining linguistic privilege.

Sociologist Peggy McIntosh, the author of a 1989 classic essay on white privilege, wrote in 2012, 'I am convinced that work against racism cannot be effective without understanding of its upside, white privilege.'[6] By analogy, it makes sense to assume that linguistic justice cannot be effectively advanced without understanding linguistic privilege. However, with the exception of some work in multicultural education that also considers language,[7] there is currently no concerted research effort to examine the nature of linguistic privilege.

Privilege relates to the unearned benefits of socially dominant groups in systems of oppression. Privilege works in two ways: first, by sparing the privileged from discrimination, and, second, by awarding them unjust benefits. One key aspect of social privilege is that the social category itself may remain relatively hidden to the privileged: where men may remain oblivious to the workings of gender, the category is salient for women; where white people may remain oblivious to the workings of race, the category is salient for people of color. Similarly, the linguistically dominant can remain oblivious to the workings of linguistic diversity: 'language' obviously will seem less important to those who never felt the necessity to learn another language in order to get an education, to find a job, or to participate in the life of a community they wished to join; those who never needed to worry about how their accent might sound to a potential employer; those who never needed to contemplate whether their linguistic proficiency was adequate to participate in classroom discussions, or whether they would be considered worth listening to when trying to call emergency services.

Understanding linguistic privilege is important to understanding linguistic domination. This is particularly relevant when it comes to the fallacy of personal responsibility in language learning, which we explored in Chapter Three. It is the privilege of the dominant to see their advantages as resulting from their own personal efforts and not entangled in a system of inequality. Raising awareness of privilege can contribute to making the role of language in social stratification visible. It can also help to promote empathy with the linguistically subordinated. Furthermore, raising awareness of privilege should also go hand in hand with the promotion of so-called 'ally behaviors.' Many of the people we have met throughout this book and who suffered linguistic disadvantage would have needed effective allies—employers, colleagues, lawyers, teachers, peers, policy makers, and so on—who could have articulated language as a source of disadvantage and who were capable of standing with them in solidarity to work for positive change.

REAL LINGUISTIC UTOPIAS

Another way to examine what the content of linguistic justice might be is to examine contexts and institutions organized in a linguistically equitable manner. In his monumental treatise about utopias *Das Prinzip Hoffung* ('The principle of hope'), the philosopher Ernst Bloch stressed the importance of the vision of a 'concrete utopia' to inspire movements for social change.[8] To him, only an achievable vision inspires the kind of hope that is prerequisite for social transformation. More recently, critics of neoliberal capitalism have similarly stressed that visions of a 'real utopia' are vital to the mobilization for social change.[9] While many people may agree that alternative social arrangements are desirable, few will be motivated to take action for change unless they consider that positive vision viable and achievable. So, it is viability and achievability in addition to desirability that makes a utopia a 'concrete' or 'real' utopia.

My aim here is altogether more modest on at least two counts: first, I am exclusively focused on linguistic justice and, second, my aim is to showcase actually existing contexts and institutions where arrangements around linguistic diversity are such as to advance the common good. Case studies of seventeenth-century Isfahan and the Vienna city library are intended to demonstrate the viability and achievability of linguistically just institutional arrangements.

Let's begin with seventeenth-century Isfahan. In 1598, Shah Abbas I, also known as Shah Abbas the Great, a king of the Safavid dynasty, moved the Persian capital to Isfahan and within less than a generation the city became a splendid cosmopolitan economic and political center. The Isfahan of the time was so impressive that it earned itself the nickname *nesf-e jahan* (بضف جهاب; 'half the world').

The German scholar Adam Olearius, who visited Isfahan in 1637, described it as follows:

> There is not any nation in all Asia, not indeed almost of Europe, who sends not its merchants to Isfahan [. . .]. There are ordinarily about twelve thousand Indians in the city [. . .]. Besides these Indians, there is at Isfahan a great number of Tartars from the provinces of Khurasan, Chattai, and Bukhar; Turks, Jews, Armenians, Georgians, English, Dutch, French, Italians and Spaniards. [. . .] The Armenian merchants, who are Christians, are the richest of any, by reason of the pains they take in making voyages themselves which is more than the other Persians do; though both have an absolute freedom to traffic where they please themselves, as foreigners have the liberty to come into Persia and put off their commodities there, paying custom.[10]

Of all of Isfahan's multilingual and multicultural inhabitants, it was the Armenians who stand out as having played a special role in Isfahan's success during its golden age. And their contribution was carefully orchestrated by Shah Abbas himself.

In the winter of 1603 to 1604 Shah Abbas transferred the Armenian inhabitants of the city of Jolfa, located in what is today Iran's far northwest, to Isfahan. They were resettled in a new part of the city called New Jolfa, and the original Jolfa was razed.

This may not sound like a particularly auspicious beginning to a multicultural golden age. However, one has to bear in mind the historical context: throughout the sixteenth century the Ottoman and Safavid empires had been waging war against each other and the battleground was usually their borderlands, territory that today comprises Armenia, Azerbaijan, Georgia, northwestern Iran, northern Iraq, Lebanon, Syria, and eastern Turkey. In these borderlands, both empires repeatedly pursued a scorched earth policy, including mass killings and massive displacement of local populations into the heartlands of both empires.

Resettling the inhabitants of Jolfa was thus a scorched earth policy with a twist: Shah Abbas pursued a long-term objective in addition to the short-term objective of military advantage. The longterm objective was to gain human capital.

What exactly was it that made the Armenians attractive to Shah Abbas? Well, Armenians brought a wealth of transnational connections: as Christians, they brought valuable connections to Europe, and their trading networks extended to the far east of Asia.

[T]heir acquaintance with cultures of the region and their familiarity with the languages and traditions of the peoples of the East and West placed them in a position to perform well as the entrepreneurs of the Safavid dynasty and Shiite Persia.[11]

The transnational connections of Armenians ranged from serving as interpreters at the Moghul courts in India to being established traders in Poland, where a whole range of foreign goods came to be known as 'Armenian goods.'

In short, Shah Abbas wished to secure the national loyalty of a transnational group. The success of his plan benefitted both Armenians and the wider society, with Isfahan turning into a flourishing trade hub.

The implementation of the Shah's plan involved far-reaching concessions to the Armenians of New Jolfa in a concerted effort to gain their loyalty and even affection: religious freedom, full citizenship rights, and their own jurisdiction. One of the more intriguing rights they enjoyed was the right to curse and cuss during bazaar disputes in the same manner as Muslims.

Shah Abbas would often visit New Jolfa, even attending Christmas and Easter Mass, and took a deep interest in the new citizens' welfare. When accused of favoring his new subjects, non-Muslims to boot, over the majority population, he would respond that the Armenians had given up their homeland to live in Isfahan and so should be treated as valued guests. Furthermore, he went on to say, their relocation had cost him 1,000 tomans per head, an investment he had made not for the Armenians but for Iran.

As a result of Shah Abbas' practical and liberal approach both the minority and the wider society of which they were a part flourished.

In the 1630s, Isfahan's Armenians established their own bilingual university focusing on the liberal arts and metaphysics. This institute of higher learning produced many notable graduates including Hovhannes Vardapet, who later went to study printing in Italy and consequently introduced the printing press to Iran. The first book ever printed in Iran was an Armenian translation of the *Book of Psalms* in 1638.

Even today, more than four centuries on, Iranian Armenians maintain their own schools and churches and the level of language maintenance of Armenians is very high. A recent study of Armenians in Tehran found that 100% of respondents claimed to know and use Armenian regularly, and to value their bilingualism.[12]

For our purposes, it is instructive to study not only the golden age of cosmopolitan, multilingual, and multicultural Isfahan, but also its decline. Not all rulers were as enlightened as Shah Abbas the Great. Some of his successors mostly saw the wealth of New Jolfa as a cash cow from which they could extract taxes. However, even if no regime ever again went to such lengths to secure the loyalty of Armenians as Shah Abbas had done, their religious freedom, their full citizenship rights, and their right to bilingual education have been continuously upheld over more than four centuries.

The alliance between the Iranian state and the transnational minority for the benefit of both has thus never ceased. However, it ceased to be effective in the face of a new set of global forces that came from outside: with the expansion of the British Empire, the Iranian state was forced into a set of humiliating and debilitating capitulation treaties, and Armenians lost much of their economic base in the overland trade between Asia and Europe as Britain opened up and controlled the sea route.

From seventeenth-century Isfahan, let's now move to contemporary Vienna and visit its central public library. The library is a public space where visitors can enjoy books, computer access, and events, where they can study, surf the web, or simply hang out.

The Viennese central library holds an amazingly multilingual collection: in addition to German, full collections are also available in Bosnian/Croatian/Serbian, English, and Turkish. Additionally, there are collections of at least 500 items each in Albanian, Czech, French, Hungarian, Italian, Polish, Portuguese, Romanian, Russian, Slovak, Slovene, and Spanish. Smaller collections are held in Arabic, Catalan, Chinese, Classical Greek, Dutch, Esperanto, Finnish, Ladino, Latin, Norwegian, Romani, Swedish, and Yiddish. Furthermore, language learning materials are available for all these and a number of other languages.

In ethnographic research by sociolinguist Birgitta Busch it emerged that the establishment of collections in languages other than German was generally guided by two principles: one was to build collections in important foreign languages such as English or French, and the other was to build collections in Vienna's migrant languages such as Bosnian/Croatian/Serbian or Turkish.[13] These broad considerations were followed by personnel considerations, which means that at least one person needs to be able to curate a language collection, and by availability considerations. Availability considerations means that only a sufficient number of items and a regular flow of new items make a collection in a particular language viable and keep it interesting. Some of this can be quite accidental. For example, when a retired professor of sinology became a volunteer, the Chinese section could be established. Conversely, the library recognizes a need to establish a Chechen collection but has not been able to act on that need because there are no established book trade connections with war-torn Chechnya.

The librarians in charge of a specific language section also shape language policy with reference to their own beliefs. The librarian in charge of the Russian section, for instance, closely listens to the needs and wishes of the users of Russian language materials. The Russian language collection thus caters for 'Russian ladies' and their love of crime fiction on the one hand, and asylum seekers from various parts of the former Soviet Union on the other. The latter prefer nonfiction and German language learning materials with Russian as the source language.

In contrast to the pragmatic approach of the Russian librarian, the Turkish librarian sees it as her mission to focus on the 'quality' of the collection. For her, quality means only stocking materials sourced from Turkey and not from Germany, where a flourishing Turkish language publishing industry has developed around the newspaper *Hürriyet*. In an interview with the researcher, she explained her reasoning as follows:

> [Turkish language publishing in Germany] is a guest worker culture that has emerged there, they write about the factory, about poverty, about the difficulties they have experienced. This is not Turkish, not Turkish culture like the one I grew up in, that happens in Turkey. (. . .) They have a culture in between.[14]

This purist attitude and conservative acquisition policy notwithstanding, youths of Turkish backgrounds love the library, and many go there to do their homework. While solving mathematical problems, they chat with each other in German and Turkish and access Internet sites with their favorite music in English, German, and Turkish, the latter both diasporic and Turkey-based.

International migrants account for a quarter of the population of Vienna and possibly a larger portion of the users of the central library. For asylum seekers, it is a space where they can access the Internet and German language learning materials for free; for youths of migrant backgrounds, it is a space to hang out with friends; and tourists go there because of the architectural interest of the building and to gain free Internet access. The public library has thus become a truly democratic multicultural space.

The central library in Vienna is a space where a language policy that fosters social cohesion is negotiated: there are no barriers to access, linguistic diversity is valued, and language policy is ultimately seen as a negotiation process between the users of the library and the staff. The researcher concludes that the library's inclusive language policy is not the result of some grand plan hatched by a central bureaucracy but the result of civic engagement. It is also conditional upon the existence of noncommercial public space that is publicly funded and accessible and open to all:

> The example of the Vienna library shows that initiatives which provide open access to spaces in which communication between linguistically and culturally diverse groups can take place publicly can contribute substantially towards inclusive language policies.[15]

In sum, as discussed in Chapter Two, human mobility and language contact has been a central aspect of social organization throughout history. Paying close attention to golden ages of multiculturalism such as seventeenth-century Isfahan can help us to broaden our imagination of linguistic justice to see that equitable institutional arrangements are not only desirable but also viable and achievable. For the same reason, attention to contemporary institutions such as the Vienna central library where linguistic diversity is valued and where 'multiculturalism works' is vital. As we are bombarded almost daily with media stories about the 'failure of multiculturalism' and the difficulties and challenges that highly diverse societies present, the dissemination of positive examples constitutes an essential counter-discourse of hope. Overall, what these 'real utopias' can teach us, similarly to the public toilets in Chapter Three, is that the most inclusive spaces and institutions are those that are linguistically least dogmatic.

THE STRUGGLE FOR LINGUISTIC JUSTICE

Social justice is rarely achieved without a fight. The great social justice issues related to class, gender, and race are inextricably linked to social movements—the labor movements, the women's liberation movements, the anti-colonial and civil rights movements—and their ongoing struggles. As Pierre Bourdieu, whose ideas loom large in this book, has repeatedly observed, language is a key terrain where all social struggle plays out.[16] The final section of this book will therefore explore the content of linguistic justice as a site of social struggle.

In response to previous publications about the disparity between educational qualifications and employment outcomes faced by select country of origin groups in Australia, as here discussed in Chapter Four, sociologist Val Colic-Peisker once reminded me that there is a more optimistic way of looking at the intersection between ethnicity and class: with specific reference to Australia, this more positive way of looking at things foregrounds social transformations over the past half-century that have led to the decoupling of 'non-Anglo identity' from 'working class.' Australia today has something that few other countries have been equally successful in achieving: a linguistically and culturally diverse middle class.

In the postwar period, almost all migrants from continental Europe ended up in Australia's working class, irrespective of their pre-migration qualifications and experience. As a result, what emerged in postwar Australia was an almost complete overlap between being of non-English-speaking background and being working class.

This one-to-one mapping has started to fracture since the 1980s. In Sydney's most affluent suburbs, for instance, around 20% to 30% of the population were born overseas and a similar number claimed a home language other than English in the 2011 census. The contemporary multicultural middle class feeds from two sources: skilled migrants and the Australia-born children of migrants.[17] Many of the Australia-born and Australia-educated children of migrants from non-English-speaking backgrounds are educational high achievers. The sons and daughters not only of the postwar migrants from continental Europe but also of the early Asian migrants from the 1970s onward have by now entered the workforce and have become a key group that feeds the multicultural middle class.

This group has also entered the struggle over representation. By claiming a legitimate space in the imagined nation, they contribute to making the image of what it means to be Australian a more inclusive one. Similar struggles over what it means to belong to the nation can be observed in all liberal democracies that have become highly diverse over the past half-century. As an example, I will briefly examine two recent books of personal experience published by second-generation Australians and Germans, who make a strong argument for reimagining the nation as diverse. One is *Growing Up Lebanese Muslim in Australia* and the other is *Wir neuen Deutschen* ('Us new Germans'); both are authored by successful journalists Nadia Jamal and Taghred Chandab, and Özlem Topçu, Alice Bota, and Khuê Pham, respectively.[18]

In both books, childhood memories of feeling left out feature strongly. Jamal and Chandab begin their book with all the 'typical Australian' things they were not allowed to do as children:

> We have quite a few nevers to our names. We never went on a school camp, we never wore a swimming costume and we never slept over at a friend's place. As Muslims, we were told it was haram (forbidden, in Arabic) to do these things.[19]

Topçu, Bota, and Pham, who were born in Germany to Turkish, Polish, and Vietnamese parents, respectively, similarly describe how, as children, they used to fantasize about having German parents, who they imagined as 'stronger' than their own parents. It is often little things that seem to stick in their memories, such as Topçu's parents not knowing how to dress her up for carnival in preschool and their idea of what a clown costume might look like turning out to be 'all wrong.'

However, as they grow older, all of them come to embrace these differences as a source of strength. Jamal and Chandab conclude:

> As young girls, these things seemed important and fun, but now that we are older and can reflect on them, we believe that the caution exercised by our parents—whether motivated by religion or culture or both—brought a valuable kind of discipline into our lives. [. . .] Our cultural reference points might be

different in some areas, for example, our parents didn't read us fairy-tales at bedtime, but we don't feel that we have missed out. We are rich in other ways, such as having a second language.[20]

What matters to them now is to claim a legitimate space in Australian society where they can be Australian *and* Muslim *and* Lebanese.

Wir neuen Deutschen articulates the claim that it is necessary to reimagine what it means to be German even more strongly. As young adults, Topçu, Pham, and Bota, too, find strength in the fact that they have learned to live with difference. What they grapple with now is the fact that, despite having been socialized in Germany, despite having established successful careers in Germany, and despite 'feeling German,' they continue to be imagined as somehow 'not German' or 'less German' in dominant discourses. By staking a claim to a broader imagination of what it means to be German, their book, too, is part of the ongoing struggle over cultural representation.

Whenever new cultural representations emerge, there is inevitable blowback. At the same time that liberal democracies are obviously becoming more diverse and as those who are subordinated by the current arrangements struggle for recognition, discourses of the nation as homogeneous have also made an incredible comeback.

For instance, since I first came to Australia in the mid-1990s one of the most noticeable changes has been an increase in displays of national ardor: displays of the flag and the national colors have increased, particularly on Australia Day; there has been a resurgence in ANZAC Day ceremonies after decades of decline; and citizenship testing has been introduced, as discussed in Chapter Six. I often discuss these changes with my students as we try to understand why Australia has become a more nationalistic place in the past two decades. The best argument is usually put forward by those who argue that nationalism is a reaction to globalization and increased immigration, where the imagined homogeneous cultural nation becomes a symbol of stability in times of rapid change.

Conversely, an argument can be made that people in more diverse nations such as Australia are less ethnocentric, less patriotic, and less inclined to fight for their countries than their counterparts in less globalized nations. Some researchers have even argued that nationalism is not a reaction to globalization but that globalization actually serves to reduce nationalism. Globalization and the obvious diversity it brings will eventually be the end of nationalism—or so this line of argument goes.[21]

Both globalization and nationalism are notoriously broad concepts and the contradiction between claims that globalization increases or decreases nationalism must be sought somewhere in how the concepts are understood. If we define 'globalization' not as the level of diversity present in a society but as the latest phase of capitalist expansion under the ideological banner of neoliberalism, a convincing case can be made that globalization is likely to lead to an increase in state-sponsored nationalism, as sociologists Cory Blad and Banu Koçer do in a case study of the rise of Islamism as a political legitimation strategy in Turkey over the past decades. Specifically, they argue that

[. . .] contrary to analyses that point to political Islam as a cultural reaction to modernity or Western imperialism and facilitated by an ever-weakening state in the globalization era, we argue that the rise of political Islam in Turkey is tied to strategies to bring the state more in line with neoliberal, modernist governance and is a function of sustained state authority.[22]

Neoliberal economic globalization has meant that states are increasingly losing their economic legitimacy. For most of the twentieth century, the legitimacy of the Turkish state, like that of many other states around the globe, had rested in the fact that it was seen to protect its population from the negative effects of economic inequality. It offered state-led development and with it social security. However, in the 1970s Turkey's foreign debt began to catch up with it and it needed to turn to the International Monetary Fund for a bailout. In exchange it was forced to devalue its currency and accept a range of austerity measures, which were intended to bolster production for export and to curb public spending. The latter in particular meant that the Turkish state largely lost its ability to ensure social stability through the remediation of economic inequality. Initially, the 1980 military coup ensured stability at gunpoint but then the problem for the state became how to return to democratic governance after having lost the ability to offer economic protection. And that is where 'culture' comes in:

> The neoliberal Turkish state clearly required authority to maintain stability if its economic reforms were to have any efficacy. However, it also needed to remove the state from its position of protectionist authority. The solution was an integration of cultural—that is, Islamist—legitimation strategies in two exemplary areas. The first was the Islamization of Turkish labor through the state advocacy of cultural, rather than the traditional class-based, trade union organizations. The second was the reduction of state-managed social service provision and the privatization of these services under Islamist patronage.[23]

This means that the Turkish state willfully adopted Islamism as a means to maintain state legitimacy while allowing for state withdrawal from the economic sphere. The latter is a direct requirement of the imposition of neoliberalism as a global ideology that requires the state to give up its economic regulatory capacity while still maintaining social stability.

The Turkish case is not unique. While there are local specifics, of course, the capacity of the state to ensure economic stability has been compromised the world over. Consequently, the legitimacy of the state as a system to ensure social stability is under threat almost everywhere. The resulting turn to 'cultural legitimacy' can also be observed in numerous places. What this means is that the struggle for linguistic justice is always also an economic struggle. As the imagined homogeneous nation has become tied to neoliberal capitalism, imagining diversity as normal, natural, and legitimate can only be tied to an order where the most powerful economic institutions and governance structures do not have a fundamental philosophy that elevates competition and inequality to its defining feature.

As more and more people seek ways to overcome neoliberal capitalism, I close with the story of Joe Hill, a role model for social activism and language learning, whose poetry came to inspire the US-American union movement.[24] Although his name is rather forgotten today, Joe Hill was arguably one of the most influential American songwriters of the twentieth century. As a Swedish immigrant, he was also a second language writer.

Joe Hill was known as 'the troubadour of the working class' and is the poet and songwriter of most of the songs in *The Little Red Songbook*, a collection of folk songs published and sung by the Industrial Workers Union of the World during its heyday in the first half of the twentieth century. He is the author of classics such as 'The Preacher and the Slave,' 'The Tramp,' or 'Casey Jones, the Union Scab.' Joe Hill's particular talent was to write activist lyrics and set them to well-known traditional folk songs and hymns.

Joe Hill was born Joel Hägglund in a small town in Sweden, and after the death of his parents bought passage to America, arriving in 1902 as a twenty-three-year-old with high hopes for a better future. While little is known about his early life, it seems he had learned some English before he left Sweden by attending some classes and by studying a dictionary. Overall his English must have been largely self-taught.

The migration experience that changed Joel Hägglund into Joe Hill ran deeper than the name change:

> Joel Hägglund left his native Sweden for America where he believed prosperity would be his merely for the asking and where equality of opportunity was a reality. But, for Joe Hill, America turned out to be a land specializing in the oppression of foreigners and migrant workers. It could have been nothing less

than an embittering experience. Certainly, it changed a young man raised in a conservative Christian home which taught him loyalty to 'God, King and all authority' into a 'rebel true-blue,' opposed to the existing social and economic inequalities, to the authority of the law when it sanctioned injustice, and, apparently, to Christianity.[25]

Unlike many other migrants with similar experiences, Joe Hill distinguished himself through his writing and his poetry, which was rooted in his experience and continues to be a resounding call for solidarity, equality, and justice.

In 1915, at the age of thirty-six, Joe Hill was accused of murder in Utah, tried in a controversial trial, and executed. A 2011 biography by writer William Adler argues that he was almost certainly innocent. Joe Hill was farewelled in Chicago by 30,000 mourners in one of the largest funeral processions ever. His songs were sung all the way to the crematorium and as soon as a song would die out in one place it was taken up in another. Eulogies to the man whose lyrics inspired so many to organize for solidarity, equality, and justice were delivered in nine languages.

Joe Hill is remembered today as a martyr of the workers' movement. He is also an inspiring second language writer. Despite the fact that he himself felt that his writing was limited by his lack of education and formal training, his poetry not only immortalized him but also remains an inspiration today. Joe Hill's writings challenge us to engage with the struggle for solidarity, equality, and justice. They also serve as a role model for second language writers. To remember Joe Hill is to overcome our collective failure of imagination when it comes to linguistic diversity: the failure to recognize that linguistic diversity undergirds inequality too frequently and the failure to imagine that we can change our social and linguistic arrangements in ways that make them more equitable and just.

NOTES

Chapter 1

1. Sydney: Ting and Walters (2014); Melbourne: Butt and Worrall (2014); Canada: Murphy (2012); USA: Brombacher (2013); Manchester: J. Brown (2013); London: Buncombe and MacArthur (1999).
2. Differential employment rates in Australia: Sutton (2014); Diversity and segregation in US schools: Hefling (2014); Interpreting costs in the UK: Brooke (2014); Lintin (2014).
3. Quoted from Schelling (1892, p. 64). Here and elsewhere, I consider it pointless to hold writers of the past to the standards of contemporary political correctness. I am therefore not adding '[sic]' to Jonson's generic masculine nor to similar examples where past usage may not be in accord with contemporary sensibilities.
4. For an analysis of 'language' in Australian and European social inclusion policy debates, see Musgrave and Bradshaw (2014) and Piller and Takahashi (2011) respectively.
5. Asscher and Widger (2008); Fraser (2012).
6. Fraser (1995, 2005).
7. Fraser (2012); Sen (2009).
8. 'The International Forum for Social Development. Social Justice in an Open World. The Role of the United Nations' (2006, p. 6); Barry (2005, p. 261).
9. 'The International Forum for Social Development. Social Justice in an Open World. The Role of the United Nations' (2006, p. 17ff.). The document also identifies distribution of income and assets as two additional

areas where inequalities are rife. While clearly critical to the dominance of the super-rich or 'the one percent,' income and asset distribution have been excluded from the present enquiry because linguistic dimensions to inequities in these areas are not readily apparent.

10. See Soutphommasane (2012) for a detailed discussion, particularly Chapters One and Two.

11. 'The International Forum for Social Development. Social Justice in an Open World. The Role of the United Nations' (2006, p. 12).

Chapter 2

1. One of the finest books about linguistic discrimination, Lippi-Green (2012) is concerned with the social consequences of diversity within American English.

2. The Council of Europe suggests the term 'plurilingualism' to capture the fact that languages are not neatly compartmentalized in the individual ('Common European Framework of Reference for Languages: Learning, Teaching, Assessment,' 2001). Others have coined a variety of terms to alert readers to fluidity in language such as 'translanguaging' (García, 2009b) or 'metrolingualism' (Otsuji and Pennycook, 2011).

3. Relationship between Afrikaans and Dutch: Berdichevsky (2004, Chapter Ten); Relationship between Wu and Mandarin Chinese: Thurgood and LaPolla (2003)

4. History and current global popularity of biltong: Witepski (2006).

5. Reck (1964, p. 359).

6. Lack of foreign languages stifling Anglophone nations: Swain (2014). Lack of languages diminishing employment opportunities: Codrea-Rado (2014); Hyslop (2012). Lack of languages as economic problem: Apps (2014); Brann and Locke (2012). Lack of languages as problem of international influence and national security: Boffey (2013); Crotty (2012). Language prerequisite for study abroad scholarships not feasible: Trounson (2014).

7. How do you explain the contradiction between media reports that brag about the large numbers of languages being spoken in the cities of Anglophone countries and media reports that bemoan a lack of proficiency in languages other than English in Anglophone countries? Join the conversation at www.languageonthemove.com/language-migration-social-justice/language-deficit-in-super-diversity.

8. Cited in Swain (2014).

9. In addition to the classic study by C. A. Ferguson (1959) about diglossia in Arabic, Haeri (2003) and Suleiman (2011) make fascinating contemporary reading about linguistic diversity in the Arab world.

10. 'Main Language by Ethnic Group, 2011' (2013).
11. de Swaan (2001, p. 4).
12. See the Internet Movie Database at www.imdb.com/title/tt0907831/ for details.
13. Data are adapted from '2011 Census of Population and Housing: Basic Community Profile, Auburn' (2012). I have substituted the 'Iranic languages' category in the census data with 'Persian' (see Chapter Six for further discussion) and excluded various 'Other' categories for the sake of simplicity.
14. See www.designa.com/int/home.html.
15. Join the conversation about this case study at http://www.languageonthemove.com/language-migration-social-justice/multilingual-mismatch. You may also wish to research the local language pyramid in a context you are familiar with.
16. This and the following quote are from 'Terminology and Concepts: Principles of Multiculturalism' (n.d.).
17. 'What if a CALD Client Should Walk in Our Door? A Guide for Service Providers' (n.d.).
18. See Anthias (2013) for a detailed exploration of the ideological work performed by diversity policies and the relationship between diversity discourses and inequality.
19. I will not reference the article in question because citation would serve no purpose other than to embarrass the author. I will mention, though, that the article was published in a peer-reviewed journal and thus the usage must have seemed unremarkable not only to the author but also to the peer reviewers and the editors.
20. Katz (1996); Skinner (2003).
21. See Holmes (1991), who argues that generally British history is not conceived as a history of immigration. Furthermore, the focus of the scant literature on the history of immigration to Britain is on non-European rather than European immigrants, although the latter have, obviously, been historically predominant.
22. It seems perfectly natural to consider the descendants of Jewish, Muslim, and Sikh migrants to Britain as examples of diversity, but to consider the descendants of Anglo-Saxon, Celtic, Norman, Roman, Viking, or Huguenot migrants to Britain as exponents of diversity seems quite wrong. Join the conversation about diversity discourses that may be well-intentioned but contribute to legitimizing some groups and delegitimizing others at http://www.languageonthemove.com/language-migration-social-justice/the-diversity-of-the-other.
23. Homer (1996, Book Nineteen, ll. 172–175); cited in the 1996 translation by Robert Fagles.

24. Goodenough (1976).
25. The article where the term 'super-diversity' was first used is Vertovec (2007). The quotes are from the entry about 'super-diversity' on Vertovec's website at www.mmg.mpg.de/research/all-projects/super-diversity.
26. Grin, Sfreddo and Vaillancourt (2010, p. 12).
27. Czaika and de Haas (2014).
28. Available at http://data.worldbank.org/data-catalog/global-bilateral-migration-database.
29. Czaika and de Haas (2014, p. 32). Read about Montevideo, the capital of Uruguay, at the turn of the twentieth century as a 'super-diverse' society and join the conversation about super-diversity as a Euro-centric concept at http://www.languageonthemove.com/language-globalization/superdiversity-another-eurocentric-idea.
30. Romónum is one island in a group of sixteen known today as the Chuuk Islands, formerly as Truk Islands or Hogoleu Islands. They are part of the Federated States of Micronesia in the Western Pacific. In 2010, all sixteen Chuuk Islands combined had a population of 48,654 ('Chuuk Islands,' 2013). When Ward Goodenough conducted his fieldwork on Romónum in the 1940s to the 1960s, the island had a few hundred inhabitants. For a review of anthropological research on the Chuuk Islands during this period, see Kiste and Marshall (1999).
31. Knirk (1999); Svärdström (1970).
32. D'Amato (2010).
33. A special issue of *Multilingua* devoted to 'Researching multilingualism and super-diversity: Grassroots actions and responsibilities' offers a sample of sociolinguistic research employing the 'super-diversity' concept (Li, 2014).
34. Rautman (2006, p. 85).
35. Runciman (2012, p. 56).
36. From a contemporary account by the historian Aşıkpaşazade, quoted from Feldman (2008, p. 109).
37. Ergin (2009).
38. Lewis (1999).
39. Lewis (1999).
40. Enjoy pictures of Istanbul's linguistic landscape and join the conversation about homogeneity as an invented tradition at http://www.languageonthemove.com/language-globalization/erasing-diversity.

Chapter 3

1. Bourdieu (1993, p. 53); Clyne (2005); Ellis, Gogolin, and Clyne (2010); Gogolin (1994).

2. Lumby (2006, De incolarum linguis. Capitulum quinquagesimum nonum); Modern English translations from 'Middle English Dictionary' (2001).
3. 'Constitution de la République Française [Constitution of the French Republic]' (1958).
4. For details on the Belgian language territories and a map see Tabouret-Keller (1999). For details on 'non-traditional' linguistic diversity in Belgium, with a focus on the city of Ghent, see De Bock (2014).
5. 'European Charter for Regional and Minority Languages' (1992a); 'European Charter for Regional and Minority Languages: Explanatory Report' (1992b). For a legal analysis of the provisions in the Charter see Mowbray (2012).
6. The European Committee of Experts has criticized Finland for this practice and asserted that under European legislation Finland has obligations to all Russian speakers (Mowbray, 2012, p. 48). For an extended discussion of the relationship between nationalism and minority language rights see also May (2011).
7. Polish refugees in Iran: Antolak (n.d.); Faruqi (2000). Biographical entry for Stanisław Kościałkowski: 'Stanisław Kościałkowski' (2015). History of Polish-Iranian relationship: Kościałkowski (1943). Polish cemeteries in Iran: Przewoźnik (2002). For the grave-mapping project of the Tehran Catholic Cemetery visit www.doulabcemetery.com.
8. For pictures and a more detailed description of the linguistic landscape of Tehran's Doulab Cemetery complex and to join the conversation visit www.languageonthemove.com/intercultural-communication/polish-cemetery-in-tehran. You might also wish to visit a cemetery in your city and conduct your own research: can you observe a similar segregation of the dead by faith, nation, and language? The practice to segregate old-timers and newcomers in death is evident even in cases where the migrants come from a relatively short distance such as a city's surrounding countryside and share the same religion and ethnicity, as was found in a study of medieval Danish burial sites (Petersen, Boldsen, and Paine, 2006). Eckert (2002, 2006) presents a fascinating case study of language and identity in Czech cemeteries in Texas.
9. Quoted from Fuller (2012, p. 23).
10. The example is based on research by Subtirelu (2013). Join the conversation about the language ideologies implicit in the congressional debate about Section 203 at http://www.languageonthemove.com/language-migration-social-justice/is-speaking-english-a-civic-duty.
11. Quoted from Subtirelu (2013, p. 54).
12. Quoted from Subtirelu (2013, p. 53).
13. The following account is based on these media sources: 'California Valedictorian Gives Speech in Spanish, Sparking Debate' (2012);

'Graduation Speech in Spanish Riles O'Reilly' (2012); 'Newman Teen Taking Heat for Giving Valedictorian Speech in Spanish' (2012); Starnes (n.d); Wise (2012). Join the conversation about this case study at http://www.languageonthemove.com/language-learning-gender-identity/monolingual-media-beat-up.

14. The following is based on an analysis of 701 Facebook comments on two separate pages: https://www.facebook.com/photo.php?fbid=1015092 2980055000&set=a.153347189999.117346.68751504999& type=1 and http://radio.foxnews.com/toddstarnes/top-stories/student-delivers-graduation-speech-in-spanish.html. Quotes are direct copies from Facebook and no changes to spelling, grammar, or other linguistic aspects have been made. For further reading on debates about linguistic diversity in new media see Androutsopoulos and Juffermans (2014).

15. For language-related service denials at US airports and on planes see Baron (2010). For service denial to Persian speaker in Atlanta Apple store see http://www.languageonthemove.com/language-migration-social-justice/shopping-while-bilingual-can-make-you-sick, where you can also join the conversation. For survey of Asian-Americans who had experienced language discrimination see H. C. Yoo, Gee, and Takeuchi (2008).

16. Kiffmeier (2010); my translation.

17. Foreign Service Institute estimates: Archibald et al. (2006). Meta-studies of time it takes to acquire academic proficiency in an immersion context: Collier (1989); Hakuta, Butler, and Witt (2000). For further discussion of adult and child immersion language learning see also Chapters Four and Five, respectively.

18. For the '10,000-hour-rule' see Eaton (2011, 2012). For UK estimates see de Castella (2013). For Australian estimates see Moore, Nicholas, and Deblaquiere (2008).

19. Collier (1989, p. 513). Emphasis in the original.

20. Age: Birdsong (2006). Prior education: Bigelow (2010). Socioeconomic status: Block (2014). Gender: Pavlenko and Piller (2001). Race: J. Miller (2003). Religion: H. Han (2011); Luck: G. C.-L. Chang (2015).

21. Barry (2005).

22. For an analysis of the stigmatization of obesity as a social justice issue see Puhl and Heuer (2010). Join the conversation about the cult of personal responsibility in language learning at http://www.languageonthemove.com/language-migration-social-justice/the-cult-of-personal-responsibility.

23. Interactional opportunities of international students: G. C.-L. Chang (2015); Takahashi (2013). Interactional opportunities at work: H. Han (2011); Major, Terraschke, Major, and Setijadi (2014); Yates (2011).

24. The case study is based on H. Han (2013). See Fauna (2011) for further demographic background. Join the conversation about

grassroots language learning in Guangzhou's Africa Town at http://www.languageonthemove.com/language-globalization/grassroots-multilingualism.

25. The term 'grassroots multilingualism' draws on Blommaert (2008) and 'fragmented,' 'truncated,' and 'incomplete' repertoires on Blommaert (2010).

26. Quoted from H. Han (2013, p. 90).

27. Bourdieu (1977, p. 652).

28. Rubin (1992); Rubin and Smith (1990). For an overview of the research on performance and perception in intercultural communication see Piller (2011). For a recent ethnographic study of the ways in which the English language proficiency of Asian and European speakers is judged in Australia see Butorac (2011, 2014). Join the conversation about perceptions of the English language proficiency of Asian speakers at www.languageonthemove.com/language-globalization/seeing-asians-speaking-english.

29. The following account is based on these media reports: Cochrane (2012); Colvin (2009); Kelly (2010); 'Tamil Asylum Seekers Caught in Indonesian Waters Say They Face Genocide in Sri Lanka' (2009); 'What Happened to the Oceanic Viking Refugees?' (2010). Join the conversation about this case study at http://www.languageonthemove.com/recent-posts/when-your-english-is-too-good.

30. Colvin (2009).

31. 'Tamil Asylum Seekers Caught in Indonesian Waters Say They Face Genocide in Sri Lanka' (2009).

32. You can view this and similar signs, and join the conversation about multilingual prohibitions at www.languageonthemove.com/recent-posts/multilingual-prohibitions.

33. You can view a selection of the toilet signage in my corpus and join the conversation about this case study at http://www.languageonthemove.com/recent-posts/toiletology.

34. Pavlenko (2005); Villenas (2001).

35. Carrick (2014).

Chapter 4

1. The International Forum for Social Development (2006, p. 33 f.).

2. Lester (2011); Lester and Young (2011); 'Patriots and Traitors' (2011). Join the conversation about this example at http://www.languageonthemove.com/language-migration-social-justice/patriots-and-traitors.

3. For an analysis of the ways in which a discourse about the alleged language deficit of migrants serves to hide systemic barriers and helps to form migrants as flexible neoliberal subjects, see Haque (2014).

4. Booth, Leigh, and Varganova (2009); Pinkerton (2013); Schneider (2014). Read about ethnic names in politics and join the conversation about discrimination against bearers of ethnic names at www.languageonthemove.com/language-migration-social-justice/whats-in-a-name.
5. Mencken (1980, p. 280).
6. Biavaschi, Giulietti, and Siddique (2013).
7. Arai and Skogman Thoursie (2009).
8. Gamba and Makeny (2007).
9. Humor as a way to escape from uncomfortable situations is highly valued in Australia, as Goddard (2009) argues.
10. Roberts (2013). Join the conversation at http://www.language onthemove.com/language-migration-social-justice/patriots-and-traitors.
11. This structure of a conventional narrative was first described by Labov and Waletzky (1967). Labov and Waletzky (1967) also identified abstract, resolution, and coda as optional elements of a conventional narrative structure.
12. Roberts (2013, p. 87).
13. Roberts (2013, pp. 91 f.).
14. Roberts, Davies, and Jupp (1992, p. 366).
15. For an overview of the research into intersectionality at work see Browne and Misra (2005); Case, Iuzzini, and Hopkins (2012); Kirk (2009).
16. Colic-Peisker (2011a). Join the conversation about the intersection of language proficiency and other identity aspects in the labor market at http://www.languageonthemove.com/language-migration-social-justice/human-capital-on-the-move.
17. The Australian census interview asks respondents who record a home language other than English to self-assess their English proficiency as 'very well,' 'well,' 'not well,' or 'not at all.'
18. This metaphor is taken from Australian and Canadian research into the labor market experiences of African migrants (Colic-Peisker, 2005; Creese and Kambere, 2003).
19. For the stock character of the overqualified migrant taxi driver see, for instance, Richard Flanagan's novel *The Unknown Terrorist* (2006). The Canadian research this section is drawing on is Creese (2011) and Creese and Wiebe (2012). Join the conversation about the social consequences of survival employment at http://www.languageonthemove.com/language-migration-social-justice/bad-faith-migration-programs.
20. Creese and Wiebe (2012, p. 61).
21. Creese and Wiebe (2012, p. 63 f.).

22. Creese and Wiebe (2012, p. 59).
23. Labor opposition immigration spokesman Tony Burke in 2007; Quoted in Hart (2007).
24. Schumann (1978).
25. Schumann (1978, p. 97). Contemporary researchers such as Block (2005) or Norton (2013) have pointed out that taking a second job instead of attending language classes may not have been a 'choice' for Alberto but the result of his precarious economic circumstances.
26. Perdue (1993b, p. 227). For further details about the research see also Perdue (1993a).
27. 'World Migration in Figures' (2013).
28. Piller and Lising (2014). Join the conversation about language learning on the job at www.languageonthemove.com/migration/is-language-learning-on-the-job-the-best-way-to-learn-a-new-language.
29. Cited from Piller and Lising (2014, p. 48).
30. Goldstein (1996) offers a workplace ethnography of a Canadian factory with a workplace English language training program.
31. Lahti and Valo (2013).
32. Alcorso (2003, p. 31).
33. Döhner, Mertens, Carstensen, Korol, and Stallbaum (2014).
34. Alcorso (2003, p. 30).
35. Jaleco (2010); Mongaya (2010); Relos (2011); Reyes (2010); 'US Hospital Settles with Pinay Nurses Fired for Speaking Tagalog' (2012). Join the conversation about the hospital's English-only policy at http://www.languageonthemove.com/recent-posts/english-only-at-bon-secours.
36. Reyes (2010).
37. Relos (2011).
38. For discussions of discrimination cases on the basis of language brought against US employers see Lippi-Green (2012). The 'language at work' chapter in Mowbray (2012) focuses on European cases.
39. Cameron (1995, p. 12).
40. '6 Sa 158/09' (2009); '8 AZR 48/10 Diskriminierung— Ethnische Herkunft—Deutschkurs' (2011); 'Keine Diskriminierung: Zum Deutschkurs Aufgefordert' (2010); 'Rechtsprechung BAG, 22.06.2011—8 AZR 48/10' (2011); 'Rechtsprechung LAG Schleswig-Holstein, 23.12.2009—6 Sa 158/09' (2009). Join the conversation about this case at www.languageonthemove.com/recent-posts/linguistic-discrimination-at-work.
41. '6 Sa 158/09' (2009). My translation.
42. For general reading on the disproportionate amount of unpaid reproductive work performed even by women in full-time paid employment see Hochschild (2003) and Latshaw (2011).

43. 'Ist das Bad noch offen Dienst?' instead of 'Gehört das Bad noch zum öffentlichen Dienst?' ('6 Sa 158/09,' 2009, p. 6). German *öffentlich* ('public') is a derivation of *offen* ('open') and the two words are thus formally similar.
44. Lindemann (2002); Lindemann and Subtirelu (2013).
45. This case study is based on Eckstein and Nguyen (2011). Join the conversation about the sociolinguistics of nail care at http://www. languageonthemove.com/language-migration-social-justice/the-sociolinguistics-of-nail-care.
46. Tran (2008).
47. 'Nail Technician' (2015).
48. Eckstein and Nguyen (2011, p. 654).
49. Eckstein and Nguyen (2011, p. 666).
50. 'Fairwork Ombudsman' (2015); 'Labour Trafficking in Australia' (2013).
51. S. Brown (2015); Mitchell and Graham (2015).
52. For average 2014 salaries in Australia by sector see 'Employees Paid by Award Only' (2014). For average 2014 salaries in China see Kuo (2014).
53. This example is based on Sabaté i Dalmau (2014). Join the conversation about language work in the *locutorio* at http://www. languageonthemove.com/language-globalization/language-work-in-the-internet-cafe.
54. Sabaté i Dalmau (2014, p. 170).

Chapter 5

1. '11th EFA (Education for All) Global Monitoring Report' (2014, p. 19).
2. Hymes (1996, p. 84).
3. 'Der monolinguale Habitus der multilingualen Schule' (Gogolin, 1994). See also Chapter Three above. Bourdieu and Passeron (1990) is a foundational text about the education system as a means of social reproduction.
4. The case study is based on Kiss (2011) and additional demographic information from Árus (2009) and 'Populatia Stabila Dupa Etnie—Judete, Municipii, Orase, Comune [Resident Population by Ethnicity—Counties, Cities, Towns, Communities]' (2011). Join the conversation about bilingual education in Székely Land at http://www.languageon themove.com/language-learning-gender-identity/bilingualism-bane-or-boon.
5. Quoted from Kiss (2011, p. 256).
6. Baker (2006, p. 219).
7. 'Lau v. Nichols' (1974).

8. Green (2014). Join the conversation about the 'sink-or-swim' approach to education at http://www.languageonthemove.com/language-globalization/sink-or-swim-for-international-students.
9. Green (2014, p. 8).
10. Collier (1989).
11. Levin and Shohamy (2007, 2008).
12. Based on Takenoshita, Chitose, Ikegami, and Ishikawa (2014). Join the conversation about the educational outcomes of migrant children in Japan at http://www.languageonthemove.com/language-migration-social-justice/educational-outcomes-of-migrant-children.
13. For an in-depth analysis of the intergenerational transmission of disadvantage see Barry (2005).
14. Takenoshita et al. (2014, p. 95).
15. The relevant literature is immense. For recent collections that bring together examinations of a wide diversity of international contexts I would recommend García (2009a), García, Skutnabb-Kangas, and Torres-Guzman (2006), McCarty (2011), Menken and García (2010), Shin (2013), and Tollefson (2013). Exemplary book-length ethnographies of heterogeneous schooling include Heller (2006), Martín Rojo (2010), and J. Miller (2003).
16. 'Statutory Framework for the Early Years Foundation Stage: Setting the Standards for Learning, Development and Care for Children from Birth to Five' (2014). The analysis here is based on Robertson, Drury, and Cable (2014). For an in-depth exploration of linguistic diversity in early childhood education in Australia see also Benz (2015). Join the conversation about the ways in which the Statutory Framework for Learning in the Early Years undermines linguistic diversity at http://www.languageonthemove.com/multilingual-families/paying-lip-service-to-diversity.
17. 'Statutory Framework for the Early Years Foundation Stage: Setting the Standards for Learning, Development and Care for Children from Birth to Five' (2014, p. 9).
18. 'Statutory Framework for the Early Years Foundation Stage: Setting the Standards for Learning, Development and Care for Children from Birth to Five' (2014, p. 9).
19. The story is sourced from Winerip (2010). Join the conversation about Oscar's reading performance at www.languageonthemove.com/recent-posts/refugee-children-left-behind-as-eagle-lands-on-the-moon.
20. For an overview of the ways in which standardized testing contributes to the stigmatization of children living in marginalized and disadvantaged communities see Ruairc (2009).

21. See Bigelow (2010) and Tetteh (2015) for research on the educational experiences of Africans with refugee backgrounds in the USA and Australia respectively.

22. 2012 NAPLAN results are based on 'National Assessment Program—Literacy and Numeracy Achievement in Reading, Persuasive Writing, Language Conventions and Numeracy: National Report for 2012' (2012). The linguistic analysis of NAPLAN data is based on Wigglesworth, Simpson, and Loakes (2011) and additional comment regarding 'underperforming schools' and 'socioeconomic disadvantage' on H. Hughes and Hughes (2012) and Fogarty (2012) respectively. Join the conversation about literacy and numeracy testing that is really language testing at http://www.languageonthemove.com/language-migration-social-justice/language-test-masquerading-as-literacy-and-numeracy-test.

23. For an overview of Aboriginal ways of speaking English in Australia see Eades (2013).

24. This examination of 'LBOTE' and other language data held by schools is based on Dixon and Angelo (2014). Join the conversation at http://www.languageonthemove.com/recent-posts/dodgy-data-and-language-misdiagnosis.

25. Dixon and Angelo (2014, p. 229).

26. See Menken and Kleyn (2010) and Menken, Kleyn, and Chae (2012) for further details. Join the conversation about long-term English language learners at www.languageonthemove.com/language-learning-gender-identity/long-term-english-language-learners.

27. Such the title of a classic article in the field, Wong Fillmore (1991).

28. W.-J. Han and Huang (2010). Join the conversation about bilingualism and mental health at www.languageonthemove.com/language-migration-social-justice/bilingualism-is-good-for-your-mental-health.

29. Kouritzin (1999).

30. Agirdag (2013). Join the conversation about the long-term economic benefits of home language maintenance at http://www.languageonthemove.com/language-migration-social-justice/monolingualism-is-bad-for-the-economy.

Chapter 6

1. Details of this case study are based on 'Azizi v. the Queen' (2012); 'DPP v. Azizi' (2013); Jones (2010); 'R v. Azizi' (2010). Join the conversation about domestic violence in a multilingual society at http://www.languageonthemove.com/language-migration-social-justice/domestic-violence-in-a-multilingual-world.

2. All Australian census data are quoted from the Australian Bureau of Statistics on the basis of the databases available at 'Census Home' (2012).
3. See Chapter Four above for details on self-assessed English language proficiency in Australian census data.
4. Originally called the Telephone Interpreter Service, the national translating and interpreting service was first established in 1973. For further details about the services provided by the translating and interpreting service see 'Multicultural Language Services Guidelines for Australian Government Agencies' (2013).
5. 'R v Azizi' (2010, §11).
6. Raymond (2014). Join the conversation about emergency service provision in linguistically diverse societies at http://www.languageonthemove.com/language-migration-social-justice/emergency-service-provision-in-linguistically-diverse-societies.
7. 'A Long Way to Equal: An Update of 'Quarter Way to Equal: A Report on Barriers to Legal Services for Migrant Women'' (2007).
8. 'On average, in 2014, over 96% of the gap in health outcomes, 94% of the gap in educational attainment, 60% of the gap in economic participation and 21% of the gap in political empowerment has been closed. No country in the world has achieved gender equality.' (Schwab et al., 2014, p. 46).
9. 'World Migration Report 2013' (2013).
10. Butorac (2011). Schwab et al. (2014) rank Australia 24/142 internationally in terms of gender equality and the origin countries represented in the study between 54/142 (Serbia) and 137/142 (Islamic Republic of Iran).
11. For overviews see Extra, Spotti, and Van Avermaet (2009) and Shohamy and McNamara (2009).
12. McNamara and Ryan (2011, p. 175).
13. K. Ryan (2012).
14. Beaudrie and Fairclough (2012, p. 13). This collection also provides a useful general overview of the Spanish language in the United States.
15. Indigenous women from Latin America, who may not have had the opportunity to learn Spanish pre-migration, may be even more isolated, as Semple (2014) reports.
16. Dreby and Schmalzbauer (2013); Schmalzbauer (2009). Join the conversation about migrant women's empowerment in the city at http://www.languageonthemove.com/language-migration-social-justice/migrant-womens-empowerment-in-the-city.
17. The account is based on Chu (2005) with additional demographic data from 'Census Home' (2012). Join the conversation about postnatal depression in migrant mothers at www.languageonthemove.com/language-migration-social-justice/postnatal-depression-and-language-proficiency.
18. H. C. Yoo et al. (2008).

19. The story is based on R. Hughes (1986). Join the conversation about language-related violence at http://www.languageonthemove.com/recent-posts/can-foreign-languages-drive-you-crazy.

20. R. Hughes (1986, p. 227).

21. R. Hughes (1986, p. 188). Join the conversation about the history of religious and linguistic exclusion in Australia at www.languageonthemove.com/language-migration-social-justice/muslims-catholics-foreign-language-speakers-and-other-traitors.

22. Quoted from R. Hughes (1986, p. 188).

23. Medhora (2015).

24. A video of the incident is available on YouTube (Nayna, 2012). The incident was also widely covered in the media (e.g., Ivett, 2012; Lowe, 2012; 'Man Questioned About Racist Rant on Bus,' 2012; Pearson, 2012; Rourke, 2012), as was news of the subsequent court proceedings (e.g., Cooper, 2014; 'Pair in Bus Rant Face Possible Jail,' 2014). Join the conversation about this case study at http://www.languageonthemove.com/language-migration-social-justice/speak-english-or-die.

25. Butler (Since 2003, s.v. 'ding').

26. Pearson (2012).

27. The attacker was subsequently sentenced to eight month in prison ('Theresa Maree Hillier to Give Birth Behind Bars for Racial Attack on Asylum Seeker in Hobart,' 2013).

28. Grin (2013).

29. Sue et al. (2007, p. 271).

30. Sue et al. (2007, p. 274).

31. Basford, Offermann, and Behrend (2014, p. 341).

32. Sue (2010).

33. G. C.-L. Chang (2015); Takahashi (2013). Join the conversation about micro-aggressions as a means to enact the linguistic domination of international students at www.languageonthemove.com/language-globalization/exclusion-on-campus.

34. Quoted from G. C.-L. Chang (2015, p. 122).

35. S. Wright and Lander (2003, p. 237).

36. Yosso, Smith, Ceja, and Solórzano (2009).

37. Quoted from Yosso et al. (2009, p. 667).

38. L. Ryan and Sales (2013). For additional demographic information see Sherwood (2014). Join the conversation at http://www.languageonthemove.com/language-learning-gender-identity/learn-english-make-friends.

39. Quoted from L. Ryan (2011, p. 716).

40. Qureshi (2012). Join the conversation about bodies on the move and belonging at www.languageonthemove.com/language-migration-social-
justice/home-is-where-im-alienated.
41. Qureshi (2012, p. 486).
42. Quoted from Qureshi (2012, p. 498).
43. Kim (2011a, 2011b). Join the conversation about belonging and media
use at www.languageonthemove.com/recent-posts/where-is-home.
44. Quoted from Kim (2011a, pp. 139; 142; 148).
45. Bourdieu (1991, p. 55). Emphasis in the original.

Chapter 7

1. For a detailed argument why internal and external social justice need
to be considered together, particularly with reference to language, see
Piller (2012). Further relevant readings include Djité (2008), Reinert
(2008), and Sassen (2001).
2. The circles model of global English was first developed by Kachru
(1985). For recent refinements and critiques see Kachru, Kachru, and
Nelson (2009) and Jenkins (2003).
3. Taylor and Hudson (1972).
4. Pool (1990).
5. This includes media coverage of the socioeconomic benefits of English
language learning such as de Lotbinière (2011) and reports that promote
English for development such as 'Partners for Change: English for Development' (2013). For recent academic examinations of the relationship
between English and development see Bolton, Graddol, and Meierkord
(2011), Coleman (2011), Erling and Seargeant (2013), and Widin (2010).
6. Phillipson (1992, p. 47). See also Mohanty, Panda, Phillipson, and
Skutnabb-Kangas (2009) and Phillipson (2009a).
7. Based on S. Clayton (2008) and additional background information
from Bruthiaux (2008), 'Cambodia' (2014), 'Cambodia' (2015), and
T. Clayton (2002). Join the conversation about English language
teaching as development aid for Cambodia at http://www.language
onthemove.com/language-globalization/free-language-choice.
8. Based on Karmani (2005). For additional background see 'Arab Human
Development Report 2009: Challenges to Human Security in the Arab
Countries' (2009), and on the 'resource curse' see Reinert (2008).
Join the conversation about 'Petro-English' at http://www.language
onthemove.com/language-globalization/happy-birthday-uae.

9. A rentier state is a state where the economy relies largely on external rent, usually derived from the sale of natural resources. As a result, the productive sector in rentier states remains underdeveloped and the proportion of the population engaged in productive work is small. The state is the principal recipient of the external rent income (Beblawi 1990).

10. Reinert (2008, p. 116).

11. Wei Ru is a pseudonym. This case study is based on Zhang (2011, forthcoming). For background information on the Nainan/Hezhe see Schwarz (1984), Tsumagari, Kurebito, and Endo (2007), and Vajda (2009). Join the conversation about Wei Ru's experience with language education at www.languageonthemove.com/education/access-denied.

12. Quoted from Zhang (2011, p. 198 f.).

13. L. T. Chang (2009). Join the conversation about English language learning and height at www.languageonthemove.com/language-learning-gender-identity/language-learning-and-height.

14. L. T. Chang (2009, p. 255).

15. Kaimann (2013); B. Smith (2014).

16. Price (2014, p. 585 f.).

17. Quoted from Pasassung (2004, p. 145). Learn more about English language education in a remote village on the island of Sulawesi and join the conversation at http://www.languageonthemove.com/language-globalization/is-english-improving-lives-in-a-remote-indonesian-village.

18. Hu and Alsagoff (2010). Join the conversation about the injustices of 'English for all' at http://www.languageonthemove.com/language-globalization/english-for-everyone-is-unfair.

19. For general discussions of linguistic human rights see Mohanty et al. (2009), Skutnabb-Kangas (2001), or Skutnabb-Kangas and Phillipson (1998, 1994).

20. Hu and Alsagoff (2010, p. 375).

21. For instance, for Bangladesh see Hamid (2010); for Indonesia see Pasassung (2004); for Peru see Niño-Murcia (2003); or for Taiwan see Price (2014).

22. For a recent collection of international case studies of English medium instruction in global higher education see Doiz, Lasagabaster, and Sierra (2012).

23. 'Times Higher Education World Reputation Rankings' (2015).

24. Because of the way in which university rankings are designed, English medium provision may improve an institution's standing on university rankings. For an in-depth examination of the relationship between English medium of instruction and performance on university rankings see Piller and Cho (2013) and also below. Join the

conversation about English in ranking metrics at http://www.language
onthemove.com/language-globalization/internationalization-and-
englishization-in-higher-education.
25. For an overview of English as the global language of academia see
    Ammon (2001).
26. See, for instance, G. Ferguson, Pérez-Llantada, and Plo (2011), or Flow-
    erdew (2008).
27. Choi (2010, p. 244). Join the conversation about academic capital-
    ism and the spread of English as medium of instruction at www.
    languageonthemove.com/multilingual-academics/academic-capitalism-
    and-the-spread-of-english.
28. Based on Piller and Cho (2013). Join the conversation about the nat-
    uralization of English as a marker of academic excellence at www.
    languageonthemove.com/language-globalization/english-is-excellence.
29. Quoted in Erkkilä (2014).
30. Kang (2009). Join the conversation about how the pressure to publish
    research in English affects what kinds of research get carried out at
    http://www.languageonthemove.com/language-globalization/does-
    internationalization-change-research-content.
31. www.languageonthemove.com/multilingual-academics/academic-
    capitalism-and-the-spread-of-english/comment-page-1#comment-
    1625.
32. You can view an image of the car and join the conversation about ac-
    ademic links between the center and the periphery at http://www.
    languageonthemove.com/language-globalization/banal-nationalism-
    and-the-internationalization-of-higher-education.
33. For further information on branch campuses in Ras al-Khaimah see
    Bardsley (2008), Stripling (2009), and Swan (2010, 2014), and for sta-
    tistics about branch campuses generally see Alexander (2007), Homay-
    ounpour (2012), and M. Miller (2005).
34. Altbach and Knight (2007).
35. The International Forum for Social Development (2006, p. 35).
36. 'Korea' (2015); B. Yoo, Kim, and Kim (2011). Join the conversation
    about language costs at www.languageonthemove.com/language-
    consumerism/language-costs.
37. Phillipson (2008, p. 28).
38. Gazzola and Grin (2013). Join the conversation about the cost of
    multilingual provision at www.languageonthemove.com/language-
    globalization/multilingual-provision-is-cheaper-than-english-only.
39. For poverty and shame see Dorling (2014), Sen (1983), and Townsend
    (1979). For the psychological deformities of racism and colonialism see
    Fanon (1963, 1967) and Hook (2012).
40. Cited in Phillipson (2009b, p. 80).

41. Fanon (1967, p. 17 f.).
42. Babaii (2010). Join the conversation about the colonial cringe in academia at www.languageonthemove.com/multilingual-academics/the-colonial-cringe-in-academia.
43. Babaii (2010, p. 102).
44. Song (2010). Join the conversation about global English and mental health at www.languageonthemove.com/recent-posts/warning-global-english-may-harm-your-mental-health.
45. Quoted from Song (2010, p. 30).
46. Morarji (2010). Join the conversation about learning to be marginal at http://www.languageonthemove.com/language-learning-gender-identity/learning-to-be-marginal.
47. Morarji (2010, p. 58).
48. 'Issues in Globalisation: How Fair Is Fashion?' (2011). Join the conversation about the politics of subtitling and illegitimate English at www.languageonthemove.com/language-migration-social-justice/the-politics-of-subtitling and www.languageonthemove.com/language-globalization/illegitimate-english.
49. Minney (2008).
50. Bourdieu (1991, p. 66). Emphases in the original.
51. You can judge for yourself by viewing the film's trailer at https://globaldimension.org.uk/resources/item/1902.
52. Appleby, Copley, Sithirajvongsa, and Pennycook (2002, p. 326).
53. The articles I am referring to are Busacca and Allert (2010) and Jacobs (2010). Join the conversation about Chinglish at http://www.languageonthemove.com/recent-posts/give-chinglish-a-break.
54. Darlington and Ford (2015). The tweet said 'vinieron sólo por el aloz y el petlóleo?' ('Have they only come for the rice and oil?') where *aroz* ('rice') is substituted with *aloz* (similar to the English substitution 'lice' for 'rice') and *petróleo* ('oil') is substituted with *petlóleo* (similar to 'petloleum').
55. E.g., Rapatahana and Bunce (2012) or Mustafa (2011).
56. de Swaan, 2001; see Chapter Two above.
57. Ives (2010, p. 530).

Chapter 8

1. Fraser (2012, p. 43).
2. Van Parijs (2011). Another key political theory text about linguistic justice is the 2003 collection *Language Rights and Political Theory* (Kymlicka and Patten, 2003b).

3. This point is made in detail by most contributors to a 2014 special issue of *Language Policy* devoted to 'Language policy and political theory' (Peled, Ives, and Ricento, 2014), particularly Ricento (2014). For an in-depth examination of the language rights concept from a sociolinguistic perspective, see Wee (2010).

4. 'Universal Declaration of Human Rights' (1948).

5. Kymlicka and Patten (2003a, p. 16).

6. McIntosh (2012, p. 195); see also McIntosh (1989). For a useful overview of privilege studies see Case et al. (2012).

7. E.g., Gallagher-Geurtsen (2007).

8. Bloch wrote *Das Prinzip Hoffnung* in exile in the United States in the 1930s and early 1940s. It was first published in the German Democratic Republic in the 1950s. For an English translation see Bloch (1995).

9. See, e.g., Moss (2014), Spannos (2008), or E. O. Wright (2014).

10. Olearius (1662). For a history of Armenians in Isfahan see Gregorian (1974) and for language maintenance among Armenians in contemporary Iran see Nercissians (2001). Join the conversation about Isfahan's golden age of multiculturalism at http://www.languageonthemove. com/language-globalization/a-golden-age-of-multiculturalism.

11. Gregorian (1974, p. 662).

12. Nercissians (2001).

13. Busch (2009). Join the conversation about civic engagement for a progressive language policy at www.languageonthemove.com/recent-posts/multiculturalism-alive-and-well-in-austria.

14. Busch (2009, p. 139).

15. Busch (2009, p. 147).

16. Bourdieu (1991); Bourdieu and Passeron (1990); Sapiro (2010). Other relevant theorists include Voloshinov (1986) and Gramsci; on the latter's conceptualization of language, see, e.g., Ives (2009, 2014).

17. Colic-Peisker, 2011b. View relevant statistics and join the conversation about Australia's multicultural middle class at www. languageonthemove.com/language-migration-social-justice/rising-multicultural-middle-class.

18. Jamal and Chandab (2005); Topçu, Bota, and Pham (2012). Join the conversation about reimagining the nation as diverse at http://www. languageonthemove.com/language-migration-social-justice/growing-up-between-cultures.

19. Jamal and Chandab (2005, p. 1).

20. Jamal and Chandab (2005, pp. 1, 179 f.).

21. On the resurgence of ANZAC remembrance see Lake, Reynolds, McKenna, and Damousi (2010). For research that shows an inverse relationship between globalization and nationalism see Ariely (2012)

and Machida (2012). The discussion of economic neoliberalism and dis-cursive nationalism is based on Blad and Koçer (2012). Join the con-versation about globalization and nationalism at http://www.language onthemove.com/language-globalization/globalisation-and-nationalism.

22. Blad and Koçer (2012, p. 37). Emphasis in the original.
23. Blad and Koçer (2012, p. 45). Emphasis in the original.
24. For biographies of Joe Hill see Adler (2011), Rosemont (2003), and G. Smith (1984). Follow links to recordings of his songs and join the conversation about the legacy of Joe Hill at http://www. languageonthemove.com/language-migration-social-justice/i-dreamed-i-saw-joe-hill-last-night.
25. G. Smith (1984, p. 47).

REFERENCES

6 Sa 158/09. (2009). Landesarbeitsgericht Schleswig-Holstein. Retrieved from http://www.sit.de/lagsh/ehome.nsf/6EB33198161840A6C12576 BC0078CEE7/$file/U_6Sa158-09_23-12-2009.pdf

8 AZR 48/10 Diskriminierung—Ethnische Herkunft—Deutschkurs [Discrimination—Ethnic Origin—German Language Class]. (2011). Bundesarbeitsgericht. Retrieved from http://juris.bundesarbeitsgericht. de/cgi-bin/rechtsprechung/document.py?Gericht=bag&Art=en& nr=15454

11th EFA (Education for All) Global Monitoring Report. (2014). Paris: Unesco. Retrieved from http://unesdoc.unesco.org/images/0022/ 002256/225660e.pdf

Adler, William M. (2011). *The Man Who Never Died: The Life, Times, and Legacy of Joe Hill, American Labor Icon.* London: Bloomsbury.

Agirdag, Orhan. (2013). The Long-Term Effects of Bilingualism on Children of Immigration: Student Bilingualism and Future Earnings. *International Journal of Bilingual Education and Bilingualism, 17*(4), 449–464. doi: 10.1080/13670050.2013.816264

Alcorso, Caroline. (2003). Immigrant Employees in Hotels. *Labour and Industry, 14*(1), 17–40.

Alexander, Harriet. (2007, June 14). Debt Climbing for Uni's Failed Campus. *Sydney Morning Herald.* Retrieved from http://www.smh. com.au/news/national/debt-climbing-for-unis-failed-campus/2007/ 06/13/1181414383789.html

Altbach, Philip G., & Knight, Jane. (2007). The Internationalization of Higher Education: Motivations and Realities. *Journal of Studies in International Education, 11*(3–4), 290–305. doi: 10.1177/1028315307303542

Ammon, Ulrich (Ed.). (2001). *The Dominance of English as a Language of Science: Effects on Other Languages and Language Communities* (Vol. 84). Berlin and New York: Mouton de Gruyter.

Androutsopoulos, Jannis, & Juffermans, Kasper (Eds.). (2014). *Superdiversity and Digital Language Practices [Special Issue of Discourse, Context and Media]* (Vol. 4–5). Amsterdam: Elsevier.

Anthias, Floya. (2013). Moving Beyond the Janus Face of Integration and Diversity Discourses: Towards an Intersectional Framing. *The Sociological Review, 61*(2), 323–343. doi: 10.1111/1467-954x.12001

Antolak, Ryszard. (n.d.). Iran and the Polish Exodus from Russia 1942, *Pars Times*. Retrieved from http://www.parstimes.com/history/polish_refugees/exodus_russia.html

Appleby, Roslyn, Copley, Kath, Sithirajvongsa, Sisamone, & Pennycook, Alastair. (2002). Language in Development Constrained: Three Contexts. *TESOL Quarterly, 36*(3), 323–346. doi: 10.2307/3588416

Apps, Peter. (2014, July 14). Lack of Foreign-Language Skills 'Threatens the UK Economy.' *The Independent.*

Arab Human Development Report 2009: Challenges to Human Security in the Arab Countries. (2009). New York: United Nations Development Programme (UNDP). Retrieved from http://www.arab-hdr.org/publications/other/ahdr/ahdr2009e.pdf

Arai, Mahmood, & Skogman Thoursie, Peter. (2009). Renouncing Personal Names: An Empirical Examination of Surname Change and Earnings. *Journal of Labor Economics, 27*(1), 127–147.

Archibald, John, Roy, Sylvie, Harmel, Sandra, Jesney, Karen, Dewey, Emily, Moisik, Scott, & Lessard, Pascale. (2006). *A Review of the Literature on Second Language Learning.* Calgary, Alberta: University of Calgary Language Research Centre.

Ariely, Gal. (2012). Globalisation and the Decline of National Identity? An Exploration across Sixty-three Countries. *Nations and Nationalism, 18*(3), 461–482. doi: 10.1111/j.1469-8129.2011.00532.x

Árus, Zsolt. (2009). The Szeklers and Their Struggle for Autonomy. Retrieved from http://sznt.sic.hu/en/?option=com_content&view=article&id=210

Asscher, Sue, & Widger, David (Eds.). (2008). *The Project Gutenberg Ebook of the Republic, by Plato.*

Azizi v. the Queen (2012). Supreme Court of Victoria. Retrieved from https://jade.barnet.com.au/Jade.html#article=270732

Babaii, Esmat. (2010). Opting Out or Playing the 'Academic Game'? Professional Identity Construction by Off-center Academics. *Critical Approaches to Discourse Analysis across Disciplines, 4*(1), 93–105.

Baker, Colin. (2006). *Foundations of Bilingual Education and Bilingualism* (4th ed.). Bristol: Multilingual Matters.

Bardsley, Daniel. (2008, September 15). British Rankings Upset University Opening in RAK. *The National*. Retrieved from http://www.thenational. ae/news/uae-news/education/british-rankings-upset-university-opening-in-rak

Baron, Denis. (2010). Arabic Flashcards Bump Student from Plane. Retrieved from https://illinois.edu/blog/view/25/22101

Barry, Brian. (2005). *Why Social Justice Matters*. Oxford: Polity.

Basford, Tessa E., Offermann, Lynn R., & Behrend, Tara S. (2014). Do You See What I See? Perceptions of Gender Microaggressions in the Workplace. *Psychology of Women Quarterly, 38*(3), 340–349. doi: 10.1177/0361684313511420

Beaudrie, Sara M., & Fairclough, Marta (Eds.). (2012). *Spanish as a Heritage Language in the United States: The State of the Field*. Washington, DC: Georgetown University Press.

Beblawi, Hazem. (1990). The Rentier State in the Arab World. In G. Luciani (Ed.), *The Arab State* (pp. 85–98). London: Routledge.

Benz, Victoria. (2015). *Dynamics of Bilingual Early Childhood Education: Parental Attitudes and Institutional Realisation*. PhD, Macquarie University. Retrieved from http://www.languageonthemove.com/wp-content/uploads/2015/07/CORRECTED-PhD-Thesis-Victoria-Benz-DIGITAL-COPY.pdf

Berdichevsky, Norman. (2004). *Nations, Language and Citizenship*. Jefferson, NC, and London: McFarland & Co.

Biavaschi, Costanza, Giulietti, Corrado, & Siddique, Zahra. (2013). The Economic Payoff of Name Americanization. *IZA Discussion Paper, 7725*. doi: ssrn.com/abstract = 2363212

Bigelow, Martha H. (2010). *Mogadishu on the Mississippi: Language, Racialized Identity, and Education in a New Land*. Malden, MA: Wiley-Blackwell.

Birdsong, D. (2006). Age and Second Language Acquisition and Processing: A Selective Overview. *Language Learning, 56*, 9–49.

Blad, Cory, & Koçer, Banu. (2012). Political Islam and State Legitimacy in Turkey: The Role of National Culture in Neoliberal State-Building. *International Political Sociology, 6*(1), 36–56. doi: 10.1111/j.1749-5687.2012.00150.x

Bloch, Ernst. (1995). *The Principle of Hope* (N. Plaice, S. Plaice, & P. Knight, Trans.). Cambridge, MA: MIT Press.

Block, David. (2005). *Multilingual Identities in a Global City: London Stories*. London: Palgrave Macmillan.

Block, David. (2014). *Social Class in Applied Linguistics*. London: Routledge.

Blommaert, Jan. (2008). *Grassroots Literacy: Writing, Identity and Voice in Central Africa*. London: Routledge.

Blommaert, Jan. (2010). *The Sociolinguistics of Globalization*. Cambridge: Cambridge University Press.

Boffey, Daniel. (2013, August 18). Lack of Language Skills Is Diminishing Britain's Voice in the World. *The Observer.* Retrieved from http://www.theguardian.com/education/2013/aug/17/language-skills-universities-business-hague

Bolton, Kingsley, Graddol, David, & Meierkord, Christiane. (2011). Towards Developmental World Englishes. *World Englishes, 30*(4), 459–480. doi: 10.1111/j.1467-971X.2011.01735.x

Booth, Alison, Leigh, Andrew, & Varganova, Elena. (2009). Does Racial and Ethnic Discrimination Vary across Minority Groups? Evidence from Three Experiments. *Australian Policy Online.* Retrieved from http://apo.org.au/research/does-racial-and-ethnic-discrimination-vary-across-minority-groups-evidence-three

Bourdieu, Pierre. (1977). The Economics of Linguistic Exchanges. *Social Science Information, 16*(6), 645–668.

Bourdieu, Pierre. (1991). *Language and Symbolic Power.* Cambridge: Polity.

Bourdieu, Pierre. (1993). *Outline of a Theory of Practice.* Cambridge: Cambridge University Press.

Bourdieu, Pierre, & Passeron, Jean-Claude. (1990). *Reproduction in Education, Society and Culture* (2nd ed.). London: Sage.

Brann, Matt, & Locke, Sarina. (2012, October 25). Lack of Language Skills Will Hurt Australian Trade with Indonesia. *ABC Rural.* Retrieved from www.abc.net.au/site-archive/rural/nt/content/201210/s3618677.htm

Brombacher, Britt. (2013). New York Is (Not Surprisingly) America's Most Multilingual City. Retrieved from http://blog.doortodoor.com/new-york-isnot-surprisingly-americas-most-multilingual-city/

Brooke, Chris. (2014, June 5). Farce of £5,000 Bill to Prosecute Lithuanian Who Stole Two 10p Bags: Court Hired Latvian Translator by Mistake. *Daily Mail.* Retrieved from http://www.dailymail.co.uk/news/article-2649599/Trial-Lithuanian-immigrant-stole-two-plastic-bags-worth-10p-cost-3-000-court-hired-Latvian-translator-mistake.html

Brown, Jonathan. (2013, August 13). 200 Languages: Manchester Revealed as Most Linguistically Diverse City in Western Europe, *The Independent.* Retrieved from www.independent.co.uk/news/uk/home-news/200-languages-manchester-revealed-as-most-linguistically-diverse-city-in-western-europe-8760225.html

Brown, Simon. (2015, January 21). Work at Manildra Site Suspended after CFMEU Alleges 457 Visa Abuse. *South Coast Register.* Retrieved from www.southcoastregister.com.au/story/2831710/foreign-workers-underpaid-living-in-worrigee-dosshouse-says-union/

Browne, Irene, & Misra, Joya. (2005). Labor-Market Inequality: Intersections of Gender, Race, and Class. In M. Romero & E. Margolis (Eds.), *The Blackwell Companion to Social Inequalities* (pp. 165–189). Oxford: Blackwell.

Bruthiaux, Paul. (2008). Language Education, Economic Development and Participation in the Greater Mekong Subregion. *International Journal of Bilingual Education and Bilingualism, 11*(2), 134–148. doi: 10.2167/beb490.0

Buncombe, Andrew, & Macarthur, Tessa. (1999, March 29). London: Multilingual Capital of the World. *The Independent*. Retrieved from www.independent.co.uk/news/london-multilingual-capital-of-the-world-1083812.html

Busacca, Allison, & Allert, Marcia. (2010, May 11). Strange Signs from Abroad. *New York Times*. Retrieved from http://www.nytimes.com/interactive/2010/05/11/travel/funny-signs.html

Busch, Brigitta. (2009). Local Actors in Promoting Multilingualism. In G. Hogan-Brun, C. Mar-Molinero, & P. Stevenson (Eds.), *Discourses on Language and Integration* (pp. 129–151). Amsterdam: John Benjamin Publishing.

Butler, Susan (Ed.). (Since 2003). *Macquarie Dictionary Online*. https://www.macquariedictionary.com.au/

Butorac, Donna. (2011). *Imagined Identity, Remembered Self: Settlement Language Learning and the Negotiation of Gendered Subjectivity*. PhD, Macquarie University. Retrieved from http://www.languageonthemove.com/wp-content/uploads/2012/03/DButorac_PhD.pdf

Butorac, Donna. (2014). 'Like a Fish Not in Water': How Language and Race Mediate the Social and Economic Inclusion of Women Migrants to Australia. *Australian Review of Applied Linguistics, 37*(3), 234–248.

Butt, Craig, & Worrall, Allison. (2014, July 11). Melbourne Language Study Reveals a Cacophony of Diversity. *The Age*. Retrieved from http://www.theage.com.au/victoria/melbourne-language-study-reveals-a-cacophony-of-diversity-20140711-zt4b4

California Valedictorian Gives Speech in Spanish, Sparking Debate. (2012, June 13). *Fox News Latino*. Retrieved from http://latino.foxnews.com/latino/news/2012/06/13/california-valedictorian-gives-speech-in-spanish-sparking-debate/

Cambodia. (2014). *The World Fact Book*. Washington, DC: Central Intelligence Agency.

Cambodia. (2015). *Ethnologue: Languages of the World*. Dallas, TX: SIL International.

Cameron, Deborah. (1995). *Verbal Hygiene*. London and New York: Routledge.

Carrick, Damien. (2014, May 13). Volunteering in the Justice System, *ABC Radio National*. Retrieved from http://www.abc.net.au/radionational/programs/lawreport/volunteering/5445876

Case, Kim A., Iuzzini, Jonathan, & Hopkins, Morgan. (2012). Systems of Privilege: Intersections, Awareness, and Applications. *Journal of Social Issues, 68*(1), 1–10. doi: 10.1111/j.1540-4560.2011.01732.x

Census Home. (2012). Canberra: Australian Bureau of Statistics. http://www.abs.gov.au/websitedbs/censushome.nsf/home/data?opendocument#frombanner=LN

2011 Census of Population and Housing: Basic Community Profile, Auburn. (2012). Canberra: Australian Bureau of Statistics.

Chang, Grace Chu-Lin. (2015). *Language Learning, Academic Achievement, and Overseas Experience: An Ethnography of Taiwanese Students in Australian Higher Education.* PhD, Macquarie University.

Chang, Leslie T. (2009). *Factory Girls: From Village to City in a Changing China.* New York: Spiegel & Grau.

Choi, Po King. (2010). 'Weep for Chinese University': A Case Study of English Hegemony and Academic Capitalism in Higher Education in Hong Kong. *Journal of Education Policy, 25*(2), 233–252.

Chu, Cordia. (2005). Postnatal Experience and Health Needs of Chinese Migrant Women in Brisbane, Australia. *Ethnicity and Health, 10*(1), 33–56. doi: 10.1080/1355785052000323029

Chuuk Islands. (2013). *Encyclopedia Britannica.* Chicago: Encyclopædia Britannica.

Clayton, Stephen. (2008). The Problem of 'Choice' and the Construction of the Demand for English in Cambodia. *Language Policy, 7*(2), 143–164. doi: 10.1007/s10993-008-9084-9

Clayton, Thomas. (2002). International Languages in Education in Developing Countries: Implications for Cambodia. In J. Lo Bianco (Ed.), *Voices from Phnom Penh. Development and Language: Global Influences and Local Effects* (pp. 87–102). Melbourne: Language Australia.

Clyne, Michael. (2005). *Australia's Language Potential.* Sydney: UNSW Press.

Cochrane, Liam. (2012, January 18). UN Grants Oceanic Viking Asylum Seekers Refugee Status, *ABC Radio National.* Retrieved from http://www.radioaustralia.net.au/international/radio/onairhighlights/un-grants-oceanic-viking-asylum-seekers-refugee-status

Codrea-Rado, Anna. (2014, January 30). Employers Struggle to Fill Vacancies Because of Lack of Languages, *The Guardian.* Retrieved from www.theguardian.com/education/2014/jan/30/employers-struggle-to-fill-vacancies-languages

Coleman, Hywel (Ed.). (2011). *Dreams and Realities: Developing Countries and the English Language.* London: British Council.

Colic-Peisker, Val. (2005). 'At Least You're the Right Colour': Identity and Social Inclusion of Bosnian Refugees in Australia. *Journal of Ethnic and Migration Studies, 31*(4), 615–638. doi: 10.1080/13691830500109720

Colic-Peisker, Val. (2011a). 'Ethnics' and 'Anglos' in the Labour Force: Advancing Australia Fair? *Journal of Intercultural Studies, 32*(6), 637–654. doi: 10.1080/07256868.2011.618108

Colic-Peisker, Val. (2011b). A New Era in Australian Multiculturalism? From Working-Class 'Ethnics' to a 'Multicultural Middle-Class.' *International Migration Review, 45*(3), 562–587. doi: 10.1111/j.1747-7379.2011.00858.x

Collier, Virginia P. (1989). How Long? A Synthesis of Research on Academic Achievement in a Second Language. *TESOL Quarterly, 23*(3), 509–531.

Colvin, Mark. (2009, October 19). Asylum Seekers Deny Jumping Queue, *ABC PM*. Retrieved from www.abc.net.au/pm/content/2009/s2718323.htm

Common European Framework of Reference for Languages: Learning, Teaching, Assessment. (2001). Strasbourg: Council of Europe. Retrieved from http://www.coe.int/t/dg4/linguistic/Source/Framework_EN.pdf

Constitution de la République Française [Constitution of the French Republic] (1958).

Cooper, Adam. (2014, January 17). Man Jailed for Racist Bus Rant. *The Age*. Retrieved from www.theage.com.au/victoria/man-jailed-for-racist-bus-rant-20140117-30zyx.html

Creese, Gillian. (2011). *The New African Diaspora in Vancouver: Migration, Exclusion and Belonging*. Toronto: University of Toronto Press.

Creese, Gillian, & Kambere, Edith Ngene. (2003). What Colour Is Your English? *Canadian Review of Sociology and Anthropology, 40*(5), 565–573.

Creese, Gillian, & Wiebe, Brandy. (2012). 'Survival Employment': Gender and Deskilling among African Immigrants in Canada. *International Migration, 50*(5), 56–76. doi: 10.1111/j.1468-2435.2009.00531.x

Crotty, James M. (2012, March 26). 7 Signs That U.S. Education Decline Is Jeopardizing Its National Security, *Forbes*. Retrieved from http://www.forbes.com/sites/jamesmarshallcrotty/2012/03/26/7-signs-that-americas-educational-decline-is-jeopardizing-its-national-security/

Czaika, Mathias, & de Haas, Hein. (2014). The Globalization of Migration: Has the World Become More Migratory? *International Migration Review, 48*(2), 283–323. doi: 10.1111/imre.12095

D'Amato, Raffaele. (2010). *The Varangian Guard 988–1453*. Oxford: Osprey.

Darlington, Shasta, & Ford, Dana. (2015, February 5). Argentina President Posts Tweet Mocking Chinese Accent, *CNN*. Retrieved from http://edition.cnn.com/2015/02/04/americas/argentina-president-tweet/

De Bock, Jozefien. (2014). Not All the Same after All? Superdiversity as a Lens for the Study of Past Migrations. *Ethnic and Racial Studies, 38*(4), 583–595. doi: 10.1080/01419870.2015.980290

De Castella, Tom. (2013, July 23). How Many Hours Does It Take to Be Fluent in English?, *BBC News*. Retrieved from http://www.bbc.com/news/magazine-23407265

De Lotbinière, Max. (2011, July 5). Research Backs English as Key to Development, *Guardian*. Retrieved from http://www.theguardian.com/education/2011/jul/05/research-backs-english-language-delotbiniere

De Swaan, Abram. (2001). *Words of the World: The Global Language System.* Cambridge, UK: Polity.

Dixon, Sally, & Angelo, Denise. (2014). Dodgy Data, Language Invisibility and the Implications for Social Inclusion: A Critical Analysis of Indigenous Student Language Data in Queensland Schools. *Australian Review of Applied Linguistics, 37*(3), 213–233.

Djité, Paulin G. (2008). *The Sociolinguistics of Development in Africa.* Clevedon: Multilingual Matters.

Döhner, Annette, Mertens, Beate, Carstensen, Christiane, Korol, Alla, & Stallbaum, Sabine. (2014). Abschlussdokumentation 'Komma-NRW' [Final Documentation of North-Rhine Westphalian Communication Project]. Bielefeld: Arbeiterwohlfahrt KV Bielefeld. Retrieved from http://www.komma-nrw.de/wp-content/uploads/2015/02/DEF-FEB-Abschlussdokumentation-komma-NRW.pdf

Doiz, Aintzane, Lasagabaster, David, & Sierra, Juan Manuel (Eds.). (2012). *English-Medium Instruction at Universities: Global Challenges.* Bristol: Multilingual Matters.

Dorling, Danny. (2014). *Inequality and the 1%.* London: Verso.

DPP v. Azizi (2013). High Court of Victoria. Retrieved from https://jade.barnet.com.au/Jade.html#article=289735

Dreby, Joanna, & Schmalzbauer, Leah. (2013). The Relational Contexts of Migration: Mexican Women in New Destination Sites. *Sociological Forum, 28*(1), 1–26. doi: 10.1111/socf.12000

Eades, Diana. (2013). *Aboriginal Ways of Using English.* Canberra: Aboriginal Studies Press.

Eaton, Sarah Elaine. (2011). *How Long Does It Take to Learn a Second Language? Applying the '10,000-Hour Rule' as a Model for Fluency.* Calgary, Alberta: Onate Press.

Eaton, Sarah Elaine. (2012). How Will Alberta's Second Language Students Ever Achieve Proficiency? ACTFL Proficiency Guidelines, the CEFR and the '10,000-Hour Rule' in Relation to the Alberta K-12 Language-Learning Context. *Notos, 12*(2), 2–12.

Eckert, Eva. (2002). From Moravia to Texas: Immigrant Acculturation at the Cemetery. *Markers, 19*, 174–211.

Eckert, Eva. (2006). *Stones on the Prairie: Acculturation in America.* Bloomington, IN: Slavica Publishers.

Eckstein, Susan, & Nguyen, Thanh-Nghi. (2011). The Making and Transnationalization of an Ethnic Niche: Vietnamese Manicurists. *International Migration Review, 45*(3), 639–674. doi: 10.1111/j.1747-7379.2011.00861.x

Ellis, Elizabeth M., Gogolin, Ingrid, & Clyne, Michael. (2010). The Janus Face of Monolingualism: A Comparison of German and Australian Language Education Policies. *Current Issues in Language Planning, 11*(4), 439–460.

Employees Paid by Award Only. (2014). Canberra: Australian Bureau of Statistics. Retrieved from http://www.abs.gov.au/ausstats/abs@.nsf/Latestproducts/6306.0Main%20Features5May%202014

Ergin, Murat. (2009). Cultural Encounters in the Social Sciences and Humanities: Western Émigré Scholars in Turkey. *History of the Human Sciences*, 22(1), 105–130. doi: 10.1177/0952695108099137

Erkkilä, Tero. (2014). Global University Rankings, Transnational Policy Discourse and Higher Education in Europe. *European Journal of Education*, 49(1), 91–101. doi: 10.1111/ejed.12063

Erling, Elizabeth J., & Seargeant, Philip (Eds.). (2013). *English and Development: Policy, Pedagogy and Globalization*. Bristol: Multilingual Matters.

European Charter for Regional and Minority Languages. (1992a). Strasbourg: Council of Europe.

European Charter for Regional and Minority Languages: Explanatory Report. (1992b). Strasbourg: Council of Europe. Retrieved from http://conventions.coe.int/treaty/en/Reports/Html/148.htm

Extra, Guus, Spotti, Massimiliano, & Van Avermaet, Piet (Eds.). (2009). *Language Testing, Migration and Citizenship: Cross-national Perspectives on Integration Regimes*. London: Continuum.

Fairwork Ombudsman. (2015) Retrieved from www.fairwork.gov.au/

Fanon, Frantz. (1963). *The Wretched of the Earth: The Handbook of the Black Revolution That Is Changing the Shape of the World* (C. Farrington, Trans.). New York: Grove Weidenfeld.

Fanon, Frantz. (1967). *Black Skin, White Masks*. London: Pluto Press.

Faruqi, Anwar. (2000). Forgotten Polish Exodus to Persia. Washington Post. Retrieved from www.library.cornell.edu/colldev/mideast/polsirn.htm

Fauna. (2011). Africans in Guangzhou: Opportunities and Discrimination. Retrieved from www.chinasmack.com/2011/pictures/africans-in-guangzhou-opportunities-discrimination.html

Feldman, Ruth T. (2008). *The Fall of Constantinople: Pivotal Moments in History*. Minneapolis, MN: Twenty-First Century Books.

Ferguson, Charles A. (1959). Diglossia. *Word*, 15, 325–340.

Ferguson, Gibson, Pérez-Llantada, Carmen, & Plo, Ramón. (2011). English as an International Language of Scientific Publication: A Study of Attitudes. *World Englishes*, 30(1), 41–59. doi: 10.1111/j.1467-971X.2010.01656.x

Flanagan, Richard. (2006). *The Unknown Terrorist*. Sydney: Picador.

Flowerdew, John. (2008). Scholarly Writers Who Use English as an Additional Language: What Can Goffman's 'Stigma' Tell Us? *Journal of English for Academic Purposes*, 7(2), 77–86.

Fogarty, Bill. (2012, July 3). Indigenous Education Report Misses the Big Picture. *The Conversation*. Retrieved from https://theconversation.com/indigenous-education-report-misses-the-big-picture-8024

Fraser, Nancy. (1995). From Redistribution to Recognition? Dilemmas of Justice in a 'Post-Socialist' Age. *New Left Review, 212*, 68–93.

Fraser, Nancy. (2005). Reframing Justice in a Globalizing World. *New Left Review, 36*, 69–88.

Fraser, Nancy. (2012). On Justice: Lessons from Plato, Rawls and Ishiguro. *New Left Review, 74*, 41–51.

Fuller, Janet M. (2012). *Bilingual Pre-teens: Competing Ideologies and Multiple Identities in the U.S. and Germany.* London: Taylor & Francis.

Gallagher-Geurtsen, Tricia. (2007). Linguistic Privilege: Why Educators Should Be Concerned. *Multicultural Perspectives, 9*(1), 40–44. doi: 10.1080/15210960701334094

Gamba, Barry, & Makeny, Bernard Amour. (2007). The Applicant. *Africa on Screen*. Parramatta, NSW: Information and Cultural Exchange.

García, Ofelia. (2009a). *Bilingual Education in the 21st Century: A Global Perspective.* Malden, MA, and Oxford: Wiley-Blackwell.

García, Ofelia. (2009b). Education, Multilingualism and Translanguaging in the 21st Century. In A. K. Mohanty, M. Panda, R. Phillipson, & T. Skutnabb-Kangas (Eds.), *Multilingual Education for Social Justice: Globalising the Local* (pp. 128–145). New Delhi: Orient BlackSwan.

García, Ofelia, Skutnabb-Kangas, Tove, & Torres-Guzman, Maria E. (Eds.). (2006). *Imagining Multilingual Schools.* Clevedon: Multilingual Matters.

Gazzola, Michele, & Grin, François. (2013). Is ELF More Effective and Fair Than Translation? An Evaluation of the EU's Multilingual Regime. *International Journal of Applied Linguistics, 23*(1), 93–107. doi: 10.1111/ijal.12014

Goddard, Cliff. (2009). Not Taking Yourself Too Seriously in Australian English: Semantic Explications, Cultural Scripts, Corpus Evidence. *Intercultural Pragmatics, 6*(1), 29–53.

Gogolin, Ingrid. (1994). *Der monolinguale Habitus der multilingualen Schule [The Monolingual Habitus of the Multilingual School].* Münster: Waxmann.

Goldstein, Tara. (1996). *Two Languages at Work: Bilingual Life on the Production Floor.* Berlin and New York: Mouton de Gruyter.

Goodenough, Ward H. (1976). Multiculturalism as the Normal Human Experience. *Anthropology and Education Quarterly, 7*(4), 4–7.

Graduation Speech in Spanish Riles O'Reilly. (2012, June 20). *News10*. Retrieved from http://www.abc10.com/story/news/local/my-neighborhood/2014/01/20/4688883/

Green, James. (2014). The Effect of English Proficiency and Ethnicity on Academic Performance and Progress. *Advances in Health Sciences Education*, 1–10. doi: 10.1007/s10459-014-9523-7

Gregorian, Vartan. (1974). Minorities of Isfahan: The Armenian Community of Isfahan 1587–1722. *Iranian Studies, 7*(3/4), 652–680. doi: 10.2307/4310181

Grin, François. (2013). *Questioning Tolerance: When Are Immigrant Linguistic and Cultural Rights Tolerable?* Lecture, Macquarie University.

Grin, François, Sfreddo, Claudio, & Vaillancourt, François. (2010). *The Economics of the Multilingual Workplace.* London: Routledge.

Haeri, Niloofar. (2003). *Sacred Language, Ordinary People: Dilemmas of Culture and Politics in Egypt.* Basingstoke: Palgrave Macmillan.

Hakuta, Kenji, Butler, Yuko Goto, & Witt, Daria. (2000). How Long Does It Take English Learners to Attain Proficiency? Stanford University. Retrieved from http://escholarship.org/uc/item/13w7m06g

Hamid, M. Obaidul. (2010). Globalisation, English for Everyone and English Teacher Capacity: Language Policy Discourses and Realities in Bangladesh. *Current Issues in Language Planning, 11*(4), 289–310. doi: 10.1080/14664208.2011.532621

Han, Huamei. (2011). Social Inclusion through Multilingual Ideologies, Policies and Practices: A Case Study of a Minority Church. *International Journal of Bilingual Education and Bilingualism, 14*(4), 383–398.

Han, Huamei. (2013). Individual Grassroots Multilingualism in Africa Town in Guangzhou: The Role of States in Globalization. *International Multilingual Research Journal, 7,* 83–97.

Han, Wen-Jui, & Huang, Chien-Chung. (2010). The Forgotten Treasure: Bilingualism and Asian Children's Emotional and Behavioral Health. *American Journal of Public Health, 100*(5), 831–839. doi: 10.2105/AJPH.2009.174219

Haque, Eve. (2014). Neoliberal Governmentality and Canadian Migrant Language Training Policies. *Globalisation, Societies and Education,* 1–18. doi: 10.1080/14767724.2014.937403

Hart, Cath. (2007, May 14). Refugees' Job Hunt Time Halved, *The Australian.*

Hefling, Kimberly. (2014, August 9). White students aren't going to be majority in schools, *Las Vegas Review Journal.* Retrieved from http://www.reviewjournal.com/news/education/white-students-aren-t-going-be-majority-schools

Heller, Monica. (2006). *Linguistic Minorities and Modernity: A Sociolinguistic Ethnography* (2nd ed.). London: Continuum.

Hochschild, Arlie Russell. (2003). *The Second Shift.* New York: Penguin.

Holmes, Colin. (1991). Immigrants and Refugees in Britain. In W. E. Mosse & J. Carlebach (Eds.), *Second Chance: Two Centuries of German-Speaking Jews in the United Kingdom* (pp. 11–30). Tübingen: Mohr Siebeck.

Homayounpour, Cyrus. (2012, May 3). Will They Come If You Build It? The Future of International Branch Campuses, *The evolllution.* Retrieved from www.evolllution.com/distance_online_learning/will-they-come-if-you-build-it-the-future-of-international-branch-campuses/

Homer. (1996). *Odyssey* (R. Fagles, Trans.). New York: Viking.

Hook, Derek. (2012). *A Critical Psychology of the Postcolonial: The Mind of Apartheid*. London: Routledge.

Hu, Guangwei, & Alsagoff, Lubna. (2010). A Public Policy Perspective on English Medium Instruction in China. *Journal of Multilingual and Multicultural Development, 31*(4), 365–382.

Hughes, Helen, & Hughes, Mark. (2012). Indigenous Education 2012. Sydney: Centre for Independent Studies. Retrieved from http://www.cis.org.au/app/uploads/2015/07/pm129.pdf

Hughes, Robert. (1986). *The Fatal Shore: A History of the Transportation of Convicts to Australia, 1787–1868*. London: The Harvill Press.

Hymes, Dell. (1996). *Ethnography, Linguistics, Narrative Inequality: Toward an Understanding of Voice*. London: Taylor & Francis.

Hyslop, Leah. (2012, August 31). Lack of Language Skills Is Biggest Obstacle for Expats, *The Telegraph*. Retrieved from http://www.telegraph.co.uk/expat/expatnews/9511398/Lack-of-language-skills-is-biggest-obstacle-for-expats.html

The International Forum for Social Development. (2006). Social Justice in an Open World. The Role of the United Nations. New York: United Nations. Retrieved from http://www.un.org/esa/socdev/documents/ifsd/SocialJustice.pdf

Issues in Globalisation: How Fair Is Fashion? (2011). Bristol: Pumpkin Interactive.

Ives, Peter. (2009). Global English, Hegemony and Education: Lessons from Gramsci. *Educational Philosophy and Theory, 41*(6), 661–683. doi: 10.1111/j.1469-5812.2008.00498.x

Ives, Peter. (2010). Cosmopolitanism and Global English: Language Politics in Globalisation Debates. *Political Studies, 58*(3), 516–535. doi: 10.1111/j.1467-9248.2009.00781.x

Ives, Peter. (2014). De-politicizing Language: Obstacles to Political Theory's Engagement with Language Policy. *Language Policy, 13*, 335–350.

Ivett, Alex. (2012, November 21). YouTube Video of Racist Abuse Captures Australia's Darker Side, *Australian Times*. Retrieved from http://www.australiantimes.co.uk/youtube-video-of-racist-abuse-captures-australias-darker-side/

Jacobs, Andrew. (2010, May 2). Shanghai Is Trying to Untangle the Mangled English of Chinglish, *New York Times*. Retrieved from http://www.nytimes.com/2010/05/03/world/asia/03chinglish.html

Jaleco, Rodney J. (2010, July 22). 4 Pinoys Lose US Jobs for Speaking in Tagalog, *ABS CBN*.

Jamal, Nadia, & Chandab, Taghred. (2005). *The Glory Garage: Growing Up Lebanese Muslim in Australia*. Crows Nest: Allen & Unwin.

Jenkins, Jennifer. (2003). *World Englishes: A Resource Book for Students*. London: Routledge.

Jones, Kate. (2010, April 8). Judge Slams 000 Operator's Reaction to Afghan Woman's Call for Help Days before Her Death at Hands of Husband, *Herald Sun*.

Kachru, Braj B. (1985). Standards, Codification and Sociolinguistic Realism: The English Language in the Outer Circle. In R. Quirk & H. G. Widdowson (Eds.), *English in the World: Teaching and Learning the Language and Literatures* (pp. 11–30). Cambridge: Cambridge University Press.

Kachru, Braj B., Kachru, Yamuna, & Nelson, Cecil (Eds.). (2009). *The Handbook of World Englishes*. Malden, MA, and Oxford: Blackwell.

Kaimann, Jonathan. (2013, October 22). China to Downgrade English Section of College Admissions Test, *Guardian*. Retrieved from http://www.theguardian.com/world/2013/oct/22/china-english-college-test-gaokao

Kang, Myungkoo. (2009). 'State-Guided' University Reform and Colonial Conditions of Knowledge Production. *Inter-Asia Cultural Studies*, *10*(2), 191–205. doi: 10.1080/14649370902823355

Karmani, Sohail. (2005). Petro-linguistics: The Emerging Nexus between Oil, English, and Islam. *Journal of Language, Identity, and Education*, *4*(2), 87–102. doi: 10.1207/s15327701jlie0402_2

Katz, David S. (1996). *The Jews in the History of England, 1485–1850*. Oxford: Clarendon Press.

Keine Diskriminierung: Zum Deutschkurs Aufgefordert. (2010, January 15). *taz*. Retrieved from www.taz.de/!46834/

Kelly, Joe. (2010, December 17). ASIO Rejects Sri Lankan Refugees from Oceanic Viking Stand-off, *The Australian*. Retrieved from http://www.theaustralian.com.au/national-affairs/asio-rejects-sri-lankan-refugees-from-oceanic-viking-stand-off/story-fn59niix-1225972655960

Kiffmeier, Jens. (2010, March 30). Interview with Collien Fernandes, *News*. Retrieved from www.news.de/politik/855050398/man-darf-sich-nicht-verzetteln/1/

Kim, Youna. (2011a). Diasporic Nationalism and the Media: Asian Women on the Move. *International Journal of Cultural Studies*, *14*(2), 133–151. doi: 10.1177/1367877910382184

Kim, Youna. (2011b). *Transnational Migration, Media and Identity of Asian Women: Diasporic Daughters*. London: Routledge.

Kirk, John. (2009). Using Intersectionality to Examine the New Complexities of Work Identities and Social Class. *Sociology Compass*, *3*(2), 234–248.

Kiss, Zsuzsanna Eva. (2011). Language Policy and Language Ideologies in Szekler Land (Rumania): A Promotion of Bilingualism? *Multilingua*, *30*(2), 221–264. doi: 10.1515/mult.2011.010

Kiste, Robert C., & Marshall, Mac. (1999). *American Anthropology in Micronesia: An Assessment.* Honolulu, HI: University of Hawai'i Press.

Knirk, James E. (1999). Runer i Hagia Sofia i Istanbul [Runes in Hagia Sofia in Istanbul]. *Nytt om runer, 14,* 26–27.

Korea. (2015). *Gross Domestic Product.* Washington, DC: World Bank Publications.

Kościałkowski, Stanisław. (1943). *L'Iran et la Pologne à travers les siècles [Iran and Poland through the Ages].* Tehran: Société Polonaise des Études Iraniennes.

Kouritzin, Sandra G. (1999). *Face[t]s of First Language Loss.* Mahwah, NJ: Lawrence Erlbaum Associates.

Kuo, Lily. (2014, January 24). The Average Chinese Private-Sector Worker Earns About the Same as a Cleaner in Thailand, *Quartz.* Retrieved from http://qz.com/170363/the-average-chinese-private-sector-worker-earns-about-the-same-as-a-cleaner-in-thailand/

Kymlicka, Will, & Patten, Alan. (2003a). Language Rights and Political Theory. *Annual Review of Applied Linguistics, 23,* 3–21. doi: doi:10.1017/S0267190503000163

Kymlicka, Will, & Patten, Alan (Eds.). (2003b). *Language Rights and Political Theory.* New York and Oxford: Oxford University Press.

Labour Trafficking in Australia. (2013). Brisbane: University of Queensland. Retrieved from http://www.law.uq.edu.au/labour-trafficking-in-australia

Labov, William, & Waletzky, Joshua. (1967). Narrative Analysis. In J. Helm (Ed.), *Essays on the Verbal and Visual Arts* (pp. 12–44). Seattle, WA: University of Washington Press.

Lahti, Malgorzata, & Valo, Maarit. (2013). The Development of Intercultural Relationships at Work: Polish Migrant Workers in Finland. *Journal of Intercultural Communication, 13*(31).

Lake, Marilyn, Reynolds, Henry, McKenna, Mark, & Damousi, Joy. (2010). *What's Wrong with ANZAC?* Sydney: UNSW Press.

Latshaw, Beth A. (2011). The More Things Change, the More They Remain the Same? *Sociology Compass, 5*(7), 653–665. doi: 10.1111/j.1751-9020.2011.00391.x

Lau v. Nichols (1974). Retrieved from http://www.languagepolicy.net/archives/lau.htm

Lester, Tim. (2011, June 6). 'We Couldn't Fit In. They Didn't Give Us a Chance to Fit In.' *Sydney Morning Herald.* Retrieved from http://www.smh.com.au/national/we-couldnt-fit-in-they-didnt-give-us-a-chance-to-fit-in-20110605-1fniw

Lester, Tim, & Young, Tim. (2011, June 6). Betrayed: Jobless Iraqis in Despair. *Sydney Morning Herald.* Retrieved from http://www.smh.com.au/national/betrayed-jobless-iraqis-in-despair-20110605-1fnjb.html

Levin, Tamar, & Shohamy, Elana. (2007). The Role of Academic Language in Understanding the Mathematics Achievements of Immigrant Students in Israel. In C. S. Sunal & K. Mutua (Eds.), *The Enterprise of Education: Research on Education in Africa, the Caribbean, and the Middle East* (pp. 313–336). Tuscaloosa, AL: Information Age Publishing.

Levin, Tamar, & Shohamy, Elana. (2008). Achievement of Immigrant Students in Mathematics and Academic Hebrew in Israeli School: A Large Scale Evaluation Study. *Studies in Educational Evaluation, 34,* 1–14.

Lewis, Geoffrey. (1999). *The Turkish Language Reform: A Catastrophic Success.* Oxford: Oxford University Press.

Li, Wei (Ed.). (2014). *Researching Multilingualism and Superdiversity: Grassroots Actions and Responsibilities. Special Issue of Multilingua 33 (5/6).*

Lindemann, Stephanie. (2002). Listening with an Attitude: A Model of Native-Speaker Comprehension of Non-native Speakers in the United States. *Language in Society, 31,* 419–441.

Lindemann, Stephanie, & Subtirelu, Nicholas. (2013). Reliably Biased: The Role of Listener Expectation in the Perception of Second Language Speech. *Language Learning, 48*(2), 283–323. doi: 10.1111/lang. 12014

Lintin, Alanna. (2014, August 3). Burton Queen's Hospital Translation Bill Goes up by 53 Per Cent, *Burton Mail.* Retrieved from http:// www.burtonmail.co.uk/Hospital-translation-goes-53-cent/story-22059443-detail/story.html#tPiZgkLtfCv9HBue.99

Lippi-Green, Rosina. (2012). *English with an Accent: Language, Ideology, and Discrimination in the United States* (2nd ed.). London: Routledge.

A Long Way to Equal: An Update of 'Quarter Way to Equal: A Report on Barriers to Legal Services for Migrant Women.' (2007). Sydney: Women's Legal Services NSW.

Lowe, Adrian. (2012, November 22). 'Speak English or Die'—Terror on a Suburban Bus, *Sydney Morning Herald.* Retrieved from http://www.smh.com.au/national/speak-english-or-die--terror-on-a-suburban-bus-20121121-29qex.html

Lumby, J. Rawson (Ed.). (2006). *Polychronicon Ranulphi Higden Maonachi Cestrensis; Together with the English Translations of John Trevisa and of an Unknown Writer of the Fifteenth Century; Higden, Ranulf, D. 1364.* Ann Arbor, MI: University of Michigan Library.

Machida, Satoshi. (2012). Does Globalization Render People More Ethnocentric? Globalization and People's Views on Cultures. *American Journal of Economics and Sociology, 71*(2), 436–469. doi: 10.1111/j. 1536-7150.2012.00835.x

Main Language by Ethnic Group, 2011. (2013). London: Office for National Statistics.

Major, George, Terraschke, Agnes, Major, Emily, & Setijadi, Charlotte. (2014). Working It Out: Migrants' Perspectives of Social Inclusion in the Workplace. *Australian Review of Applied Linguistics*, 37(3), 249–261.

Man Questioned about Racist Rant on Bus. (2012, November 28). *The Age*. Retrieved from http://www.theguardian.com/lifeandstyle/2008/jul/22/peopletree

Martín Rojo, Luisa. (2010). *Constructing Inequality in Multilingual Classrooms*. Berlin: Mouton de Gruyter.

May, Stephen. (2011). *Language and Minority Rights: Ethnicity, Nationalism and the Politics of Language* (2nd ed.). London: Routledge.

McCarty, Teresa L. (Ed.). (2011). *Ethnography and Language Policy*. London: Routledge.

McIntosh, Peggy. (1989). White Privilege and Male Privilege: A Personal Account of Coming to See Correspondences through Work in Women's Studies. *Wellesley College Center for Research on Women Working Papers*, 189.

McIntosh, Peggy. (2012). Reflections and Future Directions for Privilege Studies. *Journal of Social Issues*, 68(1), 194–206. doi: 10.1111/j.1540-4560.2011.01744.x

McNamara, Tim, & Ryan, Kerry. (2011). Fairness versus Justice in Language Testing: The Place of English Literacy in the Australian Citizenship Test. *Language Assessment Quarterly*, 8(2), 161–178. doi: 10.1080/15434303.2011.565438

Medhora, Shalailah. (2015, March 8). High-Risk Inmates at NSW Supermax Jail Banned from Speaking Arabic. *Guardian*. Retrieved from www.theguardian.com/australia-news/2015/mar/08/high-risk-inmates-at-nsw-super-max-jail-banned-from-speaking-arabic

Mencken, H. L. (1980). *The American Language* (4th ed.). New York: Alfred Knopf.

Menken, Kate, & García, Ofelia (Eds.). (2010). *Negotiating Language Policies in Schools: Educators as Policy Makers*. London: Routledge.

Menken, Kate, & Kleyn, T. (2010). The Long-Term Impact of Subtractive Schooling in the Educational Experiences of Secondary English Language Learners. *International Journal of Bilingual Education & Bilingualism*, 13(4), 399–417.

Menken, Kate, Kleyn, Tatyana, & Chae, Nabin. (2012). Spotlight on 'Long-Term English Language Learners': Characteristics and Prior Schooling Experiences of an Invisible Population. *International Multilingual Research Journal*, 6(2), 121–142. doi: 10.1080/19313152.2012.665822

Middle English Dictionary. (2001). Ann Arbor: University of Michigan Library.

Miller, Jennifer. (2003). *Audible Difference: ESL and Social Identity in Schools*. Clevedon: Multilingual Matters.

Miller, Meryl. (2005, August 27). Closing Time for USQ Dubai, *The Chronicle*. Retrieved from www.thechronicle.com.au/news/apn-closing-time-for-us/2315/

Minney, Safia. (2008, July 22). Fair Trade Is a Slow Process. *The Guardian*. Retrieved from http://www.theguardian.com/lifeandstyle/2008/jul/22/peopletree

Mitchell, Thom, & Graham, Chris. (2015, January 30). National Disgrace: CFMEU Forces Govt to Investigate $4 an Hour Foreign Workers. Retrieved from https://newmatilda.com/2015/01/29/national-disgrace-cfmeu-forces-govt-investigate-4-hour-foreign-workers/

Mohanty, Ajit K., Panda, Minati, Phillipson, Robert, & Skutnabb-Kangas, Tove. (2009). *Multilingual Education for Social Justice: Globalising the Local*. New Delhi: Orient BlackSwan.

Moore, Helen, Nicholas, Howard, & Deblaquiere, Julie. (2008). 'Opening the Door' Provision for Refugee Youth with Minimal/No Schooling in the Adult Migrant English Program Project 2.1: 'Modes of Delivery for SPP Youth.' Canberra: Australian Government: Department of Immigration and Citizenship. Retrieved from http://www.ameprc.mq.edu.au/docs/research_reports/research_report_series/Opening_the_door.pdf

Mongaya, Karlo Mikhail. (2010, July 15). Philippines: Discrimination against Filipinos in Baltimore Hospital, *Global Voices*. Retrieved from https://globalvoices.org/2010/07/15/philippines-discrimination-against-filipinos-in-baltimore-hospital/

Morarji, Karuna. (2010). Where Does the Rural Educated Person Fit? Development and Social Reproduction in Contemporary India. In P. McMichael (Ed.), *Contesting Development: Critical Struggles for Social Change* (pp. 50–63). London: Routledge.

Moss, Peter. (2014). *Transformative Change and Real Utopias in Early Childhood Education: A Story of Democracy, Experimentation and Potentiality*. London: Routledge.

Mowbray, Jacqueline. (2012). *Linguistic Justice: International Law and Language Policy*. Oxford: Oxford University Press.

Multicultural Language Services Guidelines for Australian Government Agencies. (2013). Belconnen, ACT: Department of Immigration and Citizenship.

Murphy, Jessica. (2012, October 24). Canadian Cities, Households Increasingly Multilingual: Census, *Toronto Sun*. Retrieved from www.torontosun.com/2012/10/24/canadian-cities-households-increasingly-multilingual-census

Musgrave, Simon, & Bradshaw, Julie. (2014). Language and Social Inclusion: Unexplored Aspects of Intercultural Communication. *Australian Review of Applied Linguistics*, 37(3), 198–212

Mustafa, Zubeida. (2011). *Tyranny of Language in Education: The Problem and Its Solution*. Karachi: Ushba Publishing.

Nail Technician. (2015). Retrieved from http://www.jobguide.thegood guides.com.au/occupation/Nail-Technician/NSW

National Assessment Program—Literacy and Numeracy Achievement in Reading, Persuasive Writing, Language Conventions and Numeracy: National Report for 2012. (2012). Sydney: Australian Curriculum, Assessment and Reporting Authority (ACARA). Retrieved from www. nap.edu.au/verve/_resources/naplan_2012_national_report.pdf

Nayna, Mike. (2012). Caught on Camera: Racist Australians Abuse Girl and Smash Bus Window. *Checkpoint Comedy*. Retrieved from https://www. youtube.com/watch?v=hp6J6PF47CM

Nercissians, Emilia. (2001). Bilingualism and Diglossia: Patterns of Language Use by Ethnic Minorities in Tehran. *International Journal of the Sociology of Language, 148*, 59–70.

Newman Teen Taking Heat for Giving Valedictorian Speech in Spanish. (2012, June 19). *CBS Sacramento*. Retrieved from http://sacramento. cbslocal.com/2012/06/19/newman-teen-taking-heat-for-giving-valedictorian-speech-in-spanish/

Niño-Murcia, Mercedes. (2003). 'English Is Like the Dollar': Hard Currency Ideology and the Status of English in Peru. *World Englishes, 22*(2), 121–141.

Norton, Bonny. (2013). *Identity and Language Learning: Extending the Conversation* (2nd ed.). Bristol: Multilingual Matters.

Olearius, Adam. (1662). *The Travels of Olearius in Seventeenth-Century Persia* (J. Davies, Trans.). Seattle, WA: Washington University Webserver.

Otsuji, Emi, & Pennycook, Alastair. (2011). Social Inclusion and Metrolingual Practices. *International Journal of Bilingual Education and Bilingualism, 14*(4), 413–426.

Pair in Bus Rant Face Possible Jail. (2014, January 18). *NineMSN*. Retrieved from http://www.9news.com.au/national/2014/01/18/09/37/ pair-in-bus-rant-face-possible-jail

Partners for Change: English for Development. (2013). London: British Council. Retrieved from https://www.britishcouncil.org/sites/default/ files/british-council-english-for-development.pdf

Pasassung, Nikolaus. (2004). *Teaching English in an 'Acquisition-Poor Environment': An Ethnographic Example of a Remote Indonesian EFL Classroom*. PhD, University of Sydney. Retrieved from http://www. languageonthemove.com/wp-content/uploads/2013/01/Pasassung_ English-language-learning-in-Indonesia.pdf

Patriots and Traitors. (2011). *SMH TV*. Retrieved from http://www.smh. com.au/interactive/2011/national/patriots_and_traitors/index.html

Pavlenko, Aneta. (2005). 'Ask Each Pupil about Her Methods of Cleaning': Ideologies of Language and Gender in Americanisation Instruction (1900–1924). *International Journal of Bilingual Education and Bilingualism, 8*(4), 275–297.

Pavlenko, Aneta, & Piller, Ingrid. (2001). New Directions in the Study of Multilingualism, Second Language Learning, and Gender. In A. Pavlenko, A. Blackledge, I. Piller & M. Teutsch-Dwyer (Eds.), *Multilingualism, Second Language Learning and Gender* (pp. 17–52). Berlin and New York: Mouton de Gruyter.

Pearson, Nick. (2012, November 20). Melbourne Comedian Films Racist, Violent Bus Abuse, *NineMSN*. Retrieved from http://www.9news.com.au/national/2012/11/20/15/49/melbourne-comedian-films-racist-violent-bus-abuse

Peled, Yael, Ives, Peter, & Ricento, Thomas. (2014). Introduction to the Thematic Issue: Language Policy and Political Theory. *Language Policy, 13*, 295–300.

Perdue, Clive (Ed.). (1993a). *Adult Language Acquisition: Cross-linguistic Perspectives (Vol. 1: Field Methods)*. Cambridge: Cambridge University Press.

Perdue, Clive (Ed.). (1993b). *Adult Language Acquisition: Crosslinguistic Perspectives (Vol. 2: The Results)*. Cambridge: Cambridge University Press.

Petersen, Hans Christian, Boldsen, Jesper L., & Paine, Richard R. (2006). Population Relationships in and around Medieval Danish Town. In G. Storey (Ed.), *Urbanism in the Preindustrial World: Cross-cultural Approaches* (pp. 110–120). Tuscaloosa, AL: University of Alabama Press.

Phillipson, Robert. (1992). *Linguistic Imperialism*. Oxford: Oxford University Press.

Phillipson, Robert. (2008). The Linguistic Imperialism of Neoliberal Empire. *Critical Inquiry in Language Studies, 5*(1), 1–43.

Phillipson, Robert. (2009a). *Linguistic Imperialism Continued*. London: Routledge.

Phillipson, Robert. (2009b). The Tension between Linguistic Diversity and Dominant English. In A. K. Mohanty, M. Panda, R. Phillipson & T. Skutnabb-Kangas (Eds.), *Multilingual Education for Social Justice: Globalising the Local* (pp. 79–94). New Delhi: Orient BlackSwan.

Piller, Ingrid. (2011). *Intercultural Communication: A Critical Introduction*. Edinburgh: Edinburgh University Press.

Piller, Ingrid. (2012). Multilingualism and Social Exclusion. In M. Martin-Jones, A. Blackledge, & A. Creese (Eds.), *The Routledge Handbook of Multilingualism* (pp. 281–296). London: Routledge.

Piller, Ingrid, & Cho, Jinhyun. (2013). Neoliberalism as Language Policy. *Language in Society, 42*(1), 23–44.

Piller, Ingrid, & Lising, Loy. (2014). Language, Employment and Settlement: Temporary Meat Workers in Australia. *Multilingua, 33*(1/2), 35–59.

Piller, Ingrid, & Takahashi, Kimie. (2011). Linguistic Diversity and Social Inclusion. *International Journal of Bilingual Education and Bilingualism,* 14(4), 371–381.

Pinkerton, Tiny. (2013). *Recruitment Discrimination against Middle Eastern People in Western Australia: The Case of Accountants.* BSc Honours, Edith Cowan University. Retrieved from http://ro.ecu.edu.au/theses_hons/119/

Pool, Jonathan. (1990). Language Regimes and Political Regimes. In B. Weinstein (Ed.), *Language Policy and Political Development* (pp. 241–261). Westport, CT, and London: Greenwood Press.

Populatia Stabila Dupa Etnie—Judete, Municipii, Orase, Comune [Resident Population by Ethnicity—Counties, Cities, Towns, Communities]. (2011). Bucharest: Romanian National Institute of Statistics.

Price, Gareth. (2014). English for All? Neoliberalism, Globalization, and Language Policy in Taiwan. *Language in Society, 43*(05), 567–589. doi: 10.1017/S0047404514000566

Przewoźnik, Andrzej. (2002). *Polskie Cmentarze Wojenne W Iranie. Polish War Cemeteries in Iran.* Warszawa: Rada Ochrony Pamięci Walk i Męczeństwa.

Puhl, Rebecca M., & Heuer, Chelsea A. (2010). Obesity Stigma: Important Considerations for Public Health. *American Journal of Public Health,* 100(6), 1019–1028. doi: 10.2105/AJPH.2009.159491

Qureshi, Kaveri. (2012). Pakistani Labour Migration and Masculinity: Industrial Working Life, the Body and Transnationalism. *Global Networks, 12*(4), 485–504. doi: 10.1111/j.1471-0374.2012.00362.x

R v. Azizi (2010). Supreme Court of Victoria. Retrieved from https://jade.barnet.com.au/Jade.html#article=140443

Rapatahana, Vaughan, & Bunce, Pauline (Eds.). (2012). *English Language as Hydra: Its Impacts on Non-English Language Cultures.* Bristol: Multilingual Matters.

Rautman, Marcus L. (2006). *Daily Life in the Byzantine Empire.* Westport, CT, and London: Greenwood Press.

Raymond, Chase Wesley. (2014). Negotiating Entitlement to Language: Calling 911 without English. *Language in Society, 43*(01), 33–59. doi: 10.1017/S0047404513000869

Rechtsprechung BAG, 22.06.2011—8 AZR 48/10. (2011). Retrieved from http://dejure.org/dienste/vernetzung/rechtsprechung?Gericht=BAG&Datum=22.06.2011&Aktenzeichen=8%20AZR%2048/10

Rechtsprechung LAG Schleswig-Holstein, 23.12.2009—6 Sa 158/09 (2009). Retrieved from http://dejure.org/dienste/vernetzung/rechtsprechung?Text=6%20Sa%20158/09

Reck, Andrew J. (Ed.). (1964). *Selected Writings of George Herbert Mead*. Chicago: University of Chicago Press.

Reinert, Erik S. (2008). *How Rich Countries Got Rich . . . And Why Poor Countries Stay Poor*. London: Constable.

Relos, Gel Santos. (20181, August 1). Fired for Speaking in Filipino: Filipina Nurses in Maryland Win Case Vs Hospital! *The Fil-Am Perspective*. Retrieved from http://gelsantosrelos.typepad.com/my-blog/2011/08/fired-for-speaking-in-filipino-filipina-nurses-in-maryland-win-case-vs-hospital.html

Reyes, Lemery. (2010, July 1). Fired for Not Speaking English, *NewsDesk*. Retrieved from http://newsdesk.org/2010/07/01/fired-for-not-speaking-english/

Ricento, Thomas. (2014). Thinking about Language: What Political Theorists Need to Know About Language in the Real World. *Language Policy*, *13*, 351–369.

Roberts, Celia. (2013). The Gatekeeping of Babel: Job Interviews and the Linguistic Penalty. In A. Duchêne, M. Moyer, & C. Roberts (Eds.), *Language, Migration and Social Inequalities: A Critical Sociolinguistic Perspective on Institutions and Work* (pp. 81–94). Bristol: Multilingual Matters.

Roberts, Celia, Davies, Evelyn, & Jupp, Tom. (1992). *Language and Discrimination*. London: Routledge.

Robertson, Leena H., Drury, Rose, & Cable, Carrie. (2014). Silencing Bilingualism: A Day in a Life of a Bilingual Practitioner. *International Journal of Bilingual Education and Bilingualism*, *17*(5), 610–623. doi: 10.1080/13670050.2013.864252

Rosemont, Franklin. (2003). *Joe Hill: The IWW & the Making of a Revolutionary Workingclass Counterculture*. Chicago, IL: C. H. Kerr Publications.

Rourke, Alison. (2012, November 22). Melbourne Racist Bus Attack Victim Speaks Out, *The Guardian*. Retrieved from http://www.theguardian.com/world/2012/nov/22/racist-bus-attack-victim-australia

Ruairc, Gerry Mac. (2009). 'Dip, Dip, Sky Blue, Who's It? Not You': Children's Experiences of Standardised Testing: A Socio-cultural Analysis. *Irish Educational Studies*, *28*(1), 47–66.

Rubin, Donald L. (1992). Nonlanguage Factors Affecting Undergraduates' Judgements of Nonnative English-Speaking Teaching Assistants. *Research in Higher Education*, *33*(4), 511–531.

Rubin, Donald L., & Smith, Kim A. (1990). Effects of Accent, Ethnicity, and Lecture Topic on Undergraduates' Perceptions of Non-native English Speaking Teaching Assistants. *International Journal of Intercultural Relations*, *14*, 337–353.

Runciman, Steven. (2012). *The Fall of Constantinople 1453* (18th ed.). Cambridge: Cambridge University Press.

Ryan, Kerry. (2012, April 16). Citizenship for Beginners. *Inside Story*. Retrieved from http://insidestory.org.au/citizenship-for-beginners/

Ryan, Louise. (2011). Migrants' Social Networks and Weak Ties: Accessing Resources and Constructing Relationships Post-migration. *The Sociological Review, 59*(4), 707–724. doi: 10.1111/j.1467-954X.2011.02030.x

Ryan, Louise, & Sales, Rosemary. (2013). Family Migration: The Role of Children and Education in Family Decision-Making Strategies of Polish Migrants in London. *International Migration, 51*(2), 90–103. doi: 10.1111/j.1468-2435.2010.00652.x

Sabaté i Dalmau, Maria. (2014). *Migrant Communication Enterprises: Regimentation and Resistance*. Bristol: Multilingual Matters.

Sapiro, Gisèle (Ed.). (2010). *Sociology Is a Martial Art: Political Writing by Pierre Bourdieu*. New York and London: The New Press.

Sassen, Saskia. (2001). *The Global City: New York, London, Tokyo* (2nd ed.). Princeton and Oxford: Princeton University Press.

Schelling, Felix E. (Ed.). (1892). *Ben Jonson: Timber, or Discoveries Made Upon Men and Matter*. Boston: Ginn & Co.

Schmalzbauer, Leah. (2009). Gender on a New Frontier: Mexican Migration in the Rural Mountain West. *Gender Society, 23*(6), 747–767. doi: 10.1177/0891243209346563

Schneider, Jan. (2014). Bewerberdiskriminierung am Ausbildungsmarkt [Discrimination against Applicants for Apprenticeships]. *HWWI Update, 6*.

Schumann, John H. (1978). *The Pidginization Process: A Model for Second Language Acquisition*. Rowley, MA: Newbury House.

Schwab, Klaus, Barth Eide, Espen, Zahidi, Saadia, Bekhouche, Yasmina, Padilla Ugarte, Paulina, Camus, Jessica, . . . Tyson, Laura D. (2014). The Global Gender Gap Report 2014. Geneva: World Economic Forum. Retrieved from http://www3.weforum.org/docs/GGGR14/GGGR_CompleteReport_2014.pdf

Schwarz, Henry G. (1984). *The Minorities of Northern China: A Survey*. Bellingham, WA: Center for East Asian Studies, Western Washington University.

Semple, Kirk. (2014, July 10). Immigrants Who Speak Indigenous Languages Encounter Isolation, *New York Times*. Retrieved from http://www.nytimes.com/2014/07/11/nyregion/immigrants-who-speak-indigenous-mexican-languages-encounter-isolation.html

Sen, Amartya. (1983). Poor, Relatively Speaking. *Oxford Economic Papers, 35*(2), 153–169.

Sen, Amartya. (2009). *The Idea of Justice*. Cambridge, MA: Harvard University Press.

Sherwood, Harriet. (2014, April 27). Ten Years On and Poles Are Glad to Call Britain Home. *Guardian*. Retrieved from http://www.theguardian.com/uk-news/2014/apr/26/polish-immigration-britain-cities-elections

Shin, Sarah J. (2013). *Bilingualism in Schools and Society: Language, Identity, and Policy*. London: Routledge.

Shohamy, Elana, & McNamara, Tim (Eds.). (2009). *Language Tests for Citizenship, Immigration, and Asylum. Special Issue of Language Assessment Quarterly, 6.*

Skinner, Patricia. (2003). *The Jews in Medieval Britain: Historical, Literary, and Archaeological Perspectives.* Martlesham, Suffolk: Boydell & Brewer.

Skutnabb-Kangas, Tove. (2001). The Globalisation of (Educational) Language Rights. *International Review of Education, 47*(3/4), 201–219.

Skutnabb-Kangas, Tove, & Phillipson, Robert. (1998). Language in Human Rights. *The International Communication Gazette, 60*(1), 27–46.

Skutnabb-Kangas, Tove, & Phillipson, Robert (Eds.). (1994). *Linguistic Human Rights: Overcoming Linguistic Discrimination.* Berlin and New York: Mouton de Gruyter.

Smith, Beckie. (2014, May 3). China: Compulsory English Testing to Be Removed from Gaokao. *The Pie News.* Retrieved from http://thepienews. com/news/china-remove-english-language-testing-gaokao/

Smith, Gibbs M. (1984). *Joe Hill.* Layton, UT: Gibbs Smith Publishing.

Song, Juyoung. (2010). Language Ideology and Identity in Transnational Space: Globalization, Migration, and Bilingualism among Korean Families in the USA. *International Journal of Bilingual Education and Bilingualism, 13*(1), 23–42. doi: 10.1080/13670050902748778

Soutphommasane, Tim. (2012). *Don't Go Back to Where You Came From: Why Multiculturalism Works.* Sydney: NewSouth.

Spannos, Chris. (2008). *Real Utopia: Participatory Society for the 21st Century.* Oakland, CA: AK Press.

Stanisław Kościałkowski. (2015) *Wikipedia.*

Starnes, Todd. (n.d). Spanish Graduation Speech Enrages Community, *Fox News Radio.* Retrieved from http://radio.foxnews.com/toddstarnes/ top-stories/student-delivers-graduation-speech-in-spanish.html

Statutory Framework for the Early Years Foundation Stage: Setting the Standards for Learning, Development and Care for Children from Birth to Five. (2014). London: Department for Education. Retrieved from https:// www.gov.uk/government/uploads/system/uploads/attachment_data/ file/335504/EYFS_framework_from_1_September_2014__with_ clarification_note.pdf

Stripling, Jack. (2009, February 7). Gulf Withdrawal. *Inside Higher Ed.* Retrieved from https://www.insidehighered.com/news/2009/02/27/ gulf-withdrawal

Subtirelu, Nicholas Close. (2013). 'English . . . It's Part of Our Blood': Ideologies of Language and Nation in United States Congressional Discourse. *Journal of Sociolinguistics, 17*(1), 37–65. doi: 10.1111/josl.12016

Sue, Derald Wing. (2010). *Microaggressions in Everyday Life: Race, Gender, and Sexual Orientation.* Hoboken, NJ: John Wiley & Sons.

Sue, Derald Wing, Capodilupo, Christina M., Torino, Gina C., Bucceri, Jennifer M., Holder, Aisha M. B., Nadal, Kevin, & Esquilin, Marta. (2007). Racial Microaggressions in Everyday Life: Implications for Clinical Practice. *American Psychologist, 62*(4), 271–286.

Suleiman, Yasir. (2011). *Arabic, Self and Identity: A Study in Conflict and Displacement.* Oxford and New York: Oxford University Press.

Sutton, Malcolm. (2014, August 5). Youths from Non-English Speaking Countries Overlooked for Australian Jobs Despite Training: Report, *ABC News.* Retrieved from www.abc.net.au/news/2014–08-05/non-english-speaking-youths-overlooked-for-australian-jobs/5649896

Svärdström, Elisabeth. (1970). Runorna i Hagia Sofia [Runes in Hagia Sofia]. *Fornvännen, 65,* 247–249.

Swain, Harriet. (2014, July 8). Lack of Languages Stifles Brits and Americans. *The Guardian.* Retrieved from http://www.theguardian.com/education/2014/jul/08/lack-of-languages-stifles-brits-americans

Swan, Melanie. (2010, August 31). RAK Free Zone Entices Overseas Colleges. *The National.* Retrieved from http://www.thenational.ae/uae/education/pakistani-university-campus-to-open-in-rak

Swan, Melanie. (2014, July 7). Pakistani University Campus to Open in RAK. *The National.* Retrieved from www.thenational.ae/uae/education/pakistani-university-campus-to-open-in-rak

Tabouret-Keller, Andrée. (1999). Western Europe. In J. Fishman (Ed.), *Handbook of Language and Ethnic Identity* (pp. 334–349). New York and Oxford: Oxford University Press.

Takahashi, Kimie. (2013). *Language Learning, Gender and Desire: Japanese Women on the Move.* Clevedon: Multilingual Matters.

Takenoshita, Hirohisa, Chitose, Yoshimi, Ikegami, Shigehiro, & Ishikawa, Eunice Akemi. (2014). Segmented Assimilation, Transnationalism, and Educational Attainment of Brazilian Migrant Children in Japan. *International Migration, 52*(2), 84–99. doi: 10.1111/imig.12057

Tamil Asylum Seekers Caught in Indonesian Waters Say They Face Genocide in Sri Lanka. (2009, October 18). *Thaindian News.* Retrieved from www.thaindian.com/newsportal/world-news/tamil-asylum-seekers-caught-in-indonesian-waters-say-they-face-genocide-in-sri-lanka_100262160.html

Taylor, Charles L., & Hudson, Michael C. (1972). *World Handbook of Political and Social Indicators* (2nd ed.). New Haven, CT: Yale University Press.

Terminology and Concepts: Principles of Multiculturalism. (n.d.) Retrieved from http://www.crc.nsw.gov.au/multicultural_policies_and_services_program_formally_eaps/terminology

Tetteh, Vera Williams. (2015). *Language, Education and Settlement: A Socio-linguistic Ethnography on, with, and for Africans in Australia.* PhD, Macquarie University. Retrieved from http://www.languageonthemove. com/wp-content/uploads/2015/07/Final-PhD-thesis_Vera-Williams-Tetteh.pdf

Theresa Maree Hillier to Give Birth Behind Bars for Racial Attack on Asylum Seeker in Hobart. (2013, December 21). *ABC News.* Retrieved from www.abc.net.au/news/2013–12-20/birth-behind-bars-for-racial-attack/5170478

Thurgood, Graham, & LaPolla, Randy J. (2003). *The Sino-Tibetan Languages.* London: Routledge.

Times Higher Education World Reputation Rankings. (2015). Retrieved from http://www.timeshighereducation.co.uk/world-university-rankings/2015/reputation-ranking/analysis/global-leaders

Ting, Inga, & Walters, Conrad. (2014, July 11). Sydney's Melting Pot of Language, *Sydney Morning Herald.* Retrieved from www.smh.com.au/datapoint/sydney-languages/index.html

Tollefson, James W. (Ed.). (2013). *Language Policies in Education: Critical Issues* (2nd ed.). London: Routledge.

Topçu, Özlem, Bota, Alice, & Pham, Khuê. (2012). *Wir neuen Deutschen: Wer wir sind, was wir wollen [Us New Germans: Who We Are, What We Want].* Hamburg: rowohlt.

Townsend, Peter. (1979). *Poverty in the United Kingdom: A Survey of Household Resources and Standards of Living.* Berkeley: University of California Press.

Tran, My-Thuan. (2008, May 5). A Mix of Luck, Polish: Vietnamese Dominance of the Manicure Trade Started with the Help of a U.S. Star. *Los Angeles Times.* Retrieved from http://articles.latimes.com/2008/may/05/local/me-nails5

Trounson, Andrew. (2014, April 2). Lack of Asian 'No Bar to Joining New Colombo Plan.' *The Australian.* Retrieved from www.theaustralian.com.au/higher-education/lack-of-asian-no-bar-to-joining-new-colombo-plan/story-e6frgcjx-1226871272846

Tsumagari, Toshiro, Kurebito, Megumi, & Endo, Fubito. (2007). Siberia: Tungusic and Palaeosiberian. In O. Miyaoka, O. Sakiyama, & M. E. Krauss (Eds.), *The Vanishing Languages of the Pacific Rim* (pp. 387–405). Oxford and New York: Oxford University Press.

Universal Declaration of Human Rights. (1948).

US Hospital Settles with Pinay Nurses Fired for Speaking Tagalog. (2012, July 10). *GMA News.* Retrieved from http://www.gmanetwork.com/news/story/264870/news/pinoyabroad/us-hospital-settles-with-pinay-nurses-fired-for-speaking-tagalog

Vajda, Edward J. (2009). Native Peoples of Russia's Maritime Province. Retrieved from http://pandora.cii.wwu.edu/vajda/ea210/maritime.htm

Van Parijs, Philippe. (2011). *Linguistic Justice for Europe and for the World*. New York and Oxford: Oxford University Press.

Vertovec, Steven. (2007). Super-diversity and Its Implications. *Ethnic and Racial Studies*, *30*(6), 1024–1054.

Villenas, Sofia. (2001). Latina Mothers and Small-Town Racisms: Creating Narratives of Dignity and Moral Education in North Carolina. *Anthropology and Education Quarterly*, *32*(1), 3–28.

Voloshinov, Valentin N. (1986). *Marxism and the Philosophy of Language* (L. Matejka & I. R. Titunik, Trans.). Cambridge: Harvard University Press.

Wee, Lionel. (2010). *Language without Rights*. New York and Oxford: Oxford University Press.

What Happened to the Oceanic Viking Refugees? (2010, September 25). *Green Left Weekly*. Retrieved from www.greenleft.org.au/node/45507

What If a CALD Client Should Walk in Our Door? A Guide for Service Providers. (n.d.) Retrieved from www.ccdn.com.au/resources/57-qwhat-if-a-cald-client-should-walk-in-our-doorq-a-guide-for-service-providers

Widin, Jacqueline. (2010). *Illegitimate Practices: Global English Language Education*. Bristol: Multilingual Matters.

Wigglesworth, Gillian, Simpson, Jane, & Loakes, Deborah. (2011). NAPLAN Language Assessments for Indigenous Children in Remote Communities: Issues and Problems. *Australian Review of Applied Linguistics*, *34*(3), 320–343.

Winerip, Michael. (2010, July 18). A Popular Principal, Wounded by Government's Good Intentions. *New York Times*. Retrieved from http://www.nytimes.com/2010/07/19/education/19winerip.html

Wise, Scott. (2012, June 20). Student Gets Heat for Giving Valedictorian Speech in Spanish. *CBS6*. Retrieved from http://wtvr.com/2012/06/20/valedictorian-speech-in-spanish/

Witepski, Lisa. (2006). Biltong Buddies. *Journal of Marketing* (August/September), 14–15.

Wong Fillmore, Lily. (1991). When Learning a Second Language Means Losing the First. *Early Childhood Research Quarterly*, *6*(3), 323–346.

World Migration in Figures. (2013). OECD. Retrieved from http://www.oecd.org/els/mig/World-Migration-in-Figures.pdf

World Migration Report 2013. (2013). Geneva: International Organization for Migration. Retrieved from http://www.oecd.org/els/mig/World-Migration-in-Figures.pdf

Wright, Erik Olin. (2014). *Envisioning Real Utopias*. London: Verso.

Wright, Sue, & Lander, Denis. (2003). Collaborative Group Interactions of Students from Two Ethnic Backgrounds. *Higher Education Research & Development, 22*(3), 237–251. doi: 10.1080/0729436032000145121

Yates, Lynda. (2011). Interaction, Language Learning and Social Inclusion in Early Settlement. *International Journal of Bilingual Education and Bilingualism, 14*(4), 457–471.

Yoo, Byungryul, Kim, Isak, & Kim, Hyekyung. (2011, September 10). 영어 교육 강화? 사교육 심화 [Strengthening English Education? Private Tutoring on the Increase]. *Hankook Ilbo.* Retrieved from news.hankooki. com/lpage/society/200903/h2009031002351922020.htm

Yoo, Hyung Chol, Gee, Gilbert C., & Takeuchi, David. (2008). Discrimination and Health among Asian American Immigrants: Disentangling Racial from Language Discrimination. *Social Science and Medicine, 68*(4), 726–732. doi: 10.1016/j.socscimed.2008.11.013

Yosso, Tara J., Smith, William A., Ceja, Miguel, & Solórzano, Daniel G. (2009). Critical Race Theory, Racial Microaggressions, and Campus Racial Climate for Latina/o Undergraduates. *Harvard Educational Review, 79*(4), 659–691.

Zhang, Jie. (2011). *Language Policy and Planning for the 2008 Beijing Olympics: An Investigation of the Discursive Construction of an Olympic City and a Global Population.* PhD, Macquarie University. Retrieved from http://www.languageonthemove.com/wp-content/uploads/2012/03/PhD-thesis-Zhang-Jie-library-copy_reduced-size.pdf

Zhang, Jie. (forthcoming). *English Desire in the Olympic Spotlight: Language Policy and Planning for the 2008 Beijing Olympics.* Berlin and New York: Mouton de Gruyter.

INDEX

Note: Locators followed by the letter 'n' refer to notes.